D1247594

HANDBOOK OF

JAPANESE GRAMMAR

REVISED EDITION

Harold G. Henderson

COLUMBIA UNIVERSITY

HOUGHTON MIFFLIN COMPANY

The Riverside Press, Cambridge

MIDDLEBURY COLLEGE
LIBRARY

PL
535
H4
1948

5/1970
Jap ss

COPYRIGHT, 1948, BY HAROLD G. HENDERSON
COPYRIGHT, 1943, BY HAROLD G. HENDERSON

ALL RIGHTS RESERVED INCLUDING THE RIGHT TO REPRODUCE
THIS BOOK OR PARTS THEREOF IN ANY FORM

The Riverside Press
CAMBRIDGE · MASSACHUSETTS
PRINTED IN THE U.S.A.

Preface

There are certain characteristics of Japanese grammar which usually present difficulties to foreign students. This is not due to the inherent difficulty of the grammar itself, which on the whole is simpler than that of many other languages. It is rather due to the fact that many Japanese grammatical constructions differ radically from those we are accustomed to find in English and in other European languages.

In Japanese, words are modified and brought into relation with each other by means of word-order, prefixes, suffixes, and various connectives.

Verbs, for example, are modified by the use of various suffixes. The modifications may often be further modified by the addition of further suffixes, and these still further modified, and so on, almost, it would seem, *ad infinitum*. Of course, in practice, there is a limit, but verb-forms containing a series of four or five modifying suffixes are by no means uncommon.

Fortunately there is no great difficulty in mastering these forms, as forms. They are built up in accordance with a few simple standard rules to which there are practically no exceptions. The real difficulty comes in understanding the use of the forms after we have them, for such verb-forms will seldom correspond exactly to the verb-forms we use in English.

As another example, nouns are brought into relation with each other and with the rest of the sentence by the addition of what are called "particles." Some of these particles are usually known as "postpositions," because they come after the nouns they are

connected with, and perform some of the functions of our prepo-
sitions. But even these "postpositions" have other functions too,
and particles in general do not correspond to European grammatical devices.

Speech and thought are of course very closely connected, and to
be a master of any language it is necessary to be able to think in
that language. But for Japanese, one may go further, and say
that it is practically necessary to think in Japanese in order to be
able to understand it at all. At the very least it is necessary to
think in the Japanese order of thought, with a full understanding
of the verb-forms and other devices used to show the connection
of one thought with another.

This book has been written in order to help the student to think
in the Japanese way. The method used is that of giving separate
treatment to each suffix, particle, or other connective, as well as
to such of their combinations as seem to have developed special
uses. I have tried to put under each heading enough material for
the student to get the "feel" of how it is used. The forms I have
attempted to cover include not only the "standard" colloquial,
literary, and epistolary styles, but also the more common collo-
quialisms and provincial forms whether or not these are strictly
grammatical. On the other hand, I have not tried to cover forms
found only in the Court language, in pre-Heian literature, etc.
A corresponding book on English forms would exclude Chau-
cerian forms and ephemeral slang, but would include the highly
literary "I would but that it were so" and the quite illiterate but
unfortunately very common "It ain't."

The main part of the book consists of several hundred headings,
put in alphabetical order to facilitate reference to them. There
have been added, however, some introductory notes on nomenclature, verbs, adjectives, foreign words, etc. It is absolutely
necessary that the student should have at his fingertips the
information contained in them. Unless he has it he will not be
able to use the information contained in the text.

In compiling this book I have felt at liberty to draw freely on
any previously published works on Japanese grammar for general
ideas and suggestions, without giving specific credit except where
direct quotations have been made. I must, however, express my

obligation to Professor Yamada Yoshio, the great pioneer among modern Japanese grammarians, whose voluminous and comprehensive works have been invaluable. Among the other Japanese authors whose works I have used I should mention particularly Mr. Matsuura Keizo, from whose *Gendai Nihongo Bumpō* I have taken a number of illustrative examples. 現代日本語文法

It is a pleasure to express my acknowledgments to Mr. Frank Hawley, with whose help this book was started in Tokyo in 1938; to Dr. Serge Elisseeff, who went over the manuscript and suggested several important emendations; and to all my colleagues at Columbia, particularly Sir George B. Sansom, who helped me during its preparation. They have all helped to make the book better, but are in no way responsible for its faults. I also wish to express my thanks to Columbia University and to the Rockefeller Foundation for generous financial assistance.

I must add one word of apology for the shortcomings of this book. It is far less complete than I had planned it to be. I had expected to have at least another year to work on it, and am publishing it now only because of the pressure of events, in the belief that even as it is it may be of some use. I shall be very grateful to any reader who will let me know of errors or omissions.

HAROLD G. HENDERSON.

Columbia University

PREFACE TO THE REVISED EDITION

In preparing the revised edition I have been much helped by the suggestions of my colleague, Mr. R. Tsunoda, and of Mr. K. Matsumiya, Principal of the School of Japanese Language and Culture in Tokyo. To both of them I wish to extend my grateful thanks.

H. G. HENDERSON.

Contents

To Students

Though this book is not written for absolute beginners, if a beginner wishes to use it, he should first of all read the Preface and the following Notes, and make sure that he understands at least the most fundamental part of the information set down in them. When he has done so he will no longer be an absolute beginner.

The main part of the book is a list of particles and suffixes, arranged alphabetically. Advanced students will know how to use it without being told; the following discussion is therefore addressed primarily to students who are practically beginners.

Suppose, for example, that the reader is a near-beginner, just starting to study the colloquial Japanese. He is puzzled, say, by the two words *yomimasu* and *yomemasu,* neither of which appears in the dictionary. As he is not an absolute beginner he will recognize that *-masu* is a suffix, and that *yomi* and *yome* are both forms of the verb *yomu* 'read'. Let us further suppose that his information stops there.

When he looks up *-masu* he finds that it is a polite but otherwise meaningless conjugated suffix. He also finds that it can be added to only one form of a verb, the Line 2 form (*renyōkei*). 連用型 Now, *yomi* is the *renyōkei* of *yomu,* so that is all right, but how about *yomemasu?*

The difficulty is that *yome* is a Line 4 form (*izenkei*) of *yomu,* and that *-masu* is added to Line 2 forms only. From the Table of Conjugations he finds that the only verb of which *yome* can be a Line 2 form is *yomeru,* but *yomeru* does not appear in the dictionary either. When he looks up either *-ru* or *-eru* (they are cross-indexed) he finds that in colloquial Japanese all verbs of the first conjugation (to which *yomu* belongs) have forms ending in *-eru,* and that *yomeru,* and hence *yomemasu,* conveys an idea of "read ability" and may be translated as either "can read" or "can be read." He will also find a discussion of such forms with examples of their use.   A slightly more advanced student would of course simply look up *-eru* directly.

This example has been discussed in detail in order to bring out the extreme importance of being able to recognize conjugated forms.   This applies not only to ordinary verbs, but also to conjugated suffixes, which may be regarded as practically equivalent to auxiliary verbs.   Unless the student can recognize them, he will have trouble with even such common colloquial forms as *yomaserareta* (*yoma-se-rare-ta*), not to speak of bungo forms like *yomashimerareniki* (*yoma-shime-rare-ni-ki*), both of which convey approximately the idea of "was caused to read."   And it is well to warn the student from the very beginning that he must expect occasionally to find certain bungo forms used even in quite ordinary colloquial speech and writing.

When it comes to looking up particles, no difficulties are presented.   One simply looks them up.   There are, however, two points on which a student should be warned.   First, if he looks up combinations like, say, *na no ni* or *tote wa,* he will probably find enough information to enable him to understand the meaning of sentences in which they are used.   He should not, however, attempt to use them himself until he has mastered the use of their component parts.   For the examples cited he will find discussions not only of *na, no, ni, to, -te,* and *wa,* but also of *na no, no ni, tote,* and *-te wa.*

Second, if he looks up certain particular particles, such as *hodo* or *mono,* he will find a statement that these words also have uses as nouns.   Approximate English equivalents of the nouns are given in the text, but to get a full understanding of their uses *as nouns,* the student should consult a dictionary.

One last general warning.   Many Japanese sentences—perhaps most—do not have their subjects expressed.   When such sentences are lifted out of context and isolated as examples the subject has to be guessed at. Furthermore, hardly a single Japanese non-technical word corresponds exactly to any one English word. English renderings of Japanese in this book are consequently often of necessity more specific in form than are the Japanese originals. Students should regard them as correct translations, but not as the only possible correct translations for every possible context.

* *

It should be noted that in this book the transcription of Japanese in Roman letters follows a system in which consonants have approximately their value in English, and vowels approximately their value in Italian. This system, a slight modification of the old Hepburn Romanization, has been adopted primarily because it is the one used in the great majority of existent dictionaries and textbooks. The student should know, however, that there are several other systems in use. Of these the most important are the *Kokutei Rōmazi* (Official Romanization) promulgated in a Japanese government decree in 1937, and the excellent phonemic modification of it recently worked out at Yale.

In most Japanese texts the words are not separated from each other, and there is no generally accepted standard for separation in Romaji transcription. It is indeed often impossible to decide whether a word or group of words is or is not to be regarded as a single unit. Consequently, in the text of this book the separation into words and the use of hyphens to indicate suffixes are both necessarily somewhat irregular. In the text headings, however, the use of a hyphen indicates use as a true suffix.

INTRODUCTORY NOTES

NOTE ON

Nomenclature

One of the difficulties in writing about the Japanese language is that no adequate system of nomenclature has as yet been developed.

For instance, in Japanese the same word-form may do duty as a verb, an adjective, and a noun; or as a noun and an adverb; and moreover, the construction of sentences is such that the same group of words may often, without any change of form, be used as a complete sentence, or attributively (adjectivally), or as a noun-equivalent.

The names of grammatical categories, such as "noun," "verb," "adjective," etc., are therefore throughout this book used in their English meanings. If, for instance, it is said that under certain circumstances a Japanese word "is a noun," and under other circumstances "is a verb," what is meant is that in the first instance it "either is a noun, or is used as if it were a noun, in the English sense," and in the second instance it "either is a verb or is used as if it were a verb, in the English sense."

Furthermore, among the various systems of nomenclature there is no accepted standard. It has therefore seemed best to avoid technical terms as much as possible. It has not been possible, however, to avoid them entirely. General terms are therefore defined in this section. Special technical terms are defined in the other Introductory Notes.

LITERARY AND COLLOQUIAL LANGUAGES

Another difficulty is that the Japanese language is at present in a state of flux. All living languages are, of course, but Japanese is changing far more rapidly than any of the others. A good case could be made out for there having been at least a dozen Japanese languages. There are certainly at least half a dozen "literary" styles, each of which uses special words and special constructions.

These do not correspond to dialects. They are specialized forms of the language, all of which will be known to a thoroughly educated person. They differ from each other not so much in the pronunciation of words as in vocabulary and the use of verb-endings.

There are perhaps as many different styles of the spoken language. There is the speech of the Court, that of the army, the "standard" Tokyo or *Kantō* speech, that of the *Kansai* (western Japan), the one used in formal public addresses, and so on. All these are in addition to the variations of phraseology which indicate various levels of politeness and culture. Some of them might come under the head of dialects, but certainly not all of them.

It is not advisable in a book of this sort to go deeply into these divisions, even if the present compiler were capable of doing so. The object of this book is to help the reader to understand the construction of such Japanese as he is likely to hear, or likely to read in modern newspapers and not too ancient books. It has seemed simplest therefore to divide Japanese constructions into two main categories.

The first category comprises all the constructions commonly met with in ordinary speech and in books which make no pretensions to literary scholarship. This is called the *kōgo* or colloquial.

The second category comprises all other constructions. It is here called the *bungo* or literary language.

The reader must be warned that this division is an arbitrary one. In the first place the line of division cannot be exactly defined, and in the second place it must be remembered that there are actually not one *kōgo* and one bungo, but several of each. Bungo forms are occasionally heard in speech, and nowadays much writing is done in the colloquial. There are many occasions in which both bungo and *kōgo* forms will be used together. Such a combination of forms is particularly prevalent in newspapers.

Students should realize that the present colloquial Japanese is a development from older forms. Modern bungo of course had the same origin, but it has had a different and slower development. In fact much of the modern bungo seems to be a fair approximation to the ordinary colloquial language of some seven hundred years ago.

GRAMMATICAL TERMS

Inasmuch as Japanese is built on a system different from that of English, it contains a certain number of constructions and parts of speech for which there are no English equivalents. It has therefore been necessary to adopt a special nomenclature. This has been kept as simple as possible, but the following four words could not be avoided:

PARTICLE — Any prefix, suffix, or word standing alone, which is not definable in all its uses as a noun, pronoun, verb, adjective, adverb, or conjunction.

POSTPOSITION[1] — Any particle used after a substantive to show its relation with other words.

SUBSTANTIVE — Any noun or pronoun, or any word or group of words used as a noun-equivalent, i.e., as the name of a subject of discourse.

SUBSTANTIVIZE — To make into or use as a substantive, to mark as being a substantive, or to join with so as to make a phrase which acts as a substantive.

In connection with the words "substantive" and "substantivize," the following is quoted from Sir G. B. Sansom's "Historical Grammar of Japanese."

[1] This word has been formed by analogy with "preposition."

"Japanese, even in its modern form, seems to retain vestiges of a condition in which there was imperfect differentiation of grammatical categories. The Indo-European languages have formal grammatical categories corresponding to certain psychological categories—word-classes, such as nouns, corresponding to the psychological category 'thing'; verbs, corresponding to the psychological category 'action' or 'state'; and adjectives, corresponding to the psychological category 'property'. In Japanese, either the psychological category is not fully differentiated, or the correspondence between grammatical and psychological categories is incomplete. The substantival or noun category seems to be the primary one and to have been retained in some cases where, in other languages, new categories have developed. This feature is difficult to explain, precisely because of its psychological aspect; but the following illustrations may serve to make it clear.

> "1. The typical form of a simple statement comprising subject and predicate in modern colloquial Japanese is shown in *otoko ga tatsu* 'the man stands'. Here functionally *tatsu* is a verb, but historically it is a substantive, and the formal equivalent of the sentence in English is 'standing of man'."

For further discussion the student is referred to the "Historical Grammar" (pp. 70*ff*. Edition: Oxford University Press, 1928).

One result of this lack of complete correspondence between grammatical and psychological categories is that any verb, clause, or sentence, which describes a state of affairs, may be used as if it were a name for that state of affairs, i.e., a noun. The name "substantive" is therefore employed in this book as meaning "any word or group of words representing a psychological 'thing'."

At the present time there is more correspondence between grammatical and psychological categories than there was in the earlier language. The modern colloquial uses far fewer substantives that are not nouns in form than the older language did.

One of the ways in which this is accomplished is by the use of the word *no*. This *no* can be put after any sentence, or after any verb in sentence-ending form, to make a phrase that grammatically acts like a compound noun. The present compiler is not sure whether this *no* should be regarded as itself a noun, or as a word that is used to put the previous substantive into noun form. The question seems to be of academic rather than of practical importance, but some word is needed to describe the action of *no*. The word "substantivize" therefore is used for this purpose.

It should be noted, however, that the word *no* is not necessary to the action of "substantivizing." It has never been used for this purpose in bungo, but was introduced into the colloquial several hundred years ago. At the present time there is an increasing tendency to drop it out of certain constructions common in ordinary conversation. This is particularly evident in sentences ending with *desu, deshita,* and other contractions of the copula, such as *shiroi (no) desu,* "it is white," or *mita (no) desu,* "I have seen (it)". In such sentences men, especially the younger men, tend to drop the *no*. Women and children, however, very often retain the *no* and drop the copula instead.

NOTE ON

Syntax

In any language the order in which words follow each other in sentences is dependent, at least to some extent, on the order in which thoughts follow each other in the mind of the speaker or writer.

The order of thought, and hence the order of words, is so different in Japanese and English that direct literal translation from one language to the other is usually impossible. In doing any translation it is therefore usually necessary first to understand clearly what idea is conveyed in one language, and then to rearrange its component thoughts for proper presentation in the other. In other words, understanding and translation are two different things, and in order to understand Japanese clearly one must keep to the Japanese order of thought.

The only real way to learn the Japanese order of thought is to practise it—that is, to take a sufficient number of examples, get their meanings perfectly clear, and then practise the forms used until the Japanese words convey their intended meanings without the necessity for mental rearrangement. However, a few general statements may be helpful.

The fundamental rule of Japanese construction is that qualifying words precede the words they qualify. Thus the adjective or genitive (or other adjectival expression) precedes the noun which it defines, the adverb precedes the verb, and explanatory or dependent clauses precede the principal clause. The object likewise precedes the verb. The predicative verb or adjective of each clause is placed at the end of that clause, the predicative verb or adjective of the main clause rounding off the entire sentence.

The above paragraph is quoted almost verbatim from Chamberlain's "Handbook of Colloquial Japanese" (Trübner & Co., London, 1888, p. 233); as it seems to me the most useful general rule I have yet come across.

There is one apparent exception to it. Postpositions and other particles follow the words or clauses to which they belong. Furthermore, in ordinary conversation there seems to be a tendency to use a particle (such as *yo, ne,* etc.) as a final word to indicate that the speaker is temporarily through speaking. It is probably best for students to consider this as a real exception, though on etymological grounds it is possible to consider the preceding words as modifying the particles.

One other point that often bothers students is the Japanese habit of omitting words from a sentence. It should not, however, bother anyone but a beginner. The reason for it is perfectly obvious, and rests on the quite logical assumption that the object of speech is to convey ideas. If the presence of a word is not needed to make the sense clear, it is not needed at all.

We often do the same thing in English. "Who is it?" "Mr. Brown"—not "It is Mr. Brown." "Whose hat is it?" "Mr. Brown's"—not "It is Mr. Brown's hat."

The Japanese, however, go even further, and often omit words which we would leave in. A subject, for instance, may be omitted because we already know what we are talking about. "Did Mr. Brown come?" "Yes, he came." But why the "he"? Isn't "Yes, came" equally clear as an answer? Furthermore, in English we often use the passive as a device to avoid naming the performer of an action—"A book was written on that subject"—obviously "by somebody." The Japanese do not have to use the passive for this purpose. They can get the same effect by saying the equivalent of "Somebody wrote a book on that subject" and simply omitting the "Somebody."

In general it may be said that the Japanese method of thought is fairly simple and direct. The student should notice, for instance, that concrete ideas are usually mentioned first, so that instead of "What is your name?" the normal thought-order is "Your name, what is it?" instead of "Perhaps he would like to go," it is "go," "like-to," "perhaps." He should also notice, as another instance, that when a series of happenings is referred to, the order of thought usually follows the actual temporal sequence.

Japanese methods of thought must of course be learned from examples rather than precepts. The purpose of what has been said here is primarily to introduce to the student the sort of thing for which he should be on the look-out. Most students have little difficulty with Japanese syntax once they realize that the mere fact of its differing from ours does not make it any the less normal, natural, and logical.

NOTE ON

Verbs

The conjugation of verbs is the only mechanical difficulty inherent in the Japanese language. It is therefore of prime importance that it be mastered as early as possible.

The basis of conjugation is comparatively simple. There are for each verb certain "line-forms" or "bases" to most of which suffixes may be added, each suffix having its own distinctive use. The language is agglutinative in that suffixes may often be added to suffixes, and sometimes further suffixes to them.

One of the purposes of the present volume is to explain the uses of these suffixes, but first it is necessary to make clear the formation of the "bases" or "line-forms" to which they are attached.[1] Japanese "conjugations" are simply lists of "line-forms." Such "conjugations," of course, do not at all correspond to European conjugations.

The following is a list of the "bases" or "line-forms," with their most common Japanese names, and some of the names used by grammarians writing in English.

---

[1] Many suffixes may themselves be conjugated. Such suffix-conjugations will be found in the main body of the text. It is of historical interest, but not within the scope of this work, to determine absolutely which of these suffixes may at one time have had the status of independent verbs. The important thing is that the compounds formed with them act as verbs.

Line	Japanese name	English name for "base" or "line-form"
1	*Mizenkei* (*Shōzenkei*)	Imperfect, Dubitative, Non-positive, Negative, Future, Conditional Indefinite
2	*Renyōkei*	Conjunctive, Continuative, Connective, Adverbial, Verbal
3	*Shūshikei*	Conclusive, Predicative, Substantive, Sentence-ending, Full-stop
3A	*Rentaikei*	Attributive, Adjectival, Substantival, "Form joined to Substantives"
4	*Izenkei* (*Kizenkei*) (*Jōkenkei*)	Perfect, Conditional, Conditional Definite
5	*Meireikei*	Imperative

It should be noted that the order and nomenclature of these forms are not yet wholly standardized among grammarians, even in Japan.

In this book the order is that of standard Japanese grammars. The enumeration of the *shūshikei* and *rentaikei* as Lines 3 and 3A is used because this book will probably be used mostly by students of the colloquial and in the colloquial there is no differentiation between these two forms. For the same reason, in treating the colloquial, reference to the *rentaikei* as a separate form is generally omitted. Owing to the great variety of English names, line-forms are identified in the text either by their Japanese names or by number.

The main text gives the uses of the suffixes which may be attached to the various line-forms, but something must be said about the uses of the line-forms by themselves, when they are not used as "bases" for suffixes:

Line 1. *Mizenkei*—This form is never used without suffixes (but see note under -TARA) .

Line 2. *Renyōkei*—This form may be used as a connective in forming compound words. When used without suffixes it performs two main functions:

(1) It may be used to end a clause, and at the same time indi-

cate that another clause is to follow.   For this use see the Special
Note in text under -TE.

   (2) It may be used as a noun.   When so used it may, like other
Japanese nouns, be used adverbially if the sense permits and the
context calls for it (e.g., *sono tōri* 'that way').   When used as a
noun it is usually written without the *kana* which show inflection.

   Line 3.   *Shūshikei*—This form is used by itself to end sentences.   When so used it is a simple declarative, and as it is not
primarily concerned with time it corresponds only approximately
to an English "present" tense.   Especially in bungo, it may also
be a substantive.   (See Introductory Note on Nomenclature.)

   Line 3A.   *Rentaikei*—The main use of this form is to modify
substantives.   Hence the name "adjectival."   It may, however,
itself act as a substantive.   It is sometimes used to end clauses and
sentences and is properly so used when these contain the particles
ka, ya, or *zo.*   It may also be used as a final verb in sentences ending with these particles or with *kana, kamo, namu,* or *wa,* and
occasionally at other times as well.

   Line 4.   *Izenkei*—In modern Japanese this form is used without suffixes only after the particle *koso.*   In old Japanese, or in
poetry, it may be used alone as a perfect tense.

   Line 5.   *Meireikei*—Strictly speaking, this always stands alone.
For certain verbs, however, the addition of exclamatory particles
such as *yo, ro,* or *i* has become so customary as to be requisite for
correct Japanese.

   For a much fuller treatment of these "bases" see G. B. Sansom's
"Historical Grammar of Japanese."

   The main use of the Line 3 form (*shūshikei*) is to end sentences.   The main use of the Line 3A form (*rentaikei*) is to
modify substantives or to act itself as a substantive.   In the colloquial, as there is no differentiation in form, the differentiation in
use tends to be obscured.

   One very obvious example of this occurs when a statement in
sentence form is followed by *no desu,* or various other phrases of
which the first component is the "substantivizer" *no* (e.g., *node,*
nonni).   From a strictly grammatical point of view it is perhaps
correct to say that the verb-form immediately preceding *no* is the
Line 3A form (*rentaikei*).   It is, however, undoubtedly the case

that many (and probably by far the most) Japanese feel that they have made a statement and then added something to it. In other words, they are treating the verb-form as if it were the Line 3 form (*shūshikei*), and it probably would not occur to one in a thousand to think about what form he actually was using. Cf. text under NO DESU, etc.

THE COLLOQUIAL CONJUGATIONS

I. Formation of "Bases"

From the manner in which their "bases" are formed, the vast majority of colloquial Japanese verbs fall into two categories. These may conveniently be distinguished as the first and second conjugations. There are only a very small number of colloquial verbs not in these categories, and such verbs can most easily be treated individually. In this book they are referred to as "irregular" verbs.

First Conjugation

The first conjugation is known to the Japanese as the *yodan* 'four-step' or 'four-vowel' conjugation, because it has four "bases" all with the same "root,"[2] but ending respectively with the four vowels *a, i, u,* and *e*. The "roots" all end with consonants.

Following is a table showing the pronunciation of the final syllables of all the "bases" of all verbs of the first conjugation. At the top of each column in parenthesis is given the final consonant with which each "root" ends.

Line		(K)	(G)	(B)	(N)	(M)	(T)	(H)	(R)	(S)
1	*Mizen*	-ka	-ga	-ba	-na	-ma	-ta	-wa	-ra	-sa
2	*Renyō*	-ki	-gi	-bi	-ni	-mi	-chi	-(h)i	-ri	-shi
3	*Shūshi*	-ku	-gu	-bu	-nu	-mu	-tsu	-(h)u	-ru	-su
4	*Izen*	-ke	-ge	-be	-ne	-me	-te	-(h)e	-re	-se

[2] "Root" is here used in a special sense, and only in default of a better word, to mean an unchanging (or practically unchanging) element which is found in all forms of a word. It is not here used with any etymological connotations.

It will be noted that except for the (H) column this table is simply a rearranged portion of the *kana* syllabary. In the (H) column the "h" seems to have been originally sounded. The present pronunciation does not sound the "h" at any time, and replaces it by "w" in the first line form. The (H) verbs are still written, however, with the *kana* symbols for *ha, hi, hu (fu)*, and *he*.

From this table we see that an (R) verb like *aru* 'be', has the four "bases" *ara, ari, aru* and *are*; a (T) verb like *matsu* 'wait', has the bases *mata, machi, matsu, mate*; an (H) verb like *omou* (*omohu*) 'think', has the bases *omowa, omoi, omou, omoe*; etc.

Second Conjugation

For the colloquial, what is here called the second conjugation[3] comprises a certain number of verbs whose Line 3 forms end in *-iru* and *-eru*.[4] Their conjugation is a somewhat shortened form of the first conjugation (R) column, in which the syllable *ra* is omitted from the Line 1 form, and *ri* from Line 2.

		-iru verbs	*-eru* verbs
Line 1 form	*Mizenkei*	*-i*	*-e*
Line 2 form	*Renyōkei*	*-i*	*-e*
Line 3 form	*Shūshikei*	*-i ru*	*-e ru*
Line 4 form	*Izenkei*	*-i re*	*-e re*

Japanese grammarians usually call these the *ichidan* 'one-step' or 'one-vowel' conjugations, distinguishing the *iru* verbs as *kami ichidan* 'upper one-step' and the *eru* verbs as *shimo ichidan* 'lower one-step'. They are so called because they are based on single vowels, *i* and *e*, and *i* comes above *e* in the *kana* table.

[3] Nomenclature of conjugations is not standardized. Often the *-iru* verbs are called the second conjugation and *-eru* verbs the third. The Japanese usually distinguish conjugations by the use of names rather than numbers.

[4] Note that not all verbs ending in *-iru* and *-eru* belong to the second conjugation. A good many (e.g., *hairu*) are (R) column verbs of the first conjugation. Comparatively few underived verbs belong to the second conjugation, but it includes all the potential, passive, and causative derived verbs. Cf. text on -ERU, -RARERU, -RERU, -SASERU, and -SERU.

TABLE I

Changes in end-syllables of the line-forms ("bases") of colloquial verbs

	First	Second Conjugation		Irregular Verbs				
	Yodan	*Kami Ichidan* (i, iru)	*Shimo Ichidan* (e, eru)	*Kuru* (come)	*Suru* (act, do)	*-masu* (polite suffix)	The five* *-aru* verbs	
Line 1 *Mizenkei*	-a	-i	-e	ko (ki)	se shi	-mase	-ara	1
Line 2 *Renyōkei*	-i	-i	-e	ki	shi	-mashi	-ari -ai	2
Line 3 *Shūshikei* (Line 3A *Rentaikei*)	-u	-iru	-eru	kuru	suru	-masu (-masuru)	-aru	3
Line 4 *Izenkei*	-e	-ire	-ere	kure	sure	-masure (-mase)	-are	4
Line 5 *Meireikei*	-e	-i (yo)	-e (yo)	koi	shi (yo) se (yo)	-mase -mashi	-are -ai	5

*The five *-aru* verbs are *gozaru* 'be', *nasaru* 'do', *kudasaru* 'give (down)', *ossharu* 'say', and *irassharu* 'be', 'be present', etc. They can hardly be properly called "irregular," and are best thought of as regular first conjugation verbs which have an additional form ending in *-ai*. This form is commonly used for the *renyōkei* and the imperative.

Examples of the use of this table show *taberu* 'eat' as having the bases or line-forms *tabe, tabe, taberu, tabere*; *iru* 'be' as having the bases *i, i, iru, ire,* etc.

Irregular Verbs

In the colloquial the only verbs which are properly called "irregular" are *suru* 'do', *kuru* 'come', and the suffix *-masu*. The five old formal and polite *-aru* verbs *gozaru, nasaru, kudasaru, ossharu,* and *irassharu* are regular *yodan* verbs which happen to have an alternative base-form. Their "base" changes are as follows:

		Suru	*Kuru*	*-masu*	The five *-aru* verbs
Line 1	*Mizenkei*	se, shi	ko (*ki*)	*-mase*	*-ara*
Line 2	*Renyōkei*	shi	ki	*-mashi*	*-ari, -ai*
Line 3	*Shūshikei*	suru	kuru	*-masu* (*-masuru*)	*-aru*
Line 4	*Izenkei*	sure	kure	*-masure* (*-mase*)	*-are*

It will be noticed that there are alternative forms for Line 1 of *suru,*[5] and *kuru.*[6] The five *-aru* verbs are conjugated as regular first conjugation (R) column verbs, with one exception, namely that there is an alternative Line 2 form *-ai.* This alternative form is the one generally used. The form *-masuru* is rather unusual, and is particularly formal and humble or "humilific." The form *-mase,* instead of *-masure,* occurs in several dialects, including the

[5] The *shi* is apparently really a Line 2 form, which acts as a Line 1 form in taking the suffixes *-nai* and *-yō.* It must also be noted that there seems to be a growing tendency in the colloquial to treat the conjugation of verbs compounded with *suru* as if it were that of a regular first conjugation verb ending in *-su.* Thus Line 1 sometimes becomes *-sa,* and Line 4 occasionally becomes *-se.* Even Line 3 may become *-su.* This development is frowned on by strict grammarians, but nevertheless seems to be taking place.

[6] The *ki* form of Line 1 is not accepted as correct by most grammarians. Nevertheless such a form as *kinai* may occasionally be heard, even from well-educated speakers.

one now used at the Peers' College. For negatives of *-masu*, such as *-masen,* see the main text under *-MASU.*

2. Imperative Forms

For verbs of the first (*yodan*) conjugation the imperative form (*meireikei*) is the same as the Line 4 form (*izenkei*).

For verbs of the second (*ichidan*) conjugation the imperative is the Line 1 form (*mizenkei*), plus some syllable which acts as a verbal exclamation mark. This syllable is usually *yo,* but may be *ro* or *i* or *ya.*

The imperative of *suru* may be *shiyo, shiro, seyo, sero* and occasionally *sei.* The common colloquial imperative of *kuru* is *koi.* For *-masu* there are two imperatives, *-mase* and *-mashi.*

The five irregular *-aru* verbs commonly have their imperative ending in *-ai.* The regular but rather old-fashioned imperative ending in *-are* is, however, still occasionally heard.

Note that the general rule requires the addition of at least one exclamatory syllable to imperatives of *kuru, suru,* and all verbs of the second conjugation. Such syllables may be added to all imperatives if desired, and sometimes more than one syllable is added.

The one exception to this rule is *kure,* which is the Line 1 form of *kureru,* and is commonly used as an imperative without an added syllable, apparently because its function is the same as that of the more polite *kudasai.*

Thus we have both standard and permissible forms, of which the following are examples:

	Standard	With extra syllable	
1st conjugation (*yodan*)	*kake*	*kake-ro*	Write!
	yobe	*yobe-yo*	Call!
2nd conjugation (*ichidan*)	*tabeyo*	*tabe-ro-ı*	Eat!
	miro	*miyo-i*	Look!
Irregular verbs	*nasai*	*nasai-yo*	
	nasare	*nasare-i*	Do!
	nasaimase	*nasaimase ya*	
	nasaimashi	*nasaimashi yo*	

Strictly speaking, the extra syllables are not part of the imperative "form," but are simply exclamatory particles. This is true
even for the second conjugation verbs. Thus the original imperative "Eat!" was simply *tabe,* and the present need for having an
extra syllable is the result of a custom which has hardened into a
rule. It should be added that even today the "rule" is not always
observed, though if plain forms like *tabe* or *mi* are employed as
imperatives the feeling is that an extra syllable has been delib-
erately omitted.

Occasionally forms like *mire* 'look!' or *tabere* 'eat!' may be
heard. It is hard to say whether these are to be regarded as imperatives in which the *re* is a verbal exclamation mark, like *yo* or
ro, or whether these are Line 4 forms used as imperatives after the
analogy of the first (*yodan*) conjugation verbs. For negative imperatives see the text under NA and NAKARE.

3. Sound Changes with the -TE and -TA Suffixes

The suffixes *-te, -ta, -tara,* and *-tari* are always added to the
Line 2 form (*renyōkei*) of verbs. In the colloquial these com-
binations are usually contracted.[7] See text for the use of -TE,
-TA, -TARA, -TARI.

"Official" Contractions

In the official (Tokyo) colloquial the following contractions
are standard. For verbs of the first conjugation ending in:

-ku,	*-kite*	and	*-kita*	contract to	*-ite*	and	*-ita*
-gu,	*-gite*	and	*-gita*	contract to	*-ide*	and	*-ida*
-bu,	*-bite*	and	*-bita*	contract to			
-nu,[8]	*-nite*	and	*-nita*	contract to	*-nde*	and	*-nda*
-mu,	*-mite*	and	*-mita*	contract to			

---

[7] The sound changes which take place are not always "contractions"
in the strict sense of the word. However, the term is in common use,
and is retained here because of its convenience. Students should note
that the standard "contractions" are written in Japanese with the same
number of *kana* as the uncontracted forms. For example, *-tte* is written
with two *kana, tsu* and *te;* *-nde* with two *kana,* n and *de;* etc.

[8] There is only one *-nu* verb in the colloquial. This is *shinu* 'die'.

-tsu,	-chite	and	-chita	contract to		
-(h)u,	-(h)ite	and	-(h)ita	contract to	-tte	and -tta
-ru,	-rite	and	-rita	contract to		

The *-tara* and *-tari* suffixes contract in the same way as *-ta*, e.g., *kakitari* contracts to *kaitari*; *aritaraba* to *attaraba*; etc. Note that there are only four types of standard contractions.

The verbs *yuku* and *iku* 'go' both contract irregularly to *itte* and *itta*, etc. These two verbs may be regarded as simply two pronunciations of the same verb. *Iku* is the present "official" pronunciation.

As examples, for the sake of simplicity taking the *-te* forms only[9]:

Line 3 form	Uncontracted -te form	Contracted -te (or -de) form
kaku 'write'	*kakite*	*kaite*
kagu 'sniff'	*kagite*	*kaide*
erabu 'choose'	*erabite*	*erande*
shinu 'die'	*shinite*	*shinde*
kamu 'bite'	*kamite*	*kande*
katsu 'win'	*kachite*	*katte*
ka(h)u 'buy'	*ka(h)ite*	*katte*
karu 'reap'	*karite*	*katte*

The five *-aru* verbs *gozaru, irassharu, kudasaru, ossharu,* and *nasaru* make their contractions as if they were regular *-ru* verbs of the first (*yodan*) conjugation.

There are, however, a good many irregular variations. For instance, we have *nasutte* or *nas'tte* for *nasatte, irashitte* or *irashite* for *irasshatte, kudasutta* or *kudass'ta* for *kudasatta*, etc. It is impossible to give here a complete list of all the local variations. If the student knows they exist and is on the lookout for them, they should cause him no trouble.

It will be noticed that for the standard Tokyo dialect there are no *-te* and *-ta* contractions for *-su* (S) verbs of the first conjuga-

---

[9] The *-te* forms, uncontracted, are found in bungo without further suffixes; the *-ta* forms, however, are derived from bungo forms which are uncontracted, but end in *-tari* or *-taru*; e.g., *kaita* from *kakitaru*.

tion, for any verbs of the second conjugation, nor for *suru, kuru,* or *-masu.*

"Non-Official" or Special Contractions

There are a few non-Tokyo contractions which should be noted. The most important of these is probably the Kyoto (*Kansai*) treatment of (H) verbs. This consists in contracting *-(h)ite* and *-(h)ita* to *-ute* and *uta,* instead of the Tokyo (*Kantō*) contractions *-tte* and *-tta.* For example, the *-te* and *-ta* forms of *kau* 'buy' become *kaute* and *kauta* (pronounced *kōte* and *kōta*) .[10]

For verbs such as *tamau* (*tama(h)u*), which are traditionally connected with the speech of the Kyoto Imperial Court, the Kyoto contraction is standard. For example, even in Tokyo, *tamaute,* not *tamatte,* is the standard contraction of *tama(h)ite.* For other (H) verbs the Kyoto contraction is not "standard," but is often used.

Other important *Kansai* contractions affect the *-riru* verbs of the second conjugation, and the *-mu* (M) verbs of the first. In the *Kansai* (i.e., Western Japan) *-rite* and *-rita* contract to *-tte* and *-tta* for second as well as first conjugation verbs. For example, the second conjugation verb *kariru* 'borrow' 'rent' in the Tokyo speech has the uncontracted *-te* form *karite,* but in Kyoto this is contracted to *katte.*

The *-mu* verbs contract *-mite* and *-mita* to *-ude* and *-uda.* For example, the uncontracted *-te* form of *yomu* 'read' is *yomite.* The standard Tokyo contraction is *yonde,* but in Kyoto one often hears the contraction *youde.*

Two other local contractions are perhaps important enough to be mentioned. Both occur in first conjugation verbs only. The *-bu, -nu,* and *-mu* (B, N, M) verbs are sometimes contracted to *-nte* and *nta* instead of the standard Tokyo *-nde* and *-nda.* The standard colloquial forms *-shite* and *-shita* will in certain Western dialects be contracted to *-ite* and *-ita.*

	Standard	Dialect
from *yomu* 'read'	*yonde*	*yonte*
from *kurasu* 'subsist'	*kurashite*	*kuraite*

[10] Note that *-ute* and *-uta* are written with the *kana* for *u,* not *(h) u.*

THE BUNGO OR "LITERARY" CONJUGATIONS

I. Formation of Bases

For bungo the first conjugation is the same as that of the collo-quial. There are, however, marked differences in the second con-jugation and in the irregular verbs.

The second conjugation in bungo consists of four parts, namely the *kami ichidan* and *shimo ichidan,* which are the same as in the colloquial (see p. 15), and also the *kami nidan* and *shimo nidan* (i.e., the "upper two-step" and "lower two-step" variations), which are slightly more complicated.

The *nidan* line-forms are:

		Kami nidan	*Shimo nidan*
Line 1	*Mizenkei*	-i	-e
Line 2	*Renyōkei*	-i	-e
Line 3	*Shūshikei*	-u	-u
Line 3A	*Rentaikei*	-uru	-uru
Line 4	*Izenkei*	-ure	-ure
Line 5	*Meireikei*	-i (*yo*)	-e (*yo*)

They are called *nidan* 'two-step' or 'two-vowel' conjugations be-cause each is based on two vowels—*i* and *u* for *kami, e* and *u* for the *shimo.*

The only common *kami ichidan* verbs in bungo are *miru* 'see,' *kiru* 'wear,' *niru* 'resemble,' *niru* 'boil,' *hiru* 'dry,' *iru* 'shoot,' and *iru* 'be.' [11] The only *shimo ichidan* verb in bungo is *keru* 'kick.' Only these verbs and verbs of the first conjugation have exactly the same forms in both bungo and the colloquial.

In bungo all other second conjugation verbs are *nidan* verbs. Nearly all of these correspond fairly closely to colloquial second conjugation (*ichidan*) verbs.

The relation of the colloquial *ichidan* (*-iru* and *-eru*) verbs and their bungo *nidan* counterparts is shown in the following table, in which the Line 3 (dictionary) form of the colloquial verb is given at the top of each column.

[11] Matsuura lists as also sometimes conjugated as *kami ichidan* verbs *iru* 'cast', *hiru* 'winnow', and under special conditions *iru* 'pour' and *hiru* 'sneeze'. Compounds like *kokoromiru* remain *ichidan*. A few verbs, e.g. *mochiiru,* may be either *ichidan* or *nidan*.

The general rule is that the Line 1, 2, and imperative forms (*mizenkei, renyōkei,* and *meireikei*) remain the same in both colloquial and bungo.

The colloquial -*iru* or -*eru* (Line 3, 3A forms) each corresponds to two bungo line-forms, namely, a Line 3 form -*u*, and a Line 3A form -*uru*. The colloquial -*ire* or -*ere* (Line 4 forms) correspond to a bungo Line 4 form -*ure*.

Line	(*Kariru*	*Ochiru*	*Mochiiru*	*Taberu*	*Mieru*)
1	*kari*	*ochi*	*mochii*	*tabe*	*mie*
2	*kari*	*ochi*	*mochii*	*tabe*	*mie*
3	*karu*	*otsu*	*mochiyu*	*tabu*	*miyu*
3A	*karuru*	*otsuru*	*mochiyuru*	*taburu*	*miyuru*
4	*karure*	*otsure*	*mochiyure*	*tabure*	*miyure*
Imp.	*kari* (*yo*)	*ochi* (*yo*)	*mochii* (*yo*)	*tabe* (*yo*)	*mie* (*yo*)

For verbs of the *ochiru* type, note that *chi* and *tsu,* as *kana,* both belong to the (T) column. The bungo counterparts of verbs like *mochiiru* and *mieru* have a "y" sound supplied before the -*u*, -*uru* and -*ure* forms, which are both written and pronounced as -*yu*, -*yuru* and -*yure*.

In bungo the irregular[12] verbs are *ku* 'come' (colloquial *kuru*), *su* 'do' (colloquial *suru*), *shinu* 'die' (colloquial *shinu,* regular), *inu* 'sleep', *ari* 'be' (colloquial *aru*), *ori* 'be' (colloquial *oru*), and *haberi* 'get'. To these may be added *nari* 'be' (*ni ari*), and *imazukari* 'be'. When *su* in combinations is pronounced in a sonant form as *zu,* it of course retains its conjugation.

The irregular conjugations are:

Line		*Ku*	*Su*	*Shinu, inu*	*Ari, ori, haberi* (*nari, imazukari*)
1	*Mizenkei*	*ko*	*se*	-*na*	-*ra*
2	*Renyōkei*	*ki*	*shi*	-*ni*	-*ri*
3	*Shūshikei*	*ku*	*su*	-*nu*	-*ri*
3A	*Rentaikei*	*kuru*	*suru*	-*nuru*	-*ru*
4	*Izenkei*	*kure*	*sure*	-*nure*	-*re*
5	*Meireikei*	*koyo*	*se* (*yo*)	-*ne*	-*re*

[12] "Irregular" is here used as meaning "not belonging to the first or second conjugations."

TABLE II

Changes in end-syllables ("bases") of bungo verbs

| | First | Second Conjugation | | | | Irregular Verbs | | | |
	Yodan	Kami Ichidan	Kami Nidan	Shimo Ichidan	Shimo Nidan	Ku (cf. with the colloquial kuru)	Su (cf. with the colloquial suru)	Inu and Shinu	Ari Ori Haberi (Nari)*
Line 1 Mizenkei	-a	-i	-i	-e	-e	ko	se	-na	-ra
Line 2 Renyōkei	-i	-i	-i	-e	-e	ki	shi	-ni	-ri
Line 3 Shūshikei	-u	-iru	-u	-eru	-u	ku	su	-nu	-ri
Line 3A Rentaikei	-u	-iru	-uru	-eru	-uru	kuru	suru	-nuru	-ru
Line 4 Izenkei	-e	-ire	-ure	-ere	-ure	kure	sure	-nure	-re
Line 5 Meireikei	-e	-i (yo)	-i (yo)	-e (yo)	-e (yo)	ko(yo)	se (yo)	-ne	-re

*Nari is equivalent to ni plus ari. Some grammarians add to this column the verb imazukari, (imasukari, imazokari), an old word now wholly obsolete.

It will be noticed that only *ku* (*kuru*), and *su* (*suru*) are irregular in both bungo and colloquial Japanese.

In bungo *masu* is an independent verb meaning "be". It is not irregular but conjugates both in the manner of *su* (*suru*) and as a regular *-su* (S) verb of the first conjugation.

Quite a number of bungo verbs belong to two conjugations. At least one (*owasu*) may be properly conjugated in three ways (i.e., like *suru, yodan,* or *shimo nidan*).

Contractions

Strictly speaking, there are no contractions of verb-forms in modern bungo.

In the older bungo, however, we do find sound changes which are very much like the modern colloquial contractions with the suffixes *-te* and *-ta*. (See pp. 19 ff.)

Sound changes with other suffixes also occur, but are comparatively rare. We may, for instance, find *-i* replacing a *-ki* or *-shi* sound, as *yarubei* for *yarubeki*. The most common is the change of a Line 2 form (*renyōkei*) *-hi* to *-u* before forms of the suffixes *-tsu, -nu, -ki, -keri,* or *-tari*, such as, *shitamaushi* for *shitama-(h)ishi,* etc.

2. Imperatives

The forms for these are given in the fifth line of the tables (*meireikei*). The addition of extra syllables (e.g., *yo, ro*) follows the same rules as for the colloquial, except that *i* is not used.

NOTE ON

Aru, Iru, and Oru

These three common colloquial verbs correspond approximately to the English verb "be." However, the correspondence is by no means exact. In English, "be" expresses two main groups of ideas, i.e., those of existence and, when used as a copula, those of equality or identity. The Japanese use special forms for the copula, and also further differentiate between *aru, iru,* and *oru.*

Oru 'be' and *iru* 'be' are very much alike, save that *oru* is somewhat more formal.[1] *Aru* 'be', however, is markedly different from the other two.

The main difference is that *iru* and *oru* not only have the meaning of "be," but also suggest certain other ideas connected with continuation and action. *Aru* means simply "be," "exist," and is wholly divorced from any of the above suggestions.

Students should take notice, however, that the above distinction has not yet been accepted by all grammarians. It is derived from a consideration of the following usages:

1. Of the three only *aru* may be used in expressing the copula in an equation idea such as "A is B," where A and B are substantives. In colloquial Japanese this is rendered by the form A *wa* B *de aru.* See DE ARU in text.

---

[1] *Oru* belongs to the first conjugation, *iru* to the second. They both, however, are written with the same Chinese character, 居.

Kore wa hon de aru[2]   This is a book.

Tanaka san wa dokushinsha   Mr. Tanaka is a bachelor.
de aru[2]

2. Of the three, only *aru* may be used to express a statement of
simple existence.

Pen ga aru[3]   There is a pen.

Ano hito ni wa pen ga aru[3]   To him there is a pen (i.e., He
                                 has a pen).

Ano hito ni wa ii musuko ga   To him there is a fine son (i.e.,
aru[3]   He has a fine son).

Iru and *oru* are used when to the statement of mere existence is
added a further idea of life or movement.

Koko ni tori ga oru   Here birds are (i.e., live).

There is consequently a certain validity in the old rule: "Use *aru*
for inanimate objects; use *iru* and *oru* for living beings." Note,
however, that strictly speaking the distinction is rather between
objects "thought of as inanimate" and those "thought of as living." Hence *aru* will be used in such sentences as:

Boku no hoka ni wa okyaku ga   There was another guest be-
atta   sides me.

[2] What is said here about *aru, oru,* and *iru* is also true of their *-masu*
forms, *arimasu, orimasu,* and *imasu.* The distinctions noted are not
always observed with absolute strictness, however, when one uses the
very polite verbs which are their approximate equivalents, e.g., *gozaru,
orareru, irassharu,* etc. For example, a woman may quite properly say
Donata sama de irasshaimasu ka as a polite form for "Who are you?"
Here *irasshaimasu* could be replaced by *arimasu,* but not by *imasu* or
orimasu. Note that *irassharu* is frequently used as if it were a "polite"
form of *iru* 'to be', though grammatically it is derived from *iraseraru*—
a "polite" form of *iru* 'to enter'.

[3] The Japanese use two Chinese characters for writing *aru.* Technically, the character which has the Sino-Japanese sound *zai* 在 should
only be used for *aru* when *aru* conveys the idea of "being somewhere."
(Cf. NI in text.) The Sino-Japanese *yu, u* 有 should be used in the
above sentences, where *aru* has its pure sense of simple "being." It is of
interest to note that this same character is often used in writing the
word *motsu* 'possess'.

or; for instance, in starting a fairy tale, as:

Mukashi mukashi ojiisan ga   Once upon a time there was
arimashita   an old man.

where the fact that the subject of the verb happens to be a living
being is not a primary fact in the mind of the speaker or writer.
If the fairy tale were continued with a sentence such as: "This
old man lived (or was) in Suruga," *iru* or *oru* would have to be
used, as *"Kono ojiisan wa Suruga ni orimashita."*

In the same way, when inanimate objects are thought of as very
intimately connected with life or movement, we may find *iru* and
oru being used, as in the common phrase:

Jidōsha ga imasu   (Your) car is (here) (i.e., has
                         arrived at the door).

Precisians say that this use of *iru* is not "good" Japanese, but it is
"good" Japanese in sentences such as:

Donna hanzai demo bassera- Any crime whatever will not
rezu ni wa inai   go unpunished.

where *iru* is used instead of *aru* because it is obvious that, whatever the form of the sentence, it is the criminal behind the crime
who will really be punished.[4]

As a further example the student is asked to compare the sentence from section 1:

Tanaka san wa dokushinsha Mr. Tanaka is a bachelor.
de aru

with:

Tanaka san wa dokushin de Mr. Tanaka lives in a state of
oru   celibacy.

3. *Oru* and *iru* may be used as true auxiliaries following the
-te and *-de* forms of other verbs. When so used they indicate
continuation of the action or state predicated.

[4] Mr. Matsumiya, of the School of Japanese Language and Culture in
Tokyo, has made the interesting suggestion that *iru* and *oru* express
"subjective being," while *aru* expresses "objective being." In other
words, that when *iru* or *oru* is used, the speaker or writer is at least to
some extent identifying himself with his subject and giving its viewpoint; when *aru* is used he is regarding it purely from his own viewpoint.

Chizu wo kabe ni kakete iru   (He) is hanging maps on the wall.

Chizu ga kabe ni kakatte iru   Maps are hanging on the wall.

Aru can never be a true auxiliary, at least in the English sense. After the *-te* or *-de* form of "transitive" verbs (e.g., *kakeru*), the two verbs do not have the same subject. The subject of the *aru* is the object of the transitive verb.

Chizu ga kabe ni kakete aru   Maps are hung on the wall (i.e., they are where hung by some outside agency).

Perhaps it is simpler to consider that in the above sentence the *kakete* is used as if it were an adverb. A perfectly good sentence remains if it is omitted.[5]

According to the dictates of strict grammarians *aru* cannot be used after the *-te* and *-de* forms of "intransitive" verbs.[6] Nevertheless it apparently is sometimes so used. It is quite possible to hear a conversation like:

Jidōsha wa doko da—Mada konai ka   Where's the car? Hasn't it come yet?

Hai—Kite arimasu   Yes, sir. It has come, and it is here.

[5] This point is controversial among Japanese grammarians, some of whom go so far as to say that in such sentences the *ga* does not mark the subject, but is simply a substitute for *wo*. They apparently mean that the original thought was of the order "(somebody) hung maps on the wall—and there they are." Note also that in such sentences it makes no difference whether the subject is animate or inanimate. E.g.:

Akambo mo kabe ni kakete aru   The baby too is hung on the wall.

[6] The conceptions of "transitive" and "intransitive" as we use them for English verbs are foreign to Japanese thought and hence not in all respects strictly applicable to Japanese verbs. The terms are used here for the sake of simplicity. As used here verbs like *deru* 'go out', *aruku* 'walk', etc., are counted as intransitive in spite of the fact that we have forms like *ie wo deru* 'go out from the house', *machi wo aruku* 'walk on the street', etc. See wo in text. The Japanese make the division between *tadōshi* 'other-moving-words', which corresponds more or less to transitive verbs, and *jidōshi* 'self-moving-words'.

In such instances, however, the *aru* form is used to make an independent statement of fact, and not as an auxiliary verb.

CONTRACTIONS OF "IRU" AND "ARU"

After a *-te* or *-de* in the colloquial the *i* of *iru* is often elided, particularly when the *iru* does not end a sentence. For example, *motte iru* becomes *motteru*, *yonde iru* becomes *yonderu*, etc.

When *-te* and *-de* forms are followed by *aru*, in certain dialects the *e* will be elided. For example, *oite aru* becomes *oitaru*. See also under -TARU in the main text.

Aru and its *-masu* form *arimasu*, including their agglutinated forms, are so constantly used with the postposition *de* that certain contractions have become standard. The most important are listed below:

Aru		Arimasu	
de aru	da (*ja*)	de arimasu	desu
de arō	darō (*jarō*)	de arimashō[7]	deshō[7]
de atta	datta	de arimashita	deshita
de attara	dattara	de arimashitara	deshitara
de atte	datte	de arimashite	deshite

It might also be of interest to list some of the contractions of *de gozarimasu*, which may be considered as a very polite form of *de aru*.

de gozaimasu	de gozesu	de gasu
de gozāsu	de gonsu	de gesu
de gozansu	de gwasu	de asu
de gozaesu	de gāsu	de esu
de go ansu	de wasu	desu
de gowansu	de gansu	dosu (Kyōto)
de go asu	de geisu	dasu (Ōsaka)
	de gosu	

[7] In these words the *-shō* is usually written with the *kana* for *se-u*. (せう.)

NOTE ON

Adjectives

Japanese grammarians class both verbs and adjectives together as *yōgen*, that is, words whose terminations may be changed. From the so-called "adjective terminations" they have even made a "conjugation" corresponding to the verb conjugations given in the last section.

Following is a table of the end-syllables of this conjugation for both colloquial and bungo adjectives. These end-syllables are added to an unchanging "adjective root."[1] The colloquial conjugation is often called the *ku-i-kere* conjugation.

			Colloquial	Bungo
Line 1	form	*Mizenkei*	(-*ku*)	-*ku*
Line 2	form	*Renyōkei*	-*ku*	-*ku*
Line 3	form	*Shūshikei*	-*i*	-*shi*
Line 3A	form	*Rentaikei*	-*i*	-*ki*
Line 4	form	*Izenkei*	-*kere*	-*kere*

[1] "Root" is here used, as with verbs, in default of a better word, to mean an unchanging (or practically unchanging) element in the present language. It does not necessarily indicate the original form. It is normally an unchanging element, e.g., *shiro* 'white', in *shiroi, shiroku, shiroshi, shiroki, shirokereba*, etc. It may, however, sometimes undergo slight euphonic changes, especially in compounds such as *shiraho* 'white sails', *shirayuki* 'white snow', etc.

Line 5, the imperative, does not exist. The bungo suffix -*shi* does not have to be added to those adjective roots which themselves end with the syllable -*shi* or -*ji*. For such adjectives the root itself may be used as a sentence-ending form in bungo.

There are certain advantages in treating adjectives in this way, and it is well for the student to know that they can be so treated. For the purpose of the present book, however, the advantages are outweighed by the disadvantages.

For foreign students it is simpler to consider pure Japanese adjectives as consisting of an unchanging root combined with certain suffixes. There are quite a number of suffixes which may be added, but only -*i*, -*ki*, -*ku*, and -*u* make words which are true adjectives in the English sense. Their use is indicated in the table below, and treated more fully in the body of the text. (See -I, -KI, -KU, -U.)

Short Table for "Adjective Roots" and a Few Common Suffixes

(Aka 'red' is used as an example.)

Root: (*aka*)	An "adjective root" is an unchanging form to which various suffixes may be added. For our purpose here it may be defined as what remains after removing the final -*i* from the dictionary form of an adjective. Some adjective roots have independent existence as nouns; others have not. All adjective roots, however, may be used without suffixes in emotional expressions such as *Aa, atsu!* 'What heat!' (from *atsui*) and *Aa, ita!* 'Oh, it hurts!' (from *itai*).
Root plus -*i*: (*akai*)	An exclusively colloquial form. A true adjective form when modifying nouns. (Cf. -*ki*, below.) When this form closes a sentence it includes the idea "be" and is equivalent to a verb in the Line 3 form (*shūshikei*) or "sentence-ending" form. (Cf. -*shi* below.)

Root plus -ku: (akaku)	The so-called adverb form. This and the -u form are the only forms used immediately before verbs, where they may be either adjectives or adverbs. At the end of clauses this acts as a continuative verb-form, and for certain words of measurement it may express a substantive idea.
Root plus -u: (akau, akō)	The regular form before certain verbs, of which the most important is gozaru. (In the Kansai -ku is regularly replaced by -u.) Regular pronunciations are:

$$
\begin{array}{ll}
-au & \bar{o} \\
-iu & \bar{u} \\
-uu & \bar{u} \\
-ou & \bar{o}
\end{array}
$$

(There is no root ending in -e except perhaps -be. See -BE in text.)

Root plus -ki: (akaki)	The standard bungo adjective form used to modify substantives. Also occasionally used as a noun. (In the colloquial -ki becomes -i.)
Root plus -shi: (akashi)	The standard bungo form for ending sentences. This includes the idea "be" and is definitely a verb, and as a verb may be considered to be in the Line 3 form or shūshikei. (In the colloquial -shi becomes -i.) Note, however, that -shi need not be added to roots which themselves end with either -shi or its sonant form -ji. For such words the root itself may be used as a verb, e.g., yoroshi, etc.
Root plus -kere: (akakere)	A contraction of the -ku form and the verb are (Line 4 form of aru). See the following Conjugation of Adjectives.

Other suffixes also may be added to adjective roots, but the resultant words will be nouns, verbs, etc., not true adjectives. See text for -GARU, -GE, -MI, -SA, etc.

The only important irregular adjective is *onaji* 'same', which is irregular in that it cannot take the colloquial suffix -*i*. For this word the root (*onaji*) is used as a true adjective. It can take the -*ku,* -*u,* and -*ki* suffixes. See also GOTOKI in text.

CONJUGATION OF ADJECTIVES

Adjective forms in -*i,* -*ku,* and -*shi* (bungo) may, as has been seen, include the idea of "be," and so be actually verbs.

Also, all adjectives in the -*ku* form may be conjugated by the addition of forms of the verb *aru* 'be'.

In the normal colloquial the various forms of *aru* (but not *arimasu*) contract with the -*ku* as shown in the following table:

	Uncontracted forms	Contracted forms	Example
Line 1	-ku ara	-kara	(*akakarau*)-*akakarō*
Line 2	-ku ari	-kari	(*akakarita*)-*akakatta*[2]
Line 3, 3A	-ku aru		See note[3]
Line 4	-ku are	-kere	(*akakereba*)

The special form -*ku arite* becomes -*kute,* e.g., (*akakarite*) -*akakute.*[2] The contraction to -*katte*[2] seems nowadays to be used almost entirely by women.

It should be added that the -*kute* form is likely to be hardened to -*kutte* in Tokyo (*Kantō*) speech, and softened to -*ute* in the Kyoto (*Kansai*) dialect. For example:

Uncontracted form	*akaku atte*
Standard contraction	*akakute*
Kantō dialect	*akakutte*
Kansai dialect	*akaute* (*akʼote*)

The negative is formed by the addition to the -*ku* form of the verb *nai,* which does not contract with it.[4]

[2] It is all right to consider these forms as contractions of *akaku atta* and *akaku atte,* if desired. The historical development is questionable.

[3] No contraction of -*ku aru* is used. In the usual colloquial the -*i* form takes its place (but see NO DESU).

[4] The negatives -*aranu* and -*arazu* are primarily bungo forms, but are occasionally used in the colloquial. When so used, the -*u* is usually elided in speech, to give the sounds -*aran* and -*araz.*

The verb *nai,* and the suffixes *-nai* and *-tai* are all adjectives in form, and may be conjugated by adding forms of *aru* to their *-ku* forms with the same contractions as above.

nakereba	if not or when not be
kikitakute	wishing to hear
kikitaku nakatta	did not wish to hear, etc.

It may be added that the negative has also the special forms *naide* and *-nanda.* See text under NAIDE and -NANDA.

QUASI-ADJECTIVES

Japanese, like English, has methods for modifying nouns by using words or phrases which are adjectival but not true adjectives. Naturally, these methods do not correspond exactly with the English ones.

One method of showing that a word or phrase is to be used to characterize a noun is to mark the fact by using the postposition *no.* See the text under NO and the Note on Foreign Words.

All verbs, as has been noted, may be used to modify nouns, and a large class of quasi-adjectives is formed by using the bungo verb *naru* 'be' (*ni aru*) or its contraction *na* as a connective. See the text under -NA and -NARU, and for a comparison of the uses of *-na, -naru* and *no* the introductory Note on Foreign Words.

It should be noted that there are certain special true adjectives which may replace their *-i* and *-ki* suffixes by *-na.* Some of these are:

oki	*-i, -ki, -na, -naru*	big
chiisa	*-i, -ki, -na, -naru*	small
yawaraka	*-i, -ki, -na, -naru*	soft
shikaku	*-i, (-ki), -na, -naru*	square
manmaru	*-i, -ki, -na, (-naru)*	round
majika	*-i, -ki, -na, -naru*	very near
kimijika	*-i, -ki, -na, -naru*	very small
tejika	*-i, -ki, -na, -naru*	nearby
tezema	*-i, -ki, -na, -naru*	narrow
tebaya	*-i, -ki, -na, -naru*	agile

It will be noted that all of these "roots" except *shikaku* are of Japanese, not foreign, origin. Strictly speaking, in *shikakui* it is the *-i* which replaces the *-na* or *-naru*. There seems to be a growing tendency in the modern language to allow the interchange of *-na* and *-i* for other adjectives also.

VERBS USED ADJECTIVALLY

When verbs are used to modify nouns they are technically in the Line 3A form *(rentaikei)*. It is a question of nomenclature whether or not they should be called true adjectives.

It is important, however, to realize that when they are so used the verb is placed in an attributive relation to a substantive, but this relation is not defined exactly. The definition of the relation is, where necessary, accomplished by other methods.

Thus *shiranai hito* merely relates the idea "not know" to the idea "person," and does not formulate the relation precisely; so that according to the context, *shiranai hito* may mean either "a person who does not know," or "a person who is not known."

For further discussion see Sir G. B. Sansom's "Historical Grammar of Japanese," pp. 133*ff*.

NOTE ON

Foreign Words

A great many foreign words have been adopted into Japanese. The vast majority of these are of Chinese origin, but in comparatively recent times there has been considerable borrowing from European languages also.

These words might be nouns, verbs, adjectives, or adverbs. Each class had to receive a special treatment before it could be successfully used as an integral part of the Japanese language.

The general methods used for adopting foreign words were, and are, the following:

1. If a foreign word is to be used as a noun, it is taken over unchanged. It is put into relation with other words in the same way as other Japanese nouns. That is, it is followed by the same postpositions, etc.

Amerika e (. . . *made, kara, ga, wo,* etc.)

When nouns are followed by the postposition *no* in Japanese it usually indicates that they are to be used to characterize another noun. (See text under NO.) Consequently when foreign words are followed by the postposition *no* the combination may be regarded as a quasi-adjective.

Amerika no jidōsha   an American automobile
totsuzen no shitsumon   a sudden question

2. If a foreign word is to be used as an adverb, it is treated in the same way as a Japanese adverb. That is, it may be used alone, but if there is likely to be any doubt or confusion about its use it should be marked as an adverb by the addition of *ni* or *to*, or sometimes *de*. (See text for NI, TO and DE.)

shizen or *shizen ni*	naturally
shinsetsu ni	kindly
totsuzen, or *totsuzen ni,* or *totsuzen to*	suddenly

3. If a foreign word is to be used as a verb it is followed by some form of the verb *suru,* or by some equivalent word or expression conveying the idea of "do."

benkyō suru	to study, etc.

(Note that in *benkyō wo suru* 'to do study', *benkyō* is treated as a noun.)

4. If a foreign word is to be used as an adjective, it is treated slightly differently in bungo and in the colloquial.

(a) In bungo it is followed by *-naru* (*-ni aru*) or, occasionally, by *-taru* (*-to aru*). In bungo both these suffixes may be conjugated. (See text on -NARU and -TARU.)

shinsetsu-naru onna	kind women
Onna shinsetsu nari	The woman is kind.
yōyō-taru kawa	a wide river

(b) In the colloquial it is usually followed by *-na*, a contraction of *-naru*, as,

shinsetsu-na hito	a kind person

The form *-naru* (unconjugated) is used after monosyllables and a few other words, as *tan-naru* 'simple'. The suffix *-taru* (unconjugated) is also used occasionally, but even more rarely than in bungo. These forms modify nouns.

At the end of sentences to make a predicate adjective, the colloquial uses some form of *de aru* or its equivalents to replace the conjugated forms of *-naru* and *-taru* which are used in bungo.

Bungo:

Kawa yōyō tari   The river is wide.
Onna shinsetsu nari   (The) women are kind.

Colloquial:

Onna wa shinsetsu desu   (The) women are kind.
Ano hito no nakunatta   His death was very sudden.
no wa totsuzen deshita

Notice that the above rules apply when a foreign word "is to be used as" a noun, adjective, etc. What the word was in its original language is not of first importance. In Chinese one form of a word might, and usually did, have several uses, and these were not always clearly understood by the Japanese.

A modern English example may make this point clear. With us the word "love" is used both as a noun and as a verb. It has been adopted as a sort of slang in Japanese. Strictly speaking, *rabu suru* should mean "to love," and *rabu wo suru* "to make love," but apparently the expressions are used interchangeably.

Similarly, *raiku suru* should mean "to like," but the present compiler has heard a shop-assistant, apparently wishing to show off his meager knowledge of English, make use of the expression *raiku wo shimasu ka.* What he meant, of course, was "Do you like it?"

It might be added that the Japanese pronunciation of foreign words is of course usually unlike the original, and foreign words written in the *kana* syllabary are often very hard to identify.

Comparison of -na and no

In general, *-na* is used when the foreign word is felt to be an adjective, and *no* when it is felt to be a noun.

As this is primarily a matter of feeling, it seems impossible to formulate strict rules. For instance, after *shinsetsu* one commonly uses *-na* (e.g., *shinsetsuna hito* "a kind person"). But one may sometimes find *shinsetsu no hito,* which is practically equivalent to "a person of kindness."

DICTIONARY OF
PARTICLES, SUFFIXES, AND
OTHER CONNECTIVES

-A, -A A. A contraction, quite common in rather low-class colloquial speech, used more by men than by women.

It is derived from the addition of *wa* to words ending in *-a, -u, -e* and *-o* sounds. E.g.:

hana wa	becomes	*hana'a*
iru wa	becomes	*ira'a*
ore wa	becomes	*ora'a*
koto wa	becomes	*kota'a*

It is quite possible, even probable, that this form is a survival from the period when the particle *wa* was actually pronounced *ha*, as it is still written in *kana*, and consequently that it is not actually "derived" from *wa*. The question of historical order, however, may be disregarded for our present purposes. (See also -YA.)

-AA, -AA-. A lengthening of an *-a* sound, quite common in colloquial speech when emphasis is desired.

For example, if one is called to by somebody, one might respond by *nan da,* an equivalent of "What's that?", "Well?", etc.

If, however, one is hailing a distant person, one might well use the expression *nan daa-i,* an equivalent of "Hey, there!", "Hallo-o!", etc.

AIDA. Literary particle meaning "because" or "since." Its use is almost entirely confined to the epistolary style. Technically, it should follow the Line 3A form (*rentaikei*) of verbs.

In the colloquial *aida* is a noun meaning "interval." The literary use has points of resemblance to the English causal use of "as long as."

Jijō kaku no gotoku ni sōrō   Since such is the case . . .
aida . . .

Kaze fuku aida . . .   Because the wind is
Kaze fuki sōrō aida . . .   blowing . . .

In the colloquial it is never used as a particle meaning "because," but like many other nouns it may be used as an adverb, with or without a following *ni*. Thus *nagai aida ni hataraita* would mean "(he) worked for a long time."

-AKU. Suffix, somewhat irregularly added to verbs, making a new noun. It seems to be normally suffixed to Line 3 forms *(shūshikei)* from which the final *-u* is elided, and not uncommonly to the *-mu* ("future") form.

> *toraku*   capture (*toru* 'seize' plus *aku*)
> *miraku*   sight (*miru* 'see' plus *aku*)
> *mimaku*   a possible seeing (*mimu* 'may see' plus *aku*)

Aston suggests that *-aku* is itself a contraction of *aru koto*. For example, *iwaku = I (h) u aru koto* 'thing that is said', or *ieraku*, which is a more colloquial expression, presumably formed in the same way. (See -KEKU.)

Wa (ha) or *ba* (the sonant form of *ha*) is sometimes suffixed to an *-aku* form. This is usually done before direct quotations.

> *ieraku ba* . . .   as for what was said . . .
> *negawaku wa (ba)* . . .   as for what is desired . . .

The use of such *-aku* forms to introduce quotations, either with or without a following *wa* or *ba*, is unquestionably due to Chinese influence.

-ARERU. A form apparently derived from the combination of *aru* 'be', and *eru* 'get', 'be possible', through the form *ari-eru* (See -RARERU, -RERU.)

-ATARI. A suffix. It combines with what precedes it to make a phrase which is substantive in form, but which is often used adverbially. It is used in two ways:

1. After words of space and time *-atari* indicates vagueness. In this usage it seems to be related to the noun *atari* 'neighborhood'.

> *tsugi no nichiyō-atari*   about next Sunday
> *kochira-atari*   around about here

2. After words referring to persons it is equivalent to "per.' In this usage it seems to be more closely related to the verb *ataru* 'reach', 'touch'.

> *hitori-atari*   per person
> *ichinin-atari*   per person

BA. A particle, which lends a certain emphasis to what it follows. It is used in both bungo and the colloquial.

It may be considered as a sonant form of *wa* (*ha*), and at present is chiefly used after the postposition *wo*. For its use after an *-aku* form see -AKU.

To what extent it is connected with the *-ba* suffixed to verbs is still an open question.

Bungo: 彼は敵をば愛すれども、また愛国者なり

Kare wa teki wo ba aisuredomo   Although he does love the
  mata aikokusha nari   enemy, on the other hand
                                       he loves his country.

Colloquial: 師の恩をば忘れるな.

Shi no on wo ba wasureru na   Do not forget the benefits
                                  received from your teachers.

Kore wo ba kurage to iu   This is what is called a
これをばくらげという   jellyfish.

It is difficult to define the exact force of *ba*. Usually it appears to strengthen an emphasis which is also independently indicated either by the context or the tone of voice. Note that *Kore wo kurage to iu* would mean simply "This is called a jellyfish."

-BA. A suffix. It is added to various verb and adjective forms to make a new verb form. It may have the effect of "if," "when," or "because."

Careful distinction must be made between its uses in bungo and in the colloquial. In all its uses, however, *-ba* marks a condition which precedes, and which usually is a prerequisite for, the doing or taking effect of something else.

Note that *-ba* always comes at the end of a clause, and that it therefore also has the force of a conjunction.

For the special use of *-ba* in the combination *-ba koso*, see under KOSO.

THE COLLOQUIAL

In the colloquial *-ba* may be added to the Line 4 form (*izenkei*) of verbs including *-kere* (= *-ku are*); also occasionally to the negative suffixes *-nu* and *-zu* (see -ZU BA), and to the so-called "adverbial" suffix *-ku*. (For the combinations *-taraba* and *-daraba* see under -TARABA and -TARA.)

> If a *-ba* is found suffixed to a Line 1 form (*mizenkei*) it will be a bungo form. (See NARABA.) Note that forms like *areba koso* (see -BA KOSO) or *nareba* (from the bungo *ni areba*) are bungo forms. When they are used in speech, which does sometimes happen, they are not to be considered as colloquial forms, but as quotations from bungo. For their meaning, see the section on bungo.

Japanese grammarians say that this *-ba* always indicates a supposition about the present or the future, and shows that what follows is thought of as a necessary consequence of the act or condition supposed. On the whole, this rule seems to be correct, at least if we interpret the term "present" in the Japanese way and include the so-called "historical present" which actually refers to the past. Certain apparent exceptions to it are referred to in the following text.

How the force of this *-ba* is to be rendered in English depends on the context. As a general rule:

> Translate *-ba* as "if," whenever the reference is to a present state of affairs, or to a definite happening in the future.

> Translate *-ba* as "when," whenever the reference is to a happening in the past, or when it occurs in a general statement referring to either repeated acts or a continued condition.

It should be noted that this *-ba* does not necessarily indicate any doubt about a supposition regarding present conditions, and hence may sometimes include a suggestion of "since" or "because."

Kimi ga ikeba boku mo iku	If you go, I will go too (reference to single act).
	When you go, I go too (reference to repeated act).
Oyu ga atsuku nakereba ocha wa yoku demasen	If the water is not hot enough, the tea won't be good.
Anata wa tsukarete ite watakushitachi to isshoni dekaketaku nai naraba uchi ni ite mo yoroshii	If you are tired and do not want to come out with us, it is all right to stay at home.

47

-BA

Sakura ga sakeba mainichi nanzen to iu hito ga hanami ni ikimasu	When the cherries are in bloom, every day thousands and thousands of people go to view the blossoms.
Dare demo homerarereba ureshiku omou mono da	When anyone is praised, he feels pleased.
ikazuba . . . *ikaneba . . .* *ikanakereba . . .*	if not go . . .
mitakuba . . . *mitakereba . . .*	if wish to see . . .
nagakuba . . .	when long . . .

In general, foreigners do not have much difficulty in getting the "feel" of *-ba*. The following paragraphs refer to certain uses which might present some slight difficulty.

1. Note that some sentences are elliptical, and that in such sentences the second part does not always seem to be a necessary consequence of the condition marked by *-ba*. E.g.:

Empitsu ga motto hoshikereba sono hikidashi ni takusan haitte imasu	If you want more pencils there are plenty in that drawer.

Here there is an obvious omission of an idea that might be expressed by inserting the words " . . . and will go to the trouble of looking for them, you will find that . . ." (Cf. NI YOREBA.)

Other elliptical uses also usually correspond to similar usages in English. For example, as an answer to someone who has asked the price:

Nedan wo kikeba jū yen desu	If you ask the price, it is ten yen.

2. Remember that a "historical present" may be considered as as actual "present" from the point of view of the narrator. Hence we may have such sentences as:

Yoku mireba yoso no inu sa   When I looked carefully (1
                                   saw that) it was a strange
                                   dog.

Note that this is translated with the use of a past tense, as the
reference actually is to a past action. Even in the English idiom,
it is possible, however, to use a "historical present" and say
"When I look carefully, it is a strange dog."

> Strict grammarians say that -*ba* should not be used before a -*ta* form,
> and that instead of using *mireba* in such a sentence as *yoku mireba
> yoso no inu datta,* one should use *mitara* or *miru to.* Nevertheless,
> whether "incorrect" or not, -*ba* . . . -*ta* sentences are unquestionably
> used by some Japanese. The student should recognize the meaning
> of such sentences, but it is probably better for him not to use them
> himself.

3. Among the forms that sometimes bother students are the
double negatives connected by -*ba.*

Benkyō shinakereba ikenai   Must study.
Ikanakereba narimasen   Must go.

Note that -*nakareba naranai* and -*nakareba ikenai* are equivalent to "If not (do something) it won't do" or "it can't go," and
so have the sense of "must." The former is often replaced in
speech by -*nebanaran.* The usual forms with *suru* are *shinakereba
(shinakeriya)* and *seneba.*

4. There is a common usage with the verb repeated and followed by *hodo* or *dake,* which is quite normal, but which needs a
special translation in English. E.g.:

Mireba miru hodo rippa desu   The more I look at it, the
                                   more splendid I find it.

Literally of course this is: "When look, look-extent-up-to splendid it is."

5. Note that -*ba,* like the English "if," may be used for all kinds
of suppositions, whether or not they are known to be contrary to
fact. It may even be used when there is no doubt whatever that
the supposition is true.

Consider such sentences as:

Sō de areba ikō	If it's that way, I'll go.
Sō de areba iku	If that's the way it is, I'm going.

Both these sentences may be used, in both English and Japanese, even when there is no doubt in the speaker's mind that things are "that way." When so used, the meaning of the *-ba* (or "if") clauses becomes almost equivalent to "since it is that way."

To take a further example, consider the sentence:

Anna ni benkyō sureba tozen seikō suru	If you study like that naturally you succeed.

Such sentences have a general application. It depends on the context whether the best English translation uses "if" or "when," what tenses for the verbs are most applicable, etc.

6. There is also a special usage which developed from sentences in which the *-ba* verb is repeated in declarative form with the addition of the particle *mo*. This usage too may require a special translation.

The following examples should make this usage clear. Note that when a double *mo* is used, the supposition is taken as definitely true.

Anata ga ikeba watakushi mo ikimasu	If you go I will go too.
Tachi ga hikareba, me mo hikaru	If the sword glittered, the eyes did too (intimating that both glittered).
Tachi mo hikareba, me mo hikaru	Both the sword and the eyes glittered.
Shinrui mo nakereba tomodachi mo arimasen	He has neither relatives nor friends.

BUNGO

In bungo there is a sharp differentiation in the use of *-ba*, depending on the form to which it is added.

1. It may be added to the Line 1 form (*mizenkei*) of verbs, to the negative suffix *-zu,* or to the so-called "adverbial" suffix *-ku.*

In very early texts we find *-ba* suffixed to *-ka* and *-ke* forms which are obviously contractions of *-ku ara.* E.g.: *tōkaba* (*tōku araba, tōkaraba*) 'if far'; *nakeba* (*naku araba, nakereba*) 'if not'; etc.

When *-ba* is so used, the condition marked by it is always to be taken as a hypothesis, "a condition not already determined." It is therefore to be translated as "if" or "when," but without any suggestion of "since" or "because."

Atai towaraba ni yen nari	If the price is asked, it is two yen.
Tsuki wo miba kokoro sumamu	If (when) you see the moon, your heart will be serene.
Kōzan ni noboraba suzushikaramu	If (when) one climbs a high mountain, it will be cool there.
Kō araba otsu aran	If there is A there will be B.
Kaze fukaba nami tatamu	When the wind blows the waves rise.
Yukamu to omowaba yuke	If you feel like going, go!

2. It may be added to the Line 4 form (*izenkei*) of verbs.

In early texts we find *-ba* suffixed to a *-ke,* which is obviously a contraction of *-ku are.* E.g.: *tōkeba* (*tōku areba*) 'since it is far'.

When *-ba* is so used the condition marked by it is to be taken as an actual fact, a "condition already determined." It is therefore to be translated either as "when" or else as "since" or "because," depending on the context.

Haru tateba kiyuru kōri . . .	Ice that melts when spring comes . . .
Hi wo tomoshite mireba rokujū bakari no hōshi nari	When he kindled a light and looked, it was a priest about sixty years old.
Aki no higan wo sugureba yoru yōyaku nagashi	When one passes the autumn equinox, gradually the nights grow long.

Akatsuki yori ame fureba   Since it has been raining from
  onaji tokoro ni tomareri   early morning, I have stayed
                                    in the same place.

Tsuki wo mireba kokoro   Since I see the moon, my heart
  sumamu   will clear (become serene).

Ame yamaneba hito wo   Since the rain has not stopped
  towazu   I will not visit anyone.

Yukamu to omoeba yuke   Since you feel like going, go!

-BAE. Suffix, added to the Line 2 form (*renyōkei*) of verbs. It forms a new substantive.

It indicates an effectiveness (i.e., an effect on an audience, etc.) when the action of the verb takes place.

Migoto no dekibae ga   It should have a splendid
  itashimashō   effect when finished (a
Migoto-na dekibae deshō   splendid "finished" effect).

Kono' kimono wa kibae ga   This kimono is effective when
  suru nē   worn, isn't it?

It is connected with the verb *haeru* 'look well'; and a Chinese character originally meaning "flower" or "flourish." Compounds with nouns, such as *kokorobae,* have a somewhat different meaning. Such compounds, however, can usually be found in dictionaries.

BAKARI (-BAKARI). A noun-form often used as a suffix.

Basically it indicates that what precedes it is to be regarded as a standard of measurement. In general, after numbers or numerical phrases, it has the effect of "approximately" or "about"; after other words it gives the sense of limitation which is usually conveyed in English by "simply," "alone," "just," "nothing but," etc. The original sense of "measure" is retained far more strongly in bungo than in the colloquial.

Usually *-bakari* unites with whatever precedes it to make a new substantive. It should be noted that when this substantive is either a subject or a direct object postpositions to mark it as such are often omitted. Like certain other substantives, it may at times be used as an adverb.

For a comparison of *bakari* with *dake, hodo* and *-gurai,* see under DAKE.

It is generally conceded that *-bakari* is derived from *hakaru* 'to measure, calculate', etc., being a Line 2 form with the initial consonant sonant *(nigori)*. It is, however, an open question just how far *-bakari* is to be regarded as a noun, and how far as simply a suffix. In bungo it may be joined with either the sentence-ending (Line 3) or the attributive (Line 3A) form of verbs. It is found after the attributive *(-ki)* form of adjectives, but I have not been able to find any example of its use with the adjectival sentence-ending *-shi* form. Under the circumstances it has not seemed possible to decide whether or not a hyphen should be used in the Romanized form.

THE COLLOQUIAL

1. In general, the limiting effect of *bakari* is much like that of the English "only," except when it occurs after numerical phrases. The best English rendering, however, will naturally differ in different sentences. This rendering will often be done by means of words or phrases such as "simply," "merely," "alone," "just," "nothing but," etc., but not infrequently special renderings will be required, such as those suggested in the following examples:

Note that after verbs in sentence-ending form (Line 3, 3A) *-bakari* is often more a suffix to a whole clause than to an individual verb. Note also that a few bungo expressions, such as *ikabakari,* in the sense of "How great!" are still in colloquial use.

Watakushi bakari ni kudasareta	(He) gave it only to me.
Watakushi ni bakari kudasareta	(He) gave it to me only.
Watakushi-bakari iku no desu ka	Is it that I go alone?
Kore bakari desu	It is only this.
Kokoro-bakari no gochisō desu	It is entertainment meant only to show my good-will. (Suggesting, "Of course it does not amount to much in itself.")
Inochi-bakari wa otasuke wo	Only spare my life!
Eigo-bakari de naku, doitsugo mo dekiru	He knows not only English, but also German.

Ano ko wa karada bakari ōkikutemo karaakambo desu	That child is big as far as his body is concerned, but is an utter baby.
Yume ka to bakari yorokonde . . .	Rejoicing with the feeling that it must be a dream . . . (Literally, "Is it a dream? that-way-just rejoicing . . .")
Are wa shinda mono to bakari omotte otta	All along I had thought of him as dead.

The following examples illustrate the uses of *-bakari* after verb-forms:

Bukka wa agaru-bakari da	The prices do nothing but rise.
Kare wa namakeru-bakari da	He is just idle.
Hito no me wo odorokasu-bakari no ōishi . . .	Big stones that simply make people's eyes pop out . . .
Ikite iru to-iu-bakari da	He is barely alive.
Bannin ga iru-bakari de iye wa aite iru	Except for the watchman, the house is empty.
Kome wa taku-bakari ni yōi-shite aru	The rice is all ready for boiling. (Cf. the English colloquial: The rice is all ready, only for the boiling.)
Togakushi renzan wa tōhoku no hō ni yobeba kotaeru-bakari chikaku sobadatte imasu	The Togakushi mountain-range rises in the northeast, so near that it is within calling distance (near so that just if one calls one gets an answer).
Tokachi no heiya wa kokoro-yuku-bakari harebareshii tokoro de aru	The plain of Tokachi is a most refreshing place. (*Kokoro-yuku-bakari* is literally "heart-go-measure."

After the *-ta* form of verbs *-bakari* retains the usual limiting effect of "only." In addition, if a time element is introduced it also limits the time, and in such sentences corresponds quite closely to the English "only just."

Yume ni mita bakari desu	(He) only dreamed it.
Ima kita bakari da	(It) has only just arrived.
Sōzōshita bakari de zotto-suru	(I) shudder at the bare idea.
Sono koro wa Bukkyō ga hajimete Nippon ni tsutawatta bakari no toki deshita	This period was the time when Buddhism had only just come to Japan (for the first time).

After the negative (*-nai, -nu, -n*) form of verbs, the idea conveyed is that of "only not" doing something. English idiom prefers such locutions as "ready to," "on the point of," "just short of," etc.

Kare wa naguran-bakari no kemmaku datta	He had a threatening attitude—ready to strike.
Futari wa kakutō-sen-bakari de atta	The two were on the point of coming to blows.
Watakushi wa atama mo waren bakari ni donatta	I shouted till my head was almost splitting.
Kuromueru wa ō to iwanu-bakari deshita	Cromwell was king in all but name (. . . only not saying so . . .).
Kare wa dete ike to iwanai bakari ni watakushi wo ijimeta	He made it too hot for me. (Literally, "He ill-treated me, only not actually saying 'get out'!")

It should be noted that, when *-bakari* is inserted in *-te iru* forms, the continuative force of the *-te iru* is broken up, and the effect is different from that of *-te iru bakari*. E.g.:

Ano hito wa jibun de hon wo yonde bakari iru	He goes on simply reading books by himself.

Here we have a simple statement of fact with no implication other than it is no great matter.

| *Ano hito wa jibun de hon wo*
yonde iru bakari (da) | He simply goes on reading
books by himself. |

Here the implication is that the action appears insufficient. This sentence might well be followed by "He ought to get a teacher to help
him," or something of the sort.

Students should also note, however, that fine distinctions are
not always accurately observed, and that *bakari* is often used at
least as loosely as the English word "only."

2. After numbers or numerical phrases *bakari* usually gives the
effect of "approximately" or "about." In certain special contexts,
however, it may give the effect of "only," and at times may even
simply indicate politeness. The context usually makes the sense
quite clear.

The reason is that "bakari" was originally "measure," and to
use a word indicating that a specified number is a measure normally indicates unexactness. If, however, from the context the
number is absurdly small a certain contempt is naturally suggested. Also, if the context indicates that there is no inexactness
and no intention of irony, as in a poor man's reference to "a
measure of two goldpieces," bakari may show only formality or
politeness.

hyaku-bakari	about a hundred
hyakunin-bakari	about a hundred men
tōka-bakari no tsukiyo	A night lit by a moon not yet at the full (i.e., a moon at about its tenth day of growth)
Ikura-bakari deshō ka	About how much may it be? (A polite way of saying "How much is it?")
Ichiri-bakari itta koro . . .	When (he) had gone about one *ri* . . .
Kare wa ni sen bakari *yarimashō*	He'll probably give about two cents! He'll probably give only two cents!

BUNGO

In bungo *bakari* may have either the limiting effect of "only," as in the colloquial, or it may be used in comparisons to give the idea of "measure" or "limit of extent." It may also be used after numerals, with much the same effect as in the colloquial, and it usually means "about" after dates.

After verbs, *bakari* may be used after either the Line 3A form (*rentaikei*) or the Line 3 form (*shūshikei*). It is generally agreed that the Line 3A form is the proper one, but the reader will come across many instances where this rule is not followed. When *bakari* is used after adjectives, however, these seem to be practically always in the attributive *-ki* form.

Examples where *bakari* is used with the limiting effect of "only," "just," etc., are:

Kyō bakari naru haru no oshisa wa	Regret for the passing of spring—which has come but today!
Ne no toki bakari ni . . .	Just at the hour of the Rat . . .
Koe bakari koso mukashi nari kere	Truly the voice alone is (the voice) of old!
. . . iro no kuroki bakari wo erabu	. . . chooses only the black ones.
Nen no tame toishi bakari nari	(I) only asked to make sure.
Wazuka ni ichimai no koromo wo mi ni matou bakari nari	He had on his body only a single garment.

Examples where *bakari* is used in comparisons to give the idea of "measure" or "limit of extent."

Kesa no kaze wa mi mo kogoyuru bakari samushi	The wind this morning is so cold that the very body is numb.
Hōshi bakari urayamashikaran mono wa araji	There are probably none so little envied as priests.
Ōkura kyō bakari mimi tōki hito wa nashi	There is nobody so hard of hearing as the Lord High Treasurer.

Kaku bakari no utsukushisa wa araji	There is no beauty equal to this.
Ika bakari ka yasukarazaru-beki	Whatever the price is, it won't be cheap.
Sono odoroki wa ika bakari	How great was his surprise!

After numerical expressions, *bakari* seems to be rather rare in bungo. The word *nomi* is usually used to express the idea of 'only," and *bakari* usually has a feeling of "only about." Thus:

| *ni san nichi bakari* | only about two or three days |

After numerical dates, *bakari* always means "about."

| *tōka bakari* | about the tenth day |

In the older bungo, *bakari* was quite frequently used to mean "about" after even non-numerical dates. In modern times, however, the word *koro* is replacing it for this meaning.

-BAKASHI, -BAKKARI, -BAKKASHI. Variations of *-bakari*. (See -BAKARI.)

-BA KOSO. After a *-ba,* the emphatic force of *koso* is very much like that of the English word "actually."

1. The Line 1 form (*mizenkei*) plus *-ba koso* occurs only in bungo or in set expressions which may be considered quotations from bungo. This *-ba* means "if," and "if actually" suggests that something is not "actually." It is probably for this reason that when *-ba koso* is used at the end of a sentence it has the effect of an expletive indicating strongly that the event is not likely.

Motoyori izon no araba koso . . .	Of course, if actually there be any objection . . .
Ikaba koso yokere	If he actually goes, it is all right. If he had actually gone, it would have been all right.
Utedomo tatakedomo ōzuru mono no araba koso	Though I knocked and knocked, never a man would answer me!

2. The Line 4 form (*izenkei*) plus *-ba koso* occurs in both bungo and the colloquial. Note that the *koso* causes the bungo meaning of this *-ba* ('since' or 'because') to be retained in the colloquial, so that even when used in speech it may be considered a quotation from bungo.

Aisureba koso . . .	Since actually I love you . . . (For the very reason that 1 love you . . .)
Chireba koso itodo sakura wa medetakere	It is just because they do fall that all the more the cherry-blossoms are esteemed.

NOTE.   Only pure bungo examples have been given above. For further discussion, and examples of *-ba koso* used in colloquial sentences, see under KOSO.

-BAMU.   Suffix, added to substantive forms, that is, nouns and the Line 2 form (*renyōkei*) of verbs. The compound becomes a regular verb of the first conjugation (*yodan*).

It indicates a "condition slightly present." In other words, it shows that a state exists, but to a small extent only. Etymologically, *-bamu* seems to be a contraction of *hajimu* 'to start or begin'.

kibanda kao . . .	a yellowish or sallow face . . .
Ki karebamu	The trees are somewhat withered.
Mori no konoha ga kibami-hajimeta	The forest leaves have begun to turn yellow.
(nanika ni) yoribamu . . .	be to some degree based (on something) . . .

This is primarily a literary suffix. It has come down in the colloquial for a few special compounds only. In the colloquial the old meaning is not always strictly adhered to. Thus *kibamu* always means "be yellowish," but *keshikibamu,* in addition to meaning "show signs of activity," may have the somewhat jocose use of "get very excited."

-BARA.   Suffix. Sign of plural, added only to substantives

denoting persons. It has a certain more or less derogatory
implication.

yatsubara	wretches, "those fellows"
tonobara	"misters"
hōshibara	monks

This suffix seems to be somehow connected with the noun *bara,*
meaning "lot," which is used in such modern phrases as *bara de kau*
'buy by the lot, or in bulk'. Note that in English we have the same
derogatory use of "a bunch of" or "a lot of" old fogies, or whatever
it may be.

BASHI. Bungo particle. Equivalent to an emphatic *wo* or *wa.*

The original form seems to have been *wo-ba-shi,* a particularly emphasized form of *wo ba* (see BA). *Bashi* was therefore first used as
an emphasized *wo.* Later on the derivation seems to have been par-
tially forgotten, and the particle thought of as a sonant *wa* (*ha*),
with *shi* added for emphasis.

| *Yumi bashi hiku na majikaku yose yo* | Don't draw your bows! Get up close! (i.e., where you can use your swords). |
| *Shōshō dono no on kokoro ni bashi chigaimairasu na* | Of all things don't upset the plans of the general! |

-BAYA. A bungo suffix, composed of the suffix *-ba* plus the
particle *ya.*

1. It may be added to the Line 1 form (*mizenkei*) of verbs, or
to the *-ku* form of adjectives. When so used it expresses desire or
hope concerning one's own actions, with the implication that the
hope is unlikely to be fulfilled. Hence it gives the effect of an
English "would that I could . . ." or "if I could only . . ."

Satobito ni wazukani nozokasebaya	If I could only let the folks at home have a peep!
Torikaebaya	If I could but change it!
Miyako ni idete fumi wo yomabaya	I wish I could go to the capital and read books.

2. When it is added to the Line 4 form (*izenkei*) it is simply
the same as *-ba* plus an element of doubt (see -BA).

Kono fumi wo yomebaya   (He) went to the capital, per-
    miyako ni idetari   haps because he read this
                                                      letter.

-BE. The theoretical "adjective root" of *-beki, -beku,* and
-beshi. Sansom notes that it is probably a true "root," as the
forms *bera* and *bemi* are found in classical literature. These
forms are abstract nouns, apparently occurring only after the
shūshikei form of verbs.

-BEE. A provincial and low-class form. It may be equivalent
to *-bei* or to *mai.*

-BEI. A suffix. Distinction must be made between its use in
bungo and Kyoto speech on the one hand, and certain local
colloquial on the other.
    1. In bungo and in Kyoto speech *-bei* is a normal contraction
of *-beki.* (See -BEKI.)
    2. When used in speech outside of the Kyoto district it may be
regarded as a provincial contraction of *-beshi.* It is not standard
in Tokyo, and in the following examples the sentences in parentheses represent the standard Tokyo colloquial used to express
the same ideas.

Mō kaerubei (Mō kaerō)   Let's be going home.
Sō dambei (Sō darō)   I suppose so.
Bei to iu koto wo iumeibei   You mustn't say "bei." (If you
    Hakata no mono ga warau-   do) the people in Hakata
    bei   will laugh at you.

-BEKARAZARU, -BEKARAZU. These are contractions of
-beku arazaru and *-beku arazu.* They are used as the negatives of
-beki and *-beshi,* respectively, and so express the ideas of "should
not," "must not," "cannot," etc. They are normally suffixed to
the Line 3 form *(shūshikei)* of verbs. (See -BEKI, -BESHI.) In
form they are, of course, the *-zaru* and *-zu* negatives of *-bekari* (see
-BEKARI) .
    They are literary forms, and in bungo seem to have a fairly
complete conjugation.

Line 1	*Mizenkei*	*-bekarazara*
Line 2	*Renyōkei*	*-bekarazari*
Line 3	*Shūshikei*	*-bekarazu*
Line 3A	*Rentaikei*	*-bekarazaru*

Some grammarians report the existence of the Line 4 form (*izenkei*) *-bekarazare,* but I have not been able to find any example of its use. The form *-bekarazari* used as a *shūshikei* is theoretically possible. (See -ZARI.)

The attributive (Line 3A) form *-bekarazaru* and the sentence ending (Line 3) form *-bekarazu* are not infrequently used in colloquial speech and writing. When so used they are not interchangeable, but follow the rules of bungo grammar. In the colloquial they usually express the ideas of "must not," "ought not" or "should not."

Yama wa ken ni shite yozu-bekarazu	The mountain is precipitous and not to be climbed.
arasoubekarazaru jijitsu	a fact not to be denied (undeniable)
Muyō no mono (wa) hairu-bekarazu	Those without business must not enter. (No admission except on business.)

-BEKARI. This is a wholly literary form, derived from *-beku* plus *ari,* and practically equivalent to *-beki* in meaning.

There seems to have been at one time a fairly complete literary (bungo) conjugation, but nowadays only the negative forms are used. (See -BEKI and -BEKARAZU.)

The conjugation is given by Yamada as:

Line 1	*Mizenkei*	(*yuku*) *bekara*
Line 2	*Renyōkei*	(*yuku*) *bekari*
Line 3	*Shūshikei*	(*yuku*) *bekari*
Line 3A	*Rentaikei*	(*yuku*) *bekaru*
Line 4	*Izenkei*	(*yuku*) *bekare*

Yamada notes that only the first two forms seem to have been much used at any time, and that he has never seen an example of the use of the *shūshikei.*

-BEKERE. The common contraction of *-beku* plus *are,* usually found in the forms *-bekereba* and *-bekeredo.* (See -BEKI, -BEKU, and -BEKARI.)

-BEKI, -BEKU, -BESHI. These are literary (bungo) suffixes used to express ideas similar to the English "ought to" or "is to." They are also not infrequently used in the colloquial, especially the *-beki* form.

They may be considered as made up of an "adjective root" *-be,* itself a suffix, to which the further suffixes *-ki, -ku,* and *-shi* are added. The *-be* is always a suffix to verb forms, usually the Line 3 form (*shūshikei*)

> There are certain exceptions to the previous statement. *-Beki, -beku,* and *-beshi* are normally attached to the Line 3A forms *aru* and *oru,* even in bungo, rather than to the *shūshikei ari* and *ori*. There are also a few other verbs for which the Line 3A form (*rentaikei*) is usually preferred as a base for these suffixes. As these are primarily bungo suffixes, technically they should be attached to the bungo forms of verbs even when they are used in the colloquial. E.g.: *subeki* instead of *surubeki; tabubeki* instead of *taberubeki,* etc. But colloquial verb-forms are often used, especially in speech. It must also be noticed that occasionally the *renyōkei* of second conjugation (*ichidan*) verbs is used as a base, e.g., *tabebeki*. Such usage, however, is frowned on by grammarians. It is hard for a foreigner to judge among conflicting Japanese opinions but the consensus seems to be that in speech such a form as *tabu-beki* sounds stilted, and that *taberu-beki* is to be preferred. *Tabe-beki* seems definitely illiterate. On the other hand there seems to be no consensus of opinion about *kami ichidan* (second conjugation *-iru*) verbs. Certainly the use of such a form as *i-beki* does not sound illiterate. The question is complicated and on the whole so academic that it seems best to recommend to the student that he take his *beki* where he finds it, and let it go at that.

Matsuura lists six uses of *-beshi,* namely, to express (1) supposition, (2) potentiality, (3) obligation, (4) propriety, (5) determination, and (6) command. Notice that all of these are somehow connected with an idea of futurity. He gives the following examples:

1. *Myōnichi wa ame furubeshi*   It ought to rain tomorrow (i.e., it looks like it, or it probably will).

2. *Kono mizu wa nomubeshi* — This water is to be drunk (i.e., can be drunk, is drinkable, etc.).

3. *Seifu wa kokumin no jiyū wo mitomubeshi* — The government ought to recognize the people's freedom (primarily moral obligation).

4. *Shinubeki toki wa ima zo* — The time to die is now! (i.e., when it is proper, when we must, when we ought to).

5. *Myōchō koso hayaku okubeshi* — Tomorrow morning truly I am (going) to get up early (i.e., I will, I am determined).

6. *Ichinichi ni sukunakutomo gojippeiji wa yomubeshi* — At least 50 pages are to be read each day (i.e., you will please read).

In the epistolary style the first and sixth uses are common. They respectively take the place of the dubitative future (*-u, -yō, -mu, -n* forms) and of the imperative.

In the colloquial, the third use, that of expressing moral obligation, is the main one but the other uses do occasionally occur.

Wareware no itasubeki shigoto de arinagara ... — While it is a work that we ought to do ...

Kotaru mono wa oya no mei ni shitagaubeshi — Children should obey their parents.

Chichi yori go aisatsu itasubeshi — I am to give you greetings from my father.

Mirubekuba yukite min — If it is to be seen (I) will go and see it.

Fune ni norubekereba ... — Since (they) must embark ...

Kisha ni chūi subeshi — Look out for the trains!

Kono hengaku wa Kōsen ga kakubeki yakusoku de arimashita — It was agreed that Kōsen was to do the writing for this tablet.

Shoku wo koubeki jinka mo nai — There was not even any human habitation at which they could beg for food.

Kono kuni wa waga shison no   This country is the soil where
  kimitarubeki·chi nari   my descendants are to be
                                   rulers.

Still another use, that of expressing simple futurity, is found in
official announcements concerning persons of very high rank.

Kōgō heika wa Hayama e   H.M. the Empress will proceed
  gyōkei araserarubeshi   to Hayama.

Special notice must be taken of a peculiar use of *-beku* which
has grown out of translations from English.   In this the English
infinitive is rendered by *-beku,* so that, for example, "to do" will
be translated as *subeku* or *surubeku.*

This has found its way into the language, especially in novels,
where the original English phrase was in the form "too (adjective)
to (verb)."   Thus the phrase "too hard to do" becomes *surubeku
amari ni muzukashii,* etc.

NOTE.   In the colloquial *-beki* may be used at the end of
sentences, either alone or followed by some form of *de aru.*

When so used the *-beki* form may be considered as performing
in the one case the function of a verb, in the other that of a substantive.   Otherwise its meaning is unchanged.

-BEU. Suffix, pronounced "-byo."   It is an "adverbial" form,
with the same meaning as *-beku.*   (See -BEKU.)

BIRU. See note under -BU.

-BU. A bungo suffix, now obsolescent.   Added to nouns or
adverbs, it forms a regular second conjugation verb of the *kami
nidan* 'upper two-vowel' type.

It serves to indicate an apparent state or condition or an
apparent attitude.

otonabitari	seemed grown-up (in his attitude toward things)
kotosarabu	be deliberate
okina-bu	have the mental attitude of an old man

It seems to have a colloquial counterpart -*biru*, which forms a regular second conjugation verb. It is apparently little used, but I have heard *otonabita*.

-BURI. Suffix added to nouns and occasionally to adjective roots, forming a new noun. It normally means an "assumption of airs" or an "acting in the manner of," etc.
It is the Line 2 form of -*buru*. (See -BURU.)

Eda-buri no ii matsu . . .	Pine trees whose branches have taken lovely shapes . . .
Dōya mo hikitsuzuite okonau to iu nesshinna shingi-buri de . . .	Taking on the appearance of being a debate so earnest as to be continued into that night also . . .

When added to words expressing time, -*buri* is used to indicate that time elapses or has elapsed.

Jūnen-buri de kyōdai ni au	(He) meets his brother after ten years (of separation).
Boku wa hisashi-buri ni sake wo nonda	I have drunk sake after a long time (of abstinence).

-BURU. Suffix added to nouns and occasionally adjective roots, forming a regular verb of the first (*yodan*) conjugation. In bungo it seems to be added to nouns only. It means "to assume the airs of."

gakusha-buru	to act pedantically
jōhin-buru	to assume genteel airs
mottai-butta yatsu	a pompous fellow
o kyakusan-buri ga yoi	play the guest well
takabutte	assuming airs of superiority (putting themselves· on a pedestal)

This suffix is usually written with the same character as *furu* 'to wag, shake', etc. Distinguish this from the bungo suffix -*bu* (see -BU). In the attributive (Line 3A) form the two are indistinguishable, and

possibly for this reason little used in that form in bungo. E.g., in
bungo:

Otonaburu ko   A child who seemed grown-up.
A child who assumes grown-up airs.

Otonaburitari   (He) seemed grown-up.
(He) assumed the airs of a grown-up person.

-CHA. Contraction of *-te wa,* used in familiar speech. In
kana it is usually written *chi-ya* *(tiya)*, ちや. (Cf. -TCHA, -JA.)
E.g.:

    Sō shicha ikenai   You mustn't act that way!

-CHATTA, -CHAU. Apparently contractions of *-te* forms
of verbs plus *shimau* 'end it' and *shimatta* 'ended it'.
Thus *itte shimatta* becomes *itchatta.*

Shitsurei shichau wa (woman's language) may mean either:

       (1) I will leave you here.
       (2) You (or he) are quite impolite.

CHŌ. When written with the *kana* for *te* and *hu (fu)*, てふ,
this may be a contraction for *to iu.*

CHŪ. This may be a contraction of *to iu,* definitely vulgar.
It is not usually found in writing.

DA. Contraction of *de aru,* used only in familiar or impolite
speech.
For other contractions of *de* and various forms of *aru,* see
introductory Note on *Aru.* (See also DE ARU and DESU.)

-DA. Sonant form of *-ta.* For method of derivation see introductory Note on Verbs. For meaning and usage, see -TA.

-DACHI. Sonant form of the plural suffix *-tachi.*

DAKE. *Dake* is closely related to the noun *take* 'height',
'stature', and so shows that what precedes it is used as a metaphorical stature, that is, either as an upper limit of extent or as
a measure of extent, or both. It always has an implication of
exactness. It is used after both substantives and verbs.

It is to be translated in various ways, depending on the context. If this indicates that the extent is small, *dake* will have the effect of "only." If the context indicates that the extent is large, *dake* will have the effect of "completely," "enough," etc. If there is neither implication, *dake* will correspond to "just," "exactly," "as much as," etc.

The effect of following *dake* with *wa, ni, de, atte,* etc. will be shown in the following examples. Please notice that the English given is not so much translation as colloquial equivalent.

Tada go yen dake aru	(I) have only five yen.
Aru kane wa kore dake da	This is all the money I have.
Kane no aru dake kasō	I will lend you as much money as I have.
Kore wo kau dake no kane ga aru ka	Have you enough money to buy this?
Sore dake attara takusan da	(If there is) that much (it) is enough.
Cha wo san yen dake katte koi	Get three yens' worth of tea!
Kore dake kaimashita	I bought this much.
Karirareru dake kane wo kariru	He borrows as much as he can.
Are dake kane ga attemo mada manzoku shinai	For all his wealth he is not yet satisfied.
Kane ga hoshii toki dake kimasu	He comes only when he wants money.
Kimi dake ni iwau (iwō, iō)	I will tell it to you only.
Sōzōshita dake de zotto suru	I shudder at the bare idea.
Boku dake wa izon wa nai	As far as I am concerned, there is no objection.
Eigo dake de nai furansugo mo dekiru	He knows not only English, but also French.
Areba aru dake hoshiku naru	The more you have, the more you want.
Nomu dake atama ga waruku naru	The more I drink, the more my head aches.
Hayakereba hayai dake yoshi	The sooner, the better

Kare wa kuru ka konai ka wakaranai ga yōi dake mo shite okō	I don't know whether he is coming or not, but I will at least make preparations for him.
Sasuga wa samurai dake atte . . .	Like the samurai that he is . . .
Kumasō no kashira dake atte . . .	Being Chief of the Kumasō (not in name only, but in all that the name implies) . . .
Kare wa yōkōshita dake no koto ga aru	He shows the expected results of his trip abroad. (He has not been abroad for nothing.)
Kono hon wa yomu dake no koto ga aru	This book is worth reading.
Tōbun dake koko ni iru	I shall stay here for the present.
Kare wa namakeru dake de ii hito da	Except for his laziness he is a good man.
Nokotte iru dake no chikara wo dashite hataraita	I worked with what (all the) strength I had left.
Izure dake benkyō shitemo . . .	However hard I study . . .

COMPARISON OF "DAKE" WITH "BAKARI," "HODO," AND "KURAI" IN COLLOQUIAL USAGE

1. Note that *dake* is always exact. After numbers or numerical phrases *bakari, hodo,* and *kurai* may mean "approximately" or "about." *Dake* can never have such a meaning.

2. *Dake* and *bakari* may be translated as "only." *Hodo* and *kurai* cannot have this meaning.

3. Properly speaking, only *kurai* may be used to mean "rank," "grade," or "class." This is because *kurai* conveys no sense of "limit." The other three do convey a sense of limitation, and hence can mean "grade" only when the grade is itself a top (or bottom) limit of something.

4. *Dake* and *hodo* both convey an idea of extent. The difference is that *dake* implies a fixed position ("height") at the limit of extent, while *hodo* implies any position or positions up to the

limit. In careless speech or writing this distinction is not always observed.

5. All these words started as nouns. In the present colloquial *dake* and *bakari* cannot be used as independent nouns. *Hodo* and *kurai* may still be so used, but are getting to be regarded as primarily suffixes. Thus the substantive form of pronouns is standard with *dake, bakari,* and *hodo* (e.g., *sore dake,* not *sono dake*). *Kurai* still normally takes the adjective form (e.g., *sono kurai*), but the use of substantive forms with *kurai* is not uncommon (i.e., *sore kurai,* etc.).

TABLE OF COMPARISONS FOR "-BAKARI," "DAKE," "HODO" AND "KURAI"

About[1]	*bakari*		*hodo*	*kurai*
Only	*bakari*	*dake*		
Grade[2]				*kurai*
Limit of extent (fixed)		*dake*	(*hodo*)	
Extent up-to (variable)			*hodo*	

DAKE NI (DAKENI). This combination, which occurs only in the colloquial, is often used to convey the idea that what precedes is a probable cause of what follows.

This is a natural development from indicating "a connection with just" that thing. It is a curious parallel to the English use of "inasmuch as."

Onna dake ni kokoro wa yasashii	Just because (inasmuch as) she is a woman, her heart is gentle.
Kushinshita dake ni dekibae wa rippa da	The final effect is splendid, just because trouble was taken.

DAMO. Apparently a contraction of *dani mo,* meaning "even," "only," "merely."

Yume ni damo mizu	Not even dreamed of.
Bidō damo senu	Does not move a jot.

[1] After numerical words or phrases or interrogatives calling for a numerical answer.

[2] See paragraph 3 above.

DANI. Particle used for emphasis, confined for the most part to the literary language. It has no exact equivalent in English. It may often be rendered by "even," or "at least," but has more properly the force of "such as." *Dani* is often written as two words, *da ni,* and has quite possibly been derived from *to ari* (= *da*) plus the particle *ni*.

> Apparently the older and more correct usage is that of the first example below, where *dani* is properly rendered by "such as." It must be noted, however, that properly or not *dani* is often used with the sense of "even," as if it were practically equivalent to *sae* or *sura,* or to the colloquial *demo*.

1. Its bungo uses are shown in the following examples:

Hito ni shite kinjū ni dani shikazarubeku ya	As they are men, they should not be inferior to such as birds and beasts.
Yadoru-beki iori nomi ka wa koromo dani nashi	It is not only a question of a place to stay, she hasn't even (such things as) clothes.
Ie no atari dani ima wa tōraji	We are probably not now passing through even the environs of the house.
Ka wo dani nusume	Steal at least the fragrance!

2. When *dani* does occur in the colloquial it is used loosely as a sort of emphatic suffix. The English rendering will depend on the context.

Ima dani ano ie wa fusagaranai	And even today that house is untenanted.
Hima ga areba itta n'dani	If I had had time I would have gone, positively!

-DANO. A suffix, serving as a conjunction between substantives, particularly nouns and pronouns.

It is a colloquial word, and seems to be always used in pairs. It gives an effect of "that sort of thing . . . and that sort of thing."

> It may possibly have come into being from a contraction of *to aru mono*.

Botan dano tsubaki dano	Peonies and camellias and the like.
Nan dano kan dano iu	Say this and that sort of thing.
Nan dano kan dano de kane ga iru	(I) need money for this and for that.

-DARA. A colloquial verb ending, indicating "if or when completed." It is the sonant form of the suffix *-tara,* used in certain standard contractions. For these contractions see the introductory Note on Verbs, and for the uses of *-dara* see under -TARA.

-DARI. A colloquial verb ending indicating continuation. It is the sonant form of the suffix *-tari,* used in certain standard contractions. For these contractions see the introductory Note on Verbs, and for its uses see -TARI.

DARŌ. A common colloquial contraction of *de arō.* Cf. -TARŌ.

-DARŲ. A colloquial contraction of *-de aru.* (See -TARU.)

-DATERA. A suffix, added to nouns describing people, personified animals, etc.

It is used when the person in question does something improper for or inappropriate to the kind of person described. In the colloquial it is nearly always followed by *ni.*

Datera ni is almost equivalent to *de aru no ni.*

Onna datera ni daisoreta koto wo shite	That she—a woman!—should do such an impudent thing!

-DATSU. A suffix, now practically obsolete.

It is added to nouns or adjective roots, and forms a verb of the first (*yodan*) conjugation.

It shows a condition, in much the same way as does *to aru* or *ni aru.*

Waruki kishoku-datsu	I feel ill.
omodatsu	be heavy (important)

DATTA, DATTARA. Common colloquial contractions of *de atta* and *de attara.* For other similar contractions see the list given in the introductory Note on *Aru, Iru,* and *Oru.*

DATTE. A colloquial word representing various contractions and having various uses.

1. It may be a contraction of *de atte.*

Nan datte sonna koto wo suru Why do you do such a thing?
no da

2. It may be a contraction of *de attemo.*

Nan datte shimasu	Whatever it is, (I) will do it.
Nichiyō datte yasumi ya	(We) have no holiday even on
shinai	Sunday.

3. It may be a contraction of *da to itte (iru).*

Nan datte	What is (he) saying?
Sō datte	So they say.

4. It is sometimes used as an equivalent of *wa,* with a somewhat more forceful effect.

Watakushi datte . . .	As for me . . .
Saru datte ki kara ochiru sa	Even monkeys fall out of trees. (Even Homer sometimes nods.)

5. As an introductory word it is used as a conjunction much like the English "but," "yet," "still," etc.

Datte kimari ga warui n'da	But it is so embarrassing (for
mono	me) !
Datte nani mo kare no sewa	No thanks. to him, though.
ni natte i wa shinai	(*i-wa-shinai* = an emphatic *inai*).

DE. A colloquial form, which has apparently developed from a verb-form into a postposition. It has uses both as a quasi-verb and as a postposition. (See DE ARU, DESU, DE WA, DEMO, NO DE.)

In its use as a quasi-verb it may if desired be regarded as a contraction of *de atte* 'being', 'be and', to which it is nearly equivalent in meaning. It should not be assumed, however, that this contraction represents the true historical development.

It does not occur in bungo. It may have been derived from *ni arite,* through *nite,* but seems to have special relations with the literary *ni shite.*

As a postposition, it normally indicates that the substantive it follows is used in the performance of an action. The one apparent exception to this rule occurs when *de* is followed by some form of *aru* 'be'. For this use of *de,* see DE ARU and the introductory Note on *Aru, Iru,* and *Oru.*

The postpositional use of *de* apparently also derives from the bungo *nite,* and always retains at least a latent feeling of "being." Some students feel that *de* indicates primarily "being," by extension "being present for use," and that it consequently may often be best translated by the English word "using." The historical development is not yet clear, and *de* may be a contraction of other *-te* forms besides *nite* (see MOTTE). The most likely origin of the postposition *de,* however, seems to be from *ni shite,* used in the sense of "acting in connection with."

Pen de tegami wo kaku	Write a letter with (using) a pen.
Inu wa ano hito ni tsue de utareta	The dog was beaten by him with a stick.
Kisha de yuku	Go by train (a train "being used").
Gyūnyū de bata wo koshiraeru	Make butter from milk (milk being used).
Ki de tsukutte sumi de nuru	Make it of wood and paint it with India ink.
Mō kore de kekkō desu	Already with this it is perfect. (Used for "No more, thank you.")
Kono kunshō wa sensō de itadaita	This medal (I) received for (my services in) war.
Kare wa mada dokushin de oru	He still lives as a bachelor.
Natsu wa hadashi de iru	In summer they go barefoot.

Oru and *iru* are not just simple "being," but have certain qualities of action. Hence "celibacy" and "bare feet" may be considered as "used in the action of living."

1. Note that there are many sentences in which *de* occurs and in which it is quite impossible to tell whether this *de* acts as a verb-form or as a postposition. However, in the vast majority of such sentences the meaning is not affected, whichever we take it to be. For example, a sentence like *Shiken de isogashii* is probably best rendered by "(I) am busy with examinations," but it is very close to "There being examinations, (I) am busy." For further discussion of this point see DE WA.

Consider also *de* as used in familiar speech at the beginning of sentences. Here it is probably a contraction of *sore de* 'that being (the case)', and it still retains some of this meaning, but is now more like "and" or "and so," or "and then."

De, omae wa dō itta no ka	And what did you say?
De, kimi wa jishitai to iu no da ne	And so you want to resign, eh?

Some grammarians consider that *de,* used alone at the beginning of a sentence, serves to relegate the whole preceding sentence to the category of a clause ending in a *-te* form verb.

Other examples in which it does not seem to make any very important difference in the meaning whether we consider *de* as a postposition or a verb are:

Nan dano kan dano de kane ga irimasu	I need money for various things (or: This and that being . . .).
Nama de tabemasu	We eat it raw.
Futari de ikimashita	The two went together (or: Being two people . . .).

Examples where *de* is equivalent to *de atte,* and so has the full force of a verb, are:

Kare wa shinkeika de (byōki de mo nai no ni) byōki no tsumori de aru	He is a nervous man and, although he hasn't any illness, always lives in the expectation of illness.

Itsumo otasshana koto de . . .   Your health being always
good . . . (This phrase as
it stands is used in greetings,
some further phrase like "it
gives me great pleasure" being understood.)

Kaze wa shizuka de nami mo   The wind was quiet, and the
oto wo tatemasen   waves too made no noise.

2. The scope of *de* as a postposition may be made clearer by consideration of instances where its uses approach those of *ni*. Take
for example a phrase like:

ryōshoku no ketsubō ni   be troubled about lack of
komaru   provisions

and compare it with:

ryōshoku no ketsubō de   be troubled by (i.e., suffer
komaru   from) a lack of provisions

The first is general and might refer to a future lack, someone else's
lack, etc.; the second is particular, and refers to an existing lack
which is "used" in the being troubled.

3. Consider also designation of places. These are generally
thought of as necessary to and hence used in any action that
occurs within their limits. Consequently the usual form is:

Tōkyō de hataraku   work in Tokyo
sanjō de tō wo tateru   erect a tower on the hilltop

If the verb use is not primarily concerned with action, *de* cannot
be used, and hence *ni* is used with *oru* 'be', *sumu* 'dwell', etc.

Tōkyō ni sunde iru   (He) lives in Tokyo.

It should be noted, however, that this mode of thought is not
always rigidly adhered to, and expressions like *sanjō ni tō wo
tateru* are not infrequent. In the latter sentence the suggestion
is that the speaker is not thinking of the action of building, but
of the presence of the tower after it has been built. Careful
speakers always do make this distinction, but of course in any

country careful speakers are a minority. Even loose speakers, however, would use *de* in such a phrase as *sanjo de to wo tatete iru* if they meant that someone was actually working there. The use of *ni* would indicate that the subject is not actually working but is having the work done for him. (Cf. NI.)

-DE. A suffix, with different uses in the colloquial and in bungo. (Cf. -IDE, -NDE, -UDE.)

1. In the colloquial it may be the common sonant or *nigori* form of the suffix *-te,* found in certain colloquial contractions of the Line 2 form (*renyōkei*) of verbs plus *-te.*

A list of these contractions is given in part 3 of "Colloquial Conjugations" in the introductory Note on Verbs.

It is also commonly added to the negatives *nai, -nai, -masen,* and *-nu,* to make the forms *naide, -naide, -masende,* and *-nude.* These forms may be taken as very nearly equivalent in meaning to the forms *nakute, -nakute.* (See -NAIDE.)

-Nude is often written and pronounced *-nde. -Masende* is sometimes written *-masenude,* but practically never so pronounced.

2. In bungo, it may be a suffix attached to the Line 1 form (*mizenkei*) of verbs. Note that *suru* becomes *sede.*

It is equivalent in meaning to a negative *-te* form, and as a matter of historical record seems to have been derived from *-zute.* Outside of poetry it is not much used nowadays.

yukade oru	be not going
aruki mo sede miru	to look without even taking a step

DE ARU, DE GOZAIMASU. In the colloquial the combination of *de* and forms of *aru* or *gozaru* may be used to show identity (as, "A is B") or as a copula (e.g., "he is kind"). But the strict rules for "standard" Japanese require that the word or phrase before *de* shall be a substantive in form at least. Deviations from this standard are referred to under DESU.

It is only a matter of nomenclature whether the *de* before *aru* and *gozaru* is regarded as a postposition or as a verb. It seems simplest to regard this *de* as essentially a verb, with a meaning similar to that of the English participial "being."

It may be of use for students to remember that Chinese words were made available for use as Japanese adjectives by the addition of *naru,* the attributive (Line 3A) form of the bungo verb *nari* 'be'. *Nari* (originally *ni ari*) has been replaced in the colloquial by *de aru.* (See introductory Note on Foreign Words.)

Kore wa hon de aru	This is a book.
Okusan wa o-ari desu ka	Have you a wife?
A san wa shinsetsuna hito de aru	Mr. A is a kind man.
A san wa shinsetsu de aru	Mr. A is kind.
Sō darō (de arō)	It is probably that way.
Sō de nakarō	It probably isn't that way.
Dare de atta ka oboenai	I don't remember who it was.
Kore wa akai no de gozaimasu	This is red. (This is a red one.)

There is a tendency, particularly among the younger Japanese, to drop a substantivizing *no* before forms of *de aru.* This *no,* however, is practically always retained before all forms of *de gozaru,* and indeed in most formal speech. Just how and where it is dropped varies so much with class, locality, etc., that it cannot be treated at length. A short discussion is given under DESU.

A list of common contractions of *de gozarimasu* and various forms of *de aru* and *de arimasu* is given in the introductory Note on *Aru, Iru,* and *Oru.*

-DEMO. Colloquial form of *-temo.* (See -TEMO.)

DEMO. This particle is found only in the colloquial. It may be written as two words, and seems to have been originally derived from the bungo verb-form *nite* 'being' plus *mo* 'even' or 'also'. In the course of time, however, special meanings and uses have been developed. (Cf. NITE, -TEMO and MO.)

1. The primary use of *demo* is as a concessive which may often be translated as "although," "even," or "even if." In this use *de* retains its verb force of "being" either completely or at least predominantly, and *mo* has the sense of "even." See -TEMO (-DEMO).

Note that whatever precedes the *demo,* whatever its form may be, is treated as if it were a substantive.

In the first series of the following examples note the very close relationship between *demo* and *de attemo.*

Kao wa hito demo kokoro wa oni da	Even though in face he is a man, in heart he is a devil.
Moto wa kimi no demo ureba hito no mono da	Even though it be yours originally, if you sell it it belongs to someone else.
Byōki demo ikō	(He) will probably go even if (he) is sick.
Iya demo shikata ga nai	Even if (you) don't like it, it can't be helped.
Ame demo iku hazu desu	(I) have to go, even if it rains
Empitsu demo ii	A pencil will do (even if it is a pencil).
Kaette kara demo ii	It will be all right (to do it) after you get back.
Chōjū demo nao hito no on wo shitte oru	Even birds and beasts recognize kindnesses received from others.
Sonna koto wa kodomo demo dekiru	Such a thing as that even a child can do.
Sore demo . . .	Nevertheless (even if that be) . . .

It has been said that what precedes *demo* is treated as a substantive. No difficulty is presented by such phrases as *kimi no* and *kaette kara* in the examples above. Obviously they suggest ideas such as *kimi no (mono)* and *kaette kara (suru koto).*

However, sometimes difficulty is found in getting the exact force of phrases ending in *wo.* Consider the following phrases:

Kore demo kawō
Kore wo demo kawō

The first is a rather light "I think I'll buy, even if it be this," intimating that one does not care much one way or the other.

The second intimates a much stronger dislike to taking the action of buying. It is a bit like "Look at it! Just the same, I think I'll buy it," but of course no one English phrase will suit all contingencies.

When *demo* starts a sentence it is concessive to what has previously been stated, and is translatable by "even so," "still," etc.

Demo okashii	Still, it's queer.
Demo, mada roku-ji ni naranai	Well, but it's not six o'clock yet.

2. A special use of *demo* is to imply "or other things of more or less the same kind." This is a very natural extension of the concessive meaning, and often a very slight one.

Ōkina hamaguri ya mategai demo toru to . . .	When (we) pick up a big clam or a razorshell or that sort of thing . . .
Ocha demo nomimashō	Let's drink tea or something.
Ikanai mono demo nai	It is not that (he) will not go, or that sort of thing (meaning "the chances are that he will go").
Empō e demo dekakeru	(He) will go off into the distance, or anywhere.
Dōshi to demo iwanakereba naran	We have to call it a verb (or some other similar name).

The concessive force is not wholly lost in the above sentence, and the implication is rather "for want of a better name."

After the Line 2 form (*renyōkei*) of verbs *demo*, when it has this special use, is usually followed by some form of *suru* such as *shitara, sureba,* etc., which gives the idea of "if."

Kaze wo hiki demo suru to ikenai	If (you) caught a cold or something, it wouldn't do. Do something like catching a cold and it will be too bad.

> *Shikarare demo shitara*   If he were scolded (or some-
> *sukoshi wa otonashiku*   thing of the sort) he would
> *naru deshō*   probably become (at least)
> a little more gentle.

3. In a special use which is a still further extension of the foregoing *demo* is used to indicate a rather polite vagueness. It is often found in sentences which are imperative in form. These it softens to suggestions rather than orders or even requests.

> *Ichido tazunete demo goran*   Do try going to see him once.
> *nasai*
> *Tonikaku chūi dake demo*   At any rate do try at least to
> *shite mite kudasai*   pay attention.
> *Myōban demo hima deshitara,*   If, say, tomorrow evening is
> *chotto, o-ide kudasai*   free for you, do drop in for
> a little while.

4. A special use with negatives to mean "not exactly" has a fairly close correspondence with the vaguenesss of *demo* as illustrated in the previous section.

> *Sō demo nai*   It's not exactly that.

5. *Demo . . . demo . . .* in parallel clauses has uses similar to *mo . . . mo.* (Cf. MO . . . MO.)

> *Rōjin demo kodomo demo*   An old man or a child or
> *dare demo ii*   anyone will do.
> *Nan demo ka demo iimasu*   (They) say all sorts of things.
> *Kore wa kin demo gin demo*   This is neither gold nor silver.
> *arimasen*
> *Isha demo sensei demo*   (He) is neither a doctor nor
> *arimasen*   a teacher.

Note that in the last two sentences the *demo arimasen* is a construction parallel to that of *de wa arimasen.*

> *Kin mo gin mo arimasen*   There is (present) neither gold
> nor silver.
> *Isha mo sensei mo orimasen*   There are (present) neither doc-
> tors nor teachers.

6. When *demo* occurs after words indicating place, or in other phrases where *de* is used more as a postposition than as a verb, *mo* usually has the effect of "also" rather than "even."

Nihon demo sō iu fū ni shimasu	(We) do it that way in Japan too.
Hikōki demo yukareru	One can go by plane also.
Wara demo sake ga tsukureru	Sake can be made out of straw too. (Here equivalent to "even out of straw.")

7. After interrogative pronouns or clauses built around interrogative pronouns *demo* (*or de attemo*) has much the effect of "soever it be" in such English phrases as "whosoever it be" or "what situation soever it be," but, of course, without the stilted and archaic flavor of such phrases. (For similar use of *-demo* see p. 290.)

Some students find it easier to think of *demo* as referring to "all the possible whos or whats considered separately." Cf. MO 1., (c), p. 162 f.

Dare demo yoroshii (no) desu	Anybody will do (whosoever it be . . .).
Dare demo sō iimasu	Everyone says so (separately).
Doko ni demo arimasu	It is (found) everywhere.
Tanaka san wa nan demo shitte orimasu	Mr. Tanaka knows everything.
Dochira demo niaimasu	Either of them will suit you.
Donna mono demo kaimasu	He will buy any sort of thing.
Nan ni demo bikkuri suru	Startle at anything whatever.
Itsu demo oide nasai	Come to see me at any time.

-DERU (-TERU). A contraction of *-de iru* (*-te iru*), common in colloquial speech. It is only used where the *-de* (*-te*) is part of a verb form.

> *Yonde iru* 'be reading'   → *yonderu*
> *Oyoide iru* 'is swimming' → *oyoideru*
> *Shinde iru* 'be dying'   → *shinderu*

DESHŌ. A contraction of *de arimashō*. Cf. DESU.

DESU (DA). Historically *desu* is a contraction of *de arimasu* or *de gozarimasu*, just as *da* is a contraction of *de aru,* and they are usually interchangeable with the uncontracted forms.

There seems to be, however, a growing tendency to treat both *desu* and *da* as if they were independent verbs meaning "be." (For conjugation see p. 30.) Consequently it is not always possible to replace *desu* by *de arimasu,* or *da* by *de aru.* For example:

> *Bōshi wa doko da*　　　　Where's my hat?
> *Bōshi wa doko desu ka*

are quite common colloquial sentences. (Purists would call them common in every sense of the word!) In polite and correct sentences, however, the postposition which precedes the verb would be *ni,* not *de.* Proper forms are:

> *Bōshi wa doko ni aru*
> *Bōshi wa doko ni arimasu ka,* etc.

Another example is the very definitely growing tendency to use *desu* or *da* directly after the *-i* form of an adjective, as:

> *Kore wa akai desu*　　This is red.

Technically, this is a contraction from the full form:

> *Kore wa akai no desu*

The contracted form is still frowned on by grammarians, but is widely used, especially by the younger men. These tend to use both forms, but with a distinction in meaning. The first or contracted form is used to mean "This is red"; the uncontracted form with *no desu* is used to mean "This is a red one." (See NO DESU.)

In such sentences as those given above *de gozaimasu* cannot be substituted for *desu* without the *no.* E.g.:

> *Kore wa akō gozaimasu*　　This is red.
> *Kore wa akai no de*　　　　This is a red one.
> *gozaimasu*

The first of these sentences cannot have any meaning other than the one given, and so corresponds to *kore wa akai (desu).*

The second might also mean "This is red," with the *no de gozaimasu* which is stuck on making the statement a little fuller and more polite. In practice, however, it usually has the meaning given here.

See the introductory Note on *Aru, Iru,* and *Oru* for a list of common contractions of *de* with other forms of *aru,* such as *deshō* for *de arimashō, datta* for *de atta,* etc. See also -TARŌ.

DE WA. A combination of *de* and *wa,* used only in the colloquial, and in speech often contracted to *ja* or *jā.* (See DE and WA.)

As the *de* may be used either as a verb-form or as a postposition it is not practicable to give examples of all possible uses of this combination. The common uses most likely to trouble students are discussed below.

1. The most common use of *de wa* is with *aru* or *gozaru* to emphasize a negative. It is often used in questions to which an affirmative answer is expected.

Aru no de wa arimasen	Emphatically, it is not.
Sō de wa nai	It's not that way.
Ikō ja arimasen ka	Let's go, shan't we?
Sore wa futsū no kangàe	That is not an ordinary
jā arimasen	thought.

It will be noted that in these sentences the *de* retains its full verb feeling, and `. . . de wa nai` has an effect very much that of "as for being . . . it is not."

Note also that while *de wa* is less often used to emphasize an affirmative than a negative, it may be so used, and with great effect.

Aru no de wa aru	It most certainly is!
Kare wa kodomo de wa aru	He is a child all right, but he
ga mujaki de wa nai	is certainly not guileless.

2. When *de wa* starts a sentence the *de* refers to an existing state of affairs which may or may not have been expressed in words by the preceding speaker, or, in books, described in the preceding

sentence. In this it differs from *sore de wa*, which practically always refers to a preceding sentence.

Some grammarians consider *sore de wa* to be a contraction of *sore de aru naraba* 'if that be so . . .'

De wa sayonara	Well then, goodbye.
De wa gozaimasu ga	I admit it is so, but . . . (as for being, it is, but . . .).

3. Other examples of the uses of *de wa* are:

Jū yen de wa taranu	Ten yen won't be enough.
Boku no kangae de wa . . .	According to my opinion . . .
Jūsan to sanjū de wa dotchi ga ōkii no desu ka	Which is the larger, thirteen or thirty?

The only difficulty is in deciding whether *de* is used with its full verb feeling, or as a postposition. In the above examples the *de* does seem to be a postposition at least as much as it is a verb.

There are, however, examples of *de wa* where the verb feeling is absolutely dominant, as in:

Moshi seken no hyōbandōri shizuka de wa kibōsha mo sadameshi okarō	If it be quiet as its reputation has it, those desirous (of going there) certainly must be many.

When the verb feeling of *de* is dominant, the use of *de wa* has much in common with that of *-te wa*. (See -TE WA.)

-DO. A suffix, primarily bungo. It is added to the Line 4 form (*izenkei*) of verbs. It is interchangeable with the bungo suffix *-domo*, and is translatable by "but" or "although." (See -DOMO.)

Yobedo kotaezu	(I) called, but (he) did not answer. (Although I called . . .).
Kono sho wo yomedo sono imi wo satorazu	Although (I) have read this book, (I) do not understand its meaning. (I have read this book but . . .)

Matedo kurasedo kaette konai   **Though** (I) waited, and time
                                   went on, (he) did not come
                                   back (home).
Ōkaredo . . .   Though (be) many . . .

DOCHI. A noun. Counted as a plural suffix by some grammarians. Apparently not used at the present time. Pierson cites:

    onna-dochi   women
    omou-dochi   they who have the same
                                             opinion

(Cf. *dōshi* in modern dictionaries.)

-DOMO. A suffix with two distinct uses and meanings.

1. It may be added to substantives which indicate people.
When so used it is normally a sign of the plural. Special exceptions to this rule are noted below.

    hitodomo   people
    shinruidomo   (my) relatives
    tsuwamonodomo   warriors

At the present time *-domo* definitely implies a humble position
of some kind. Hence, for example, the present tendency to use
it for persons connected with the speaker. Used about others it has
a rather slighting effect. It also has a certain feeling of formality.
In past times it had no such implication of low position.

It may also be used, for the sake of politeness, in reference to
oneself alone. For example, *watakushi-domo* may be used for "I"
as well as "we."

Note that there are a few words, like *kodomo* 'child' in which
the *-domo* has wholly lost its plural significance. For comparison
with other "plural" suffixes see -GATA, -RA, -TACHI, -NADO, and -TŌ,

This *-domo* is etymologically connected with *tomo* 'together'.

2. It may be added to the Line 4 form (*izenkei*) of verbs.
This is almost entirely a bungo usage. (See also -DO.) When
so used it shows a condition already determined and suggests an
adversative "but" or "although."

Hana sakedomo yukazu	The flowers have bloomed, but I am not going.
Kaze yamitaredomo nami nao takashi	Although the wind has stopped the waves are still high.
Yosukō wa suiryō tsune ni yutaka ni shite yōyō to nagaruredomo kaki wa koto ni zōsui su	The Yangtse-kiang is always full of water and flows in a wide stream but in summer the water gets especially high.
Utedomo tatakedomo ōzuru mono no araba koso	I knocked and knocked but never a man answered me.

Note the following common contractions of the *-ku* form of adjectives with *aredomo*:

> (*shiro*) *keredomo*
> (*shiro*) *keredo*
> (*shiro*) *kedo*

All three mean "although it is (white)," or "It is (white) but." The colloquial *keredomo* 'but' seems to have been derived from this form, probably through *kaku aredomo*.

-DŌRI. A suffix, added to nouns and pronouns. The combination forms a new noun.

This suffix is the sonant pronunciation of the Line 2 form (*renyōkei*) of the verb *tōru* 'go through'. It has two uses, one where its meaning is concrete and one where it is abstract. These uses are much like those of the English word "way."

1. The concrete use is in names of streets, where it is translatable by "street," "avenue," or "way."

| *Karasumaru-dōri* | Karasumaru Avenue |
| *Nihonbashi-dōri* | Nihonbashi Street |

2. In its abstract use *-dōri* means "the way of" and usually is best translated by "according to" or some similar phrase.

| *Mihon-dōri ni tsukutte kudasai* | Please make it according to the model. |

Yotei-dōri (ni) . . .   As arranged . . .
Kono kutsu wa chūmon-dōri   These shoes are not made as
  ni dekite inai   ordered.
Omoi-dōri no hito ga nai   I can't find a man to my mind.

-DORU. A contraction of *-de oru.* (Kyushu dialect)

DZ. A Romanization sometimes used instead of "z." It is
most often used in representing the sonant or *nigori* form of *tsu.*
E.g., *midzu* for *mizu* 'water', etc.

E. A particle with various uses. [See also E (HE).]

Note that the pronunciation "e" may be used in place of the standard
"i" in certain dialects, especially in those of northern Japan, e.g.,
Fukushima and Sendai.

1. It may be used like *hai* to show assent. For other modern
uses as an interjection, see any standard dictionary.

       E ikimasu   All right. I'll go!

2. In old bungo it was used as a vocative, and this use still persists in certain provincial dialects:

       Chichi-haha e   O Father and Mother!

3. Another old bungo use was as an expletive, equivalent to *aa*:

       E kurushie   Alas, how afflicting!

4. One very rare use, apparently occurring only in very old
bungo, was as a substitute for *ni*:

       Sono uchi e   Within that time.

E(HE). A postposition. (Written *he* in *kana,* but often transliterated into Romaji as *ye.*)   It indicates that the substantive it
follows is a limit towards which action takes place.

The limit is always conceived as fixed, and the action as or like
movement in space. If one is thinking primarily of the motion, *e*
is always used. If one is thinking primarily of the fixed limit,
the present tendency is to replace *e* by *ni.*

Tōkyō e iku   (He) goes to Tokyo.
Tsukue no ue e oku   (He) puts (it) on the table.

| *Zaisan wo ko e yuzuru* | (He) transfers (his) fortune to (his) son. |
| *Ojisan e tebukuro wo ageru* | (She) gives gloves to (her) uncle. |

Note that in the above sentences *ni* may replace *e* without greatly affecting the sense, but that when the verb is indefinite in regard to motion the distinction between *e* and *ni* is of great importance.

| *Dochira e irasshaimasu ka* | Where are you going? |
| *Dochira ni irasshaimasu ka* | Where do you live? |

-E. A colloquial suffix, used in familiar speech. Its function is to express a slight doubt, somewhat like the English "Eh?".

It usually comes at the end of interrogative sentences, affixed to the *-ta* (*-da*) form of verbs, to *da* (= *de aru*), or to the interrogative particle *ka*.

Dō da, omoshirokatta ka-e	Well, was it interesting? Eh?
Nanda-e	What's that again?
Dare da-e	Who's that? (I'm not sure.)
Sore kara dōshita-e	And what would we do after that?
(Q) *Mō ii ka-e*	(Q) Ready?
(A) *Mada da yo*	(A) Not yet!
Kore de yoi ka-e	Would this do it?
Iya jaa nee ka-e	Disagreeable, ain't it? (A vulgar expression.)

In the above sentences the English is an equivalent rather than a translation.

EE. The student should recognize that this combination of sounds may represent a rather low-class pronunciation of *ei* or *ai*.

There is a tendency, even among good speakers, to pronounce a final *-ei* as *-ee*.

-ERU. A colloquial suffix, attached to the consonant "root" of first conjugation (*yodan*) verbs. It combines to make a new verb expressing active ability or passive potentiality. This new verb is regularly conjugated as a second conjugation *(shimo ichidan)* verb, except that strictly speaking it has no imperative form. Grammarians sometimes refer to it as a "potential." (Cf. -RERU.)

kaku	'write'	root *kak*	becomes	*kakeru*	'can write or be written'
iu	'say'	root *i(h)*	becomes	*ieru*	'can say or be said'
uru	'sell'	root *ur*	becomes	*ureru*	'can sell or be sold'
iku	'go'	root *ik*	becomes	*ikeru*	'can go'

Some grammarians prefer to regard such an *-eru* verb as a combina tion of the Line 4 form *(izenkei)* with the suffix *-ru*. Others regard it as a contraction of the Line 1 form *(mizenkei)* and *-reru,* which it almost certainly is. (Cf. -RERU and -RU.) There are also indications that it might be a contraction of *-i-uru* or *-i-eru*. E.g., *kaki-uru* or *kaki-eru* 'can write' could contract to *kakeru*.

Note that in the colloquial there are other *-eru* verbs with similar meaning but not formed as described above. E.g., *mieru, kikoeru,* etc. Such verbs, however, will be found in dictionaries. There are also some regularly formed *-eru* verbs, nearly all of which will be found in dictionaries, which usually have a passive rather than a "potential" meaning. E.g., *mitoreru* 'look with rapture' or 'be captivated with looking'; *shireru*, which is more commonly used in the sense of "is known" than that of "can be known," etc. The ex istence of such verbs can be used as proof of the theory that the *-eru* ending is actually a contraction of *-areru*.

Students should carefully distinguish between this colloquial form and the somewhat similar bungo form obtained by adding the conjugated suffix *-ri* to a Line 4 form *(izenkei)*. Cf. -RI.

Whether these *-eru* verbs are to be translated as active or passive will be obvious from the context. E.g.:

Kore ga uremasu ka	Can this be sold?
Kore wo uremasu ka	Can (you) sell this?

In sentences such as the above, the first form is the more com mon. The *wo* puts more emphasis on the *kore* than *ga* does.

To those of us who are imbued with Occidental ideas of gram mar it would seem obvious that the *uremasu* in the first sentence is a passive verb and that the *uremasu* in the second sentence is an active one. Certainly teachers find the terms "active" and "passive" very useful in instructing elementary students. It must be remembered, however, that these terms are foreign to Japanese conceptions. When Japanese use verbs in their "potential" forms (i.e., *-eru*, or *-reru*, *-rareru* verbs used with a "potential" force) they do not think of such verbs being either "active" or "passive"—at any rate not in the full Occidental sense of the terms. In such a sentence as:

Kore wa uremasu ka   Can this be sold?
                          Can (we) sell this?

the *uremasu* may be considered as passive, or active, or neither, or both. It really does not matter to a Japanese.

Perhaps the nearest English equivalent would be to translate the *-eru* as "get." It is possible to understand how "Does this get a selling?' and "Do (we) get a selling of this?" could both convey the idea "Can this be sold?"

What postpositions are used with "potential" verbs depends largely on the context and on the shade of feeling expressed. For example, the following sentences all mean, basically, "Can you write such splendid characters as these?"

Anata wa konna kekkōna ji ga kakemasu ka
Anata ni wa konna kekkōna ji ga kakemasu ka
Konna kekkōna ji ga anata ni kakemasu ka
Konna kekkōna ji wo anata ga kakemasu ka
Konna kekkōna ji wa anata wa kakemasu ka
Konna kekkōna ji wa anata ni wa kakemasu ka
Konna kekkōna ji wa anata ga kakemasu ka

It is impossible to go into all the conditions which might make one of these forms the most appropriate. It may be said, however, that the first sentence is in the "standard" form, the one most likely to be used. The last would be used only on very rare occasions, say when someone claims to have written some very beautiful characters, and it seems impossible to believe that he was capable of it. An approximate English equivalent would be: "Is it possible for *you* to write such splendid characters as these?"

For further examples and discussion of the uses of "potential" verbs, see under the heading -RERU.

WARNING. The suffixes -*saseru* and -*rareru* cannot properly be added to a potential -*eru* verb.

In practice, -*saseru* seems never to be added, but poor speakers do sometimes get confused and so add the -*rareru* suffix.

For example, to express the idea "It is unreadable" it is correct to use either *yomenai* or *yomarenai*. Students should not be upset by hearing the incorrect *yomerarenai* used for the same purpose.

GA. A particle which functions both as a postposition and as a conjunction. The student should give particular attention to the sharp differentiation of its uses in bungo and in the colloquial. There is, however, seldom any difficulty in determining its function. As a postposition it is used only after substantives. As a conjunction it is used only after complete sentences.

The only possibility of confusion arises when, in the colloquial, *ga* marks as a subject a substantive which is not a noun in form. Normally, however, this is not done except in short phrases which the context makes perfectly clear.

In all its uses *ga* retains certain special characteristics. It lays a special stress on what it follows, holds it up for observation, and marks a very close link between two concepts.

When *ga* is used as a postposition, in the colloquial, the two concepts are usually a subject and its verb; in bungo they are usually two substantives. When *ga* is used as a conjunction it of course joins two clauses or sentences.

Note that in bungo, when *ga* is used as a conjunction it demands the Line 3A form (*rentaikei*) of verbs and the -*ki* form of adjectives.

Uses as a Postposition

As a postposition *ga* has the following uses.

1. It may mark the subject of a verb. This subject is always regarded as a substantive, but is not necessarily a substantive in form. This is the most common use of *ga* in the colloquial.

In bungo the subject is usually not marked. Thus the colloquial *yuki ga furu* 'snow falls' in bungo would simply be *yuki furu*, the subject being identified as such by its position in the sentence. Note that in general postpositions do not "form" cases, but rather "mark" them.

For a comparison of *ga* with *no* when marking the subject of a verb in attributive clauses, see the discussion under NO. For a comparison with *wa* see under WA.

Kireina hana ga aru	There are lovely flowers.
Koko ni onna ga inai	No women are here.
Dandan hi ga mijikaku naru	Bit by bit the days grow shorter.
Wasureta hō ga ii	It is best forgotten.
Kimi wa Eigo ga susunda	You have improved in your English.
Kono ie wa chichi ga tateta	As for this house, my father built it.
Chichi ga tateta ie ni sumu	Live in the house one's father built.
Aa, ano hito wa sei ga takai	And what a tall man he is!
Ano hito no hō ga sei ga takai	That man is the taller.
Boku ga an ga aru	I have a plan.

Note in all these examples how firmly *ga* links a subject with its verb, especially in phrases that are attributive or otherwise subordinate. In the last examples *an ga aru* and *sei ga takai* become practically equivalent to compound verbs.

Note also that the substantive marked as a subject is not necessarily a substantive *in form*. E.g.:

Sono baai ni wa makeru ga kachi da	In those circumstances to lose is to win.
Hayai ga ii	It is better to be early.
Son Gokū wa o itoma itashimashō to iu ga hayai ka kumo ni notte tonde ikimashita	Son Goku said, "I will take my leave," and, almost before he had said it, got on a cloud and flew away.
Boku no ga kimi no da	What is mine is yours.

(In these sentences it is obviously not necessary to use substantive *forms* such as *makeru koto, hayai hō, to iu no,* or *boku no mono.*)

There are certain expressions where *ga* unquestionably marks the subject of a verb, and yet to many foreigners it seems to mark the direct object. This error is usually due to faulty dictionaries. An example of such expressions is:

Kono bun no imi ga wakaru ka	Is the meaning of this sentence clear?

Most dictionaries give the meaning of *wakaru* as "understand" but it is really more nearly "be" or "become clear to the understanding." The word *wakaru* is etymologically connected with the word *wakeru* 'to separate' or 'divide'. By a slight extension of meaning *wakeru* can be and is used for "to separate mentally," "to distinguish between," and so "to classify." The oldest sense of *wakaru* seems to have been "be separated" or "be divided." By a natural transition it has acquired its present sense of "be separated mentally" or "be clear to the understanding." That this is its present sense is proved by such sentences as:

Jijitsu ga dandan watakushi ni wakatte kita	The facts gradually became clear to me.

There are many such examples:

Ano hito wa yumi ga taihen jōzu desu	He is very skillful with the bow.
Nihongo de tegami wo kaku koto ga dekimasu ka	Can (you) write a letter in Japanese?
Konna yasashii no ga yomenakute dō shimasu	What will you do if you can't read a thing as easy as this (. . . if a thing as easy as this cannot be read)? (Cf. -ERU.)

In bungo the subject is usually not marked. Thus the colloquial *yuki ga furu* 'snow falls' in bungo would simply be *yuki furu*. However, in comparatively rare instances *ga* does mark the subject of a verb even in bungo. E.g.:

Aoyama ni hi ga kakuraba . . .	If the sun be hidden in the blue mountains . . .

There are also certain instances where *ga* appears in bungo after verb and adjective forms, where it seems to mark the subject. In such sentences, however, *ga* performs other functions as well. See under "Uses as a Conjunction," paragraph 5.

2. It may indicate a psychological subject which is not necessarily the strict grammatical subject. (Cf. WA.) This use is confined to sentences which treat of the desires, likes or dislikes of the person to whom they refer.

Mizu ga nomitai	I want to drink water.
Watakushi wa kore ga suki desu	I like this one.
Pan ga hoshiku nai	He does not want bread.

Words like *hoshii* and *suki* are so difficult to define that it is possible that when they are used *ga* actually does mark the grammatical subject. With the *-tai* form, however, logic seems to demand *wo* in place of *ga*, and its use is becoming common in speech. Speech naturally uses forms like:

Kore wo o suki desu ka	Do you like this?

when "this" is presented to ascertain what the other person feels about it. Purists, however, still properly frown on the not unnatural reply:

Kore wo suki desu	I do like it.

It should be noted that with the *-tai* form *wo* in place of *ga* is the strict literary construction. But even in bungo we find such forms as

Fumi yomu ga tanoshi	I like reading books.

See under "Uses as a Conjunction," paragraph 5.

3. It may join two substantives. This is the standard and most usual bungo use of *ga*, and indicates that the first substantive in some way characterizes the second.

When the first substantive describes a person, the characterization usually indicates possession, but does not necessarily do so. The characterization may be of any kind. In the colloquial this function of *ga* has been almost entirely taken over by *no*. For a reasonably full discussion see under NO. Japanese usually say that *ga* is "stronger" than *no*. Sansom illustrates the difference by the phrase:

Shizuno-o ga ono no oto	The sound of the peasant's axe.

Ono ga waruki koto no zange	The confession of one's own sins.
Obana ga kaze . . .	The wind in the obana (i.e., the wind that stirs them) . . .
Kanaoka ga uma	A horse painted (drawn) by Kanaoka.
Izumotakeru ga tachi	Izumotakeru's sword.
Izumotakeru ga hakeru tachi	The sword that Izumotakeru wore.

Some grammarians say that in the above sentence *ga* marks the subject of the verb *hakeru*. It seems simpler, however, to consider that *ga* is used to show that the following substantive (*tachi*) is being characterized.

This bungo use of *ga* still persists in the colloquial in a large number of place-names and in a small number of stereotyped phrases.

Examples of place-names:

Amagasaki shi	Nun's Point Town
Hiru-ga-kojima	Leech Islet
Asama-ga-take	Mt. Asama

Examples of phrases:

Waga kuni	Our country (Japan)
Kimi ga yo	The Sovereign's reign
Man ga ichi	One out of ten thousand (a very small chance)
Kore ga yō ni	In this way
Nen ga nenjū	The whole year through
Kyō ga hi made shirazu ni ita	I was ignorant of it up to this very day

When *ga* is used, as in the last two examples, between words that are the same or that have similar meanings, the effect is simply that of strong emphasis.

Students should note that occasionally a word which cannot be inflected and so is a substantive in form may actually be used as a verb. Such words are usually of foreign origin. E.g.:

Anata ga goran no tōri desu   It is as you see.

Here *goran,* though a noun in form, has the force of a verb, of which *anata* is the subject.

It is, of course, possible that this usage derives from the bungo genitive use of *ga.*

Uses as a Conjunction

As a conjunction *ga* has the following uses:

1. It will, if there is any incongruity with a following clause, serve to emphasize the incongruity. This is one of the commonest uses in both bungo and the colloquial.

Bungo:

Takaki ni noborishi ga   (We) climbed to a high place
miezariki   but could not see (it).

Colloquial:

Kaze wa samui ga tenki wa yoi   The wind is cold but the
                                                   weather is good.

Ā iu ga kokoro de wa shinjite   That is what he says, but in
inai   his heart he does not believe
                                                   it.

Ame ga furō ga yari ga furō   It may rain rain, or it may
ga odoroku koto de nai   rain spears, but there is no
                                                   need for alarm.

Takai tokoro ni nobotta ga   (We) climbed to a high place,
mienakatta   but could not see (it).

2. It may act as a simple conjunction with the following clause, and is often used to give the speaker time to think what the next remark is going to be.

In speech the *ga* at the end of clauses is usually followed by at least a short pause. Sometimes the pause is quite long.

Bungo:

> *Nikkō ni yukishi ga sōrei*   (We) went to Nikkō and it
> *nariki*   was splendid.

Colloquial:

> *Watakushi mo shitte iru ga*   I know him too and he's a
> *shinsetsuna hito da*   very kind man.
> *Boku wa iku ga kimi wa*   I'm going—how about you?
> *Watakushi wa Tanaka de*   My name is Tanaka—is your
> *gozaimasu ga, go shujin wa*   master at home?
> *go zai-taku de irasshaimasu*
> *ka*

3. It may be used in the colloquial without any following clause. This use is very common in speech, and usually indicates politeness.

> The Japanese feel that, in talking with a person with whom one is not on familiar terms, to make a definite statement with which he might disagree smacks of rudeness. By suggesting that something may be added, *ga* gives the desired effect of a certain polite vagueness. As mentioned above, another use of this *ga* is to focus attention on a statement while the speaker takes time to think. If he decides not to say anything further there is no harm done.

> *Tonikaku sō iu hanashi ga*   At least that is what people
> *arimashita ga . . .*   said . . . (With the impli-
>   cation: "You don't have to
>   believe it," or "It is not im-
>   portant," etc.)

(Refer to WO, NO, WA, TOKORO GA, KEREDOMO.)

4. It may be used in bungo without any following clause. When so used *ga* becomes a word of emotion. It serves to make the previous sentence an expression of desire, not fact. The suggestion is: ". . . but that is not so. Would that it were!"

> In such expressions of desire *ga* is usually, but not always, combined with *mo* or *na*. (Cf. MO GA, GAMO, GANA.) Note that here *ga* follows the Line 3A form (*rentaikei*) of verbs and the *-ki* form of adjectives.

Inazuma no hikari no ma ni   Oh, to have seen you even for
   mo kimi wo miteshi ga   the time of a lightning-
                                 flash!

5. In bungo *ga* has still another use, which perhaps should not be called that of a conjunction, as here it acts also as a substantivizing particle, and seems to mark the subject.

Shiranu ga hotoke   Ignorance is bliss.
Mukō ni miyuru ga Fujisan   The one seen opposite is
   nari   Mt. Fuji.
Kotoba sukunaki ga ayashi   A dearth of words is
                                 intriguing.

Presumably the original function of *ga* in such sentences was that of a conjunction, as the sentences can also be read:

Not know (anything) but be Buddha.
Appear opposite and be Mt. Fuji.
Words few but be intriguing.

6. There is a special case of duplication (. . . *ga* . . . *ga* . . .). This is described by Matsumiya as "when two suppositional phrases of contrary meaning are followed by a clause which expresses the determination or the purpose of the speaker." In such sentences *ga* . . . *ga* . . . is equivalent to "whether . . . or . . ." It is often unnecessary to translate the *ga* at all.

This may be considered as simply a special example of uses as a conjunction, paragraph 1.

Tōkarō ga chikakarō ga   It may be far. It may be near.
   tonikaku itte mimashō   Anyway I'll try going.
Kikō ga kikumai ga hanasu   I intend to speak, whether
   tsumori desu   (they) listen or do not
                               listen.

-GAMASHII. Suffix, meaning "like," "smacking of," "-ish," etc., and usually used with a derogatory nuance.

It may be added to nouns, adverbs and the Line 2 form (*renyōkei*) of verbs. The combination then becomes a regular adjective.

It is sometimes written and pronounced -*gawashii*.

hito-gamashii	like a somebody (i.e., an important person)
tairan-gamashii	seeming extravagant
giron-gamashii	disputatious
katte-gamashii	looking or sounding selfish
ogori-gamashii	smacking of extravagance

GANA. A particle, with somewhat different uses in bungo, and in the colloquial. See also MO GANA.

BUNGO

In bungo *gana* expresses desire or the intensification of desire. It is used with the Line 3A form (*rentaikei*) of verbs, and the *ki* form of adjectives.

Aki narade
    Tsuma yobu shika wo
    Kikishi gana
	I would like to have heard the stag calling his mate when it was not fall.

Note that it may be used elliptically, when the context is such that an omitted verb can be clearly understood, as in:

Kano kimitachi wo (miteshi) *gana*	Those noble persons, would that I . . . (had seen them).

After interrogatives it gives a certain effect of indefiniteness:

Nani gana torasen to *omoedomo torasubeki* *mono nashi*	Though I felt "I would like to give something," there was nothing to give.

THE COLLOQUIAL

In the colloquial it seems to be always used with sentences which suggest or express desire on the part of the speaker.

The *gana* itself, however, gives an effect of indefiniteness, and after interrogative expressions makes them indefinites. (Cf. KA.)

When it is used, the postpositions *wa, ga* and *wo* may be omitted.

Nani gana nomitai	I want to drink something or other.
Shibai ni gana ikō	Let's go to the theatre or something.
Nan to shite gana hyakushō wo tasukeyō to omou kokoro ga atta zo	He had a heart that felt, "Somehow or other I want to help the peasants."

This last example is not modern, but is taken from a lecture on Mencius given in the Tokugawa period.

-GARI. A suffix with two possible meanings. It may be the Line 2 form (*renyōkei*) of the suffix -*garu* (see -GARU), or it may be used in bungo only, in such phrases as:

tsuma-gari yukeba . . .	when (he) goes to the place where (his) wife is . . .

Here the -*gari* seems to be equivalent to *ga ori (ni)*, although some authorities derive it from *kakari*.

-GARU. A suffix added to nouns, bases of adjectives and adverbs. It may be considered as a contraction of -*ge* and *aru*. (See -GE.) In the colloquial it forms a verb of the first (*yodan*) conjugation; in bungo it follows the irregular conjugation of *ari*.

1. When added to nouns it means "seem to think of oneself as" (chiefly used about a third person).

tsūjin-garu	seems to think he knows his way about
saishi-garu	consider himself a wit

There is a modern tendency to use -*garu* as a substitute for -*buru* 'to assume the airs of'. Strict grammarians object to this use.

2. When added to bases of adjectives or to adverbs it means "feel," or "seem to feel" a certain state of affairs to be so. This form also is chiefly used about a person other than oneself, and when so used necessarily implies that he somehow expresses his feeling.

Anna ni asonde kurashitai na to urayamashigaru	"Wouldn't I like to live playing around like that!" he says, enviously. (Thus he shows his feeling that it is an enviable state of affairs.)
okashi-garu	feel that something is funny
ita-garu	experience a feeling of pain
ikita-garu	feel a desire to go
iya-garu	(apparently) feel a dislike
samu-garu	feel cold
samu-gari	a person who is sensitive to cold
atarashi-garu	be fond of novelty (have a feeling for newness)

-GATA. A suffix. It is a sign of plurality, used only for persons. It is interchangeable with -*tachi,* but is a polite form implying respect. For comparison with other "plural" suffixes see -DOMO, -NADO, -RA, -TACHI, and -TŌ.

Kōzoku-gata	members of the Imperial family
go-fūjin-gata	ladies
anata-gata	you (plural)

-GATE (NI). Bungo suffix added to the Line 2 form (*renyōkei*) of verbs. It is used to indicate that the performance of the action described by the verb is difficult.

Karei-gate ni shite ...	Finding it difficult to return ...

-GATERA. Suffix added to nouns, including the Line 2 forms (*renyōkei*) of verbs acting as nouns.

It is used to indicate that what precedes it is the more important of two actions which are taken more or less simultaneously. In other words it marks the main performance of a person, to which any other action taken is incidental.

Imashime-gatera ni iu koto . . .	Something said in the process of admonition . . .

Sampo-gatera mizuguruma ni yotta koto mo arimashita	In the process of taking a walk, it also happened that (I) approached the water wheel.
Hanami-gatera Toda san wo hōmonshita	I went to see the cherry-blossoms and took the opportunity of calling on Mr. Toda.

Ume no hana
  Saki chiru sono ni
    Ware yukamu
Kimi ga tsukai wo
  Katamachi gatera
	Into the garden
	Where plum-blossoms fall
	  I will go . . .
	The while I unrequited
	Wait your messenger.

-GATERI. Suffix now obsolete. Equivalent to *-gatera*. (See -GATERA.)

-GAWASHII. Suffix, same as *-gamashii*.

-GE. Suffix, added to nouns, pronouns, adjective roots or the Line 2 form (*renyōkei*) of verbs. It makes a new noun.

This new noun describes a seeming condition of affairs. Hence it is not positive and could never be used about oneself except in connection with the way one seems to others.

otonage-nai	seemingly not grown up
ureshige	the appearance of being happy
mitage	the apparent desire to look

A *-ge* form may be turned into an adjective by the addition of *na* in the colloquial, *-naru* in bungo. It may also be used as an adverb with or without a following *ni*. These are the most common uses of this form.

ayashige na otoko	a suspicious-looking man
imi-arigena kao wo suru	give a knowing look
omowazuge ni shita	done apparently unintentionally
nanige naku	as if nothing were the matter; apparently unconcerned

Note that as -*ge* does not indicate a positive condition the rest
of a sentence in which it is used usually reflects this uncertainty.
This is especially true when the -*ge* form is not followed by -*na* or
ni. E.g.: one is more likely to hear *yukige desu ne* 'it looks like
snow, doesn't it?', rather than simply *yukige desu*.

In certain dialects the suffix -*ke* is sometimes given the sonant pronunciation -*ge*, but this is not standard Japanese. For the meaning
of such a -*ge*, see -KE.

-GENA. A suffix practically equivalent to -*rashii* 'seeming'. Its
use after nouns, pronouns, adjective roots, and the Line 2 form
(*renyōkei*) of verbs is treated under -GE.

There is also a special use of -*gena* after verbs in a sentence-
ending form. Here it is a contraction of -*ge nari* (bungo) and
means "the apparent condition of affairs is" as described.

This usage seems most prevalent in western Japan.

Mō kaetta-gena   (He) has already gone home, it seems.

GI. This word is usually listed in dictionaries as a noun meaning "matter" or "affair," "law," "ceremony," etc.

It has, however, a special use as a substitute for the postpositions *wa* or *ga* in a limited number of cases, chiefly documents
with a legal or semi-legal flavor. This use practically never occurs
in speech, but may be found in the epistolary style, particularly
when applied to the first person or to persons intimately related
to the first person.

Watakushi gi . . .
Watakushi wa . . .   As for me, I . . .

-GIRI. Sonant form of -*kiri*, with a slight suggestion of famili-
arity or rudeness.

Un to kotaeta-giri damatte ita He answered only "un" and
                                  remained silent.

GOTOKI, GOTOKU, GOTOSHI. A semi-adjective, which
retains many of the characteristics of a noun. It expresses the
idea of similarity or likeness.

It is perhaps best thought of as a noun, to which the suffixes

-ki, -ku, and *-shi* may be added so as to allow its use as an adjective, adverb, or verb.

It may help to realize that it was derived from the noun *koto* 'affair'. The form *goto* is found in early literature but is now obsolete except in certain dialects.

The suffixes *-ki, -ku,* and *-shi* retain their usual uses, save that the *-ku* form is not conjugated with *aru.* Other suffixes such as *-sa* or *-mi,* which are normally added to adjective roots, cannot be suffixed to *goto.*

Gotoki, gotoku and *gotoshi* are primarily bungo forms, but on account of their convenience are widely used in the colloquial.

These forms retain their substantive force on account of their meaning, "like," and are usually preceded by a *no* or *ga.*

It may help students to realize that in English we have the form "the like," and that we may sometimes use "like" and "the like of" interchangeably. E.g.:

A wa B no gotoshi	A is like B. A is the like of B.
B no gotoki hito . . .	A man like B . . . A man the like of B . . .

GURAI. (See KURAI.)   This is a sonant or "muddied" (*nigori*) form of *kurai.* Even more than *kurai* it seems to have a certain vagueness, an idea of "about" or "approximation." In speech it is generally used after nouns.

HA. One of the two common transliterations of は, the 26th syllable in the *kana gojūon* or "Table of 50 Sounds."

When this *kana* symbol comes at the beginning of a word it is usually both pronounced and transliterated as *ha.* However, when it is used either as a postposition or in the interior of a word it is usually pronounced and transliterated as *wa.*

For its uses as a postposition see WA.

HA, HAA, HAI. Interjection. A word of assent. Also used to show that one understands what the speaker has said.

Ha and *haa* are perhaps better considered as noises than as real words. They are usually used to equals or inferiors.

Hai, however, has attained the dignity of being in the dictionaries. It means "yes, sir" or "yes, ma'am," rather than simply
"yes," and is usually used by servants, women, and others who for
some reason wish to indicate that they are inferiors.

HAZU. This is a noun form with special uses as a particle. It
marks what it follows as fitting the facts as far as they are known.
It therefore indicates a strong likelihood or expectation for which
a definite reason exists.

> The original noun signified a notch, especially the notch of an arrow
> (*yahazu*). Therefore the suggestion is that "the arrow is on the
> bow-string." The idea is much like that of the English expression
> "It is on the cards" (that such and such a thing is to happen), etc.
> It has nothing to do with moral obligations.

Yamamoto san wa kyō kuru hazu desu	Mr. Yamamoto is expected to arrive today.
Ano hito wa irairashite ita hazu da	No wonder he was irritated.
Kyō Yokohama e iku hazu desu	I am (supposed) to go to Yokohama today.
Sonna hazu de wa nakatta	It could not have been like that! (judging from what I know about the facts).
Ima ni mieru hazu desu	He ought to show up presently.

As has already been noted, *hazu* does not in itself convey an idea
of moral obligation. There is, however, one use of *hazu* in which
moral obligation is strongly suggested. This occurs in sentences
where *hazu* refers to an expectation which is general, and not
merely that of a single person or a few individuals. Apparently
it occurs only in such sentences and not always then. Take as an
example:

Sore-kurai-na koto wa shitte iru hazu da	That sort of thing he ought to know.

If this sentence refers simply to the judgment and expectation
of the speaker, the idea conveyed is that the speaker has reason

to believe that the person spoken about does "know that sort of thing."

On the other hand, if this sentence refers to the general judg-ment and expectation of the community, the idea conveyed is like that of the English, "It is expected of him that he know that sort of thing." As in English, the suggestion is that it is a proper expectation, of which he must be aware, and that moral delin-quency is involved if he does not satisfy it. This suggestion is somewhat stronger in Japanese than in English, probably due to the fact that conformity to generally accepted standards is regarded in Japan as even more important than it is with us.

It may be added that the addition of a *hazu* tends to strengthen any idea of moral obligation implied by some previous form, such as *-beki* or *-te mo ii*. For example, as a very free translation:

Watashi ni uchiaketemo ii hazu da	I really think it wouldn't do any harm if he were candid with me.

Once the meaning of *hazu* has been understood, it of course depends on the context how its effect can best be given in English.

For example, the following passage occurs in a fairy-tale, in which it is related how a magic object slips from the owner's hand and is stolen by an invisible enemy. The Japanese goes on:

Ochite kita hazu no fukube ga mienaku natta node iyoiyo awatete kusa wo wakete sagashita	The bottle-gourd, which he naturally supposed had fallen to the ground, had disappeared, and so, in ever-increasing agitation, he parted the grass and searched for it.

The translation given for *ochite kita hazu* might well be ren-dered by other locutions, such as "which he had every reason to think had fallen," "which ought naturally to have fallen," etc.

HE. A particle, used as (1) a postposition and (2) an interjec-tion.

1. For its use as a postposition see under E (HE).

This postposition is written in *kana* with the 29th character of the 50-Sound Table, ∧ , the 4th character in the (H) column. It is, however, pronounced *e* (like an English "eh"). It is often transliterated in Romaji as "ye," and in fact is sometimes so pronounced. E.g., *doko ye* for *doko e* 'where to?'

2. As an interjection it is used to express assent, or to signify that the speaker has heard and understood what was said to him. It is similar in use to *haa* or *ha*.

HODO. A noun, which has also a number of uses as a particle.

The basic meaning of *hodo* seems to be something like "that which surrounds." It is used today as a noun in the various senses of physical surroundings, circumstances, bounds, moderation ("a being within bounds"), etc.

As a particle it retains a slight noun feeling, but generally performs functions like those of true adverbs. (For a comparison with *dake*, *-bakari*, and *kurai* (*-gurai*) see under DAKE.)

As a particle it has two main uses.

After Numerical Expressions

After numbers or numerical expression *hodo* has much the effect of the English "something around" or "about."

isshūkan hodo	about a week
hyakunin hodo	something around a hundred men

After Other Words

If *hodo* immediately follows a substantive, without any intervening particle, it may itself act as a particle and mark that substantive as describing a limit up to which some condition exists.

When so used it has an effect like that of the English phrases "up to the extent of," "to the extent that." The best translation will of course depend on the context.

If *hodo* immediately follows an adjective or verb in the attributive form, and is not itself followed by a particle, it acts as a particle with a similar effect.

Yama hodo takai no desu	It is as tall as a mountain (. . . tall to that extent).
Jidōsha hodo benrina mono wa nai	There is nothing so convenient as an automobile (. . . to the extent of an automobile).
Anata hodo no hito . . .	Such a man as you . . . (A person who reaches to your standard . . .)
Yomikirenai hodo hon wo moratta	I received more books than I could read (. . . to the extent that I could not finish reading them).
Kinō tsukareru hodo hataraita	Yesterday I worked till I was tired out.
Shigoto nasare yo tasuki no kireru hodo	Do your work, up to the wearing-out of your *tasuki!*
Fureba furu hodo ii desu	The more it rains the better. (If rain, to the extent that it rains it is good.)
Hayakeriya hayai hodo ii	The sooner the better.
Chimpon wa furui hodo takai	Rare books are more expensive the older they are.
Ōi hodo yoroshii	The more there are the more satisfactory it is. (It is satisfactory to the extent that there are many.)

Note that in these last four sentences the English idiom requires a special translation of a "the more . . . the more" type. It may help to understand the "feel" of the Japanese idiom if one notices that *ōi* is never used except as a predicate adjective.

The English equivalent of this type of sentence of course depends on the context. Note that one may have the same *form* and yet require a different English translation. E.g.:

Nikurashii hodo kawaii wa	She is so lovely that she inspires hatred (. . . lovely to that extent).

There is one idiomatic use of *hodo* which often puzzles foreigners. In this a substantive which precedes *hodo* is itself preceded by a modifying verb or adjective.

Bakanaru ko hodo kawaii	The more the child is a dunce the dearer he is (to his parents) .
Takai basho hodo kaze ga ōi	The higher the place, the more the wind

This seems to be a case of simple inversion. The first sentence, for instance, is practically equivalent to *ko wa bakanaru hodo kawaii,* and the second to *basho wa takai hodo kaze ga ōi.*

NOTE. If it is not at once obvious whether *hodo* is used as a noun or a particle, it usually does not matter. E.g.:

Niwa to iu hodo no niwa de nai	It is not such a garden that one calls it a "garden" (i.e., it is not much of a garden) .
Kurakute ashimoto ga mienai hodo desu	It is so dark that one cannot see what is at one's feet.
Ano yama wa ten ni todoku hodo ni takai	That mountain is so high that it reaches to heaven.
Sore hodo made ni shinakutemo ii	You need not go to that extent.
Ima made mo kusuri wo nonde iru hodo da kara . . .	Since the circumstances are such that I am still taking medicine . . .
Ano obaasan wa nasake wo shiranai ni mo hodo ga aru	That old woman goes to the limit in pitilessness.

I. 1. The sound *i* is often a substitution for an older *ki* or *shi* sound.

(a) The colloquial suffix *-i,* which is added to adjective roots, substitutes for the bungo suffixes *-ki* and *-shi.* For example, *shiroi* substitutes for both *shiroki* and *shiroshi.*

(b) The colloquial contractions of *-te* or *-ta* (*-tari*) forms show (taking the *-te* form as example) :

standard: -*ite* from -*kite,* as *kaite* from *kakite*

standard: -*ide* from -*gite,* as *oyoide* from *oyogite* (with a shift of the sonant *nigori*)

dialects: -*ite* from -*shite,* as *saite* from *sashite*

(c) Even in nouns the substitution occurs. Thus *kisaki* 'empress consort' is more common than *kisai,* but both occur. On the other hand *saiwai* 'good fortune' is the only form now used, but it was originally *sakiwai.*

2. The sound *i* is often used, in both bungo and colloquial, to replace a standard *e* sound. E.g.:

Kōya no yama i	towards Mt. Koya
Kōya no yama e	

3. The sound *i* is occasionally used, especially in the colloquial, to replace a standard *yō* sound. E.g.:

kyōjin mitai ni	like a madman
kyōjin mitayō ni	

-I. A suffix having various uses, depending on what precedes it.

1. Its most common use in the colloquial is as a suffix to adjective "roots." (See the introductory Note on Adjectives.) When it is so used the resultant word may serve either as (a) an adjective, or (b) a verb. E.g.:

(a)	*Shiroi hon desu*	It is a white book.
(b)	*Hon ga shiroi*	The book is white.

It thus performs, in the colloquial, the work of the two bungo suffixes -*ki* and -*shi.* (Cf. -KI, -SHI.)

For the sake of beginners, it is worth emphasizing the fact that in Japanese there is a close similarity between verbs and adjectives. A word like *shiroi* is usually classed as an adjective, yet when it comes at the end of a sentence, as in example (b) above, it undoubtedly performs the functions of a verb—in fact it is a verb in the English sense. In the same way, any word usually classed as a verb may be used, without differentiation from its sentence-ending form, to modify a noun and so perform the functions of an adjective. In other words, in the colloquial there is no differentiation between the Line 3 form *(shūshikei)* and the Line 3A form *(rentaikei)*.

> The adjective "root" plus *-i* may be considered as the Line 3, 3A form *(shūshikei* and *rentaikei)* of the colloquial *-ku, -i, -kere* conjugation. See the introductory Note on Adjectives.

It should be noted that there are a few forms, such as *shikakui* 'four-cornered', *netsui* 'persevering', etc., in which the *-i* has been added directly to words of Chinese origin.

2. In its other uses, both in the colloquial and in bungo, *-i* is practically equivalent to an exclamation mark. It is perhaps better to consider it as an emphatic noise, rather than a true suffix. In the colloquial it is used:

(a) After imperatives (see also introductory Note on Verbs).

Koi	Come!
Tabei	Eat!
Taberoi	Eat!

Of the above forms the first *(koi)* is standard. The others are examples of rather vulgar language.

(b) After sentences ending with verbs in the *-ta* or *-da* form.

Sō de arō to omouta-i	(I) thought it would be that way!

(c) After interrogative sentences ending with *-da* or *-ka*. When so used it has the same effect of slight doubt that is given by the suffix *-e*. (See -E.)

Dare da-i, ima waratta no wa	Who's that?—who laughed just now?

WARNING. Foreign students of the colloquial sometimes have trouble with verbs which end sentences and yet are apparently in the Line 2 form *(renyōkei)*.

They may recognize these as the bungo Line 3 forms *(shūshikei)* of the verbs *ari, ori* and *haberi* (usually in proverbs or well-known quotations from the classics). To these may be added *nari* (from *ni ari*).

In these forms -*i* is of course not a real suffix. See the bungo conjugations in the introductory Note on Verbs.

-IDA, -IDE. Verb endings, not true suffixes. (See also -IDE.) In the colloquial these are the standard contractions for the -*ta* and -*te* forms of (G) verbs of the first (*yodan*) conjugation. See introductory Note on Verbs. E.g.: *oyoide*, contracted from *oyogite* (*oyogu* 'swim').

-IDE. A suffix to the Line 1 form (*mizenkei*) of verbs. It is not "standard" either for bungo or the colloquial, but will be found in *kyōgen* and in a few local dialects. (See also -IDA, -IDE.) It is equivalent in meaning to the negative suffixes -*zute* or -*naide*.

Apparently it came into use first in Ashikaga times. Hence its retention in *kyōgen*. It may have developed from a lengthening of the vowel sound before a negative -*de*. (See -DE.) Yamada, however, considers it equivalent to -*naide*, with the -*i* taking the place of -*nai*.

Kikaide nan to seu	What shall we do if we don't hear?
Onore wa kiki mo sadameide ikioru	You are going off without making sure even by asking!
Ocha demo mairimaseide . . .	Without taking tea or anything . . .
Sanyō ga dekitemo dekiidemo . . .	Whether the calculation can be made or not . . .

-ITA, -ITE. Verb endings, not true suffixes, which occasionally give trouble to students, especially when written in Romaji. (See also -TA, -TE, and the introductory Note on Verbs.)

1. In the colloquial, if these forms are preceded by a vowel in Romaji, they may be:

(a) Standard contractions of -*kita* and -*kite* forms of (K) verbs of the first (*yodan*) conjugation. The *kana* ゐ (*i*) is used for these. E.g.:

kaita, contracted from *kakita* (*kaku* 'write')

(b) Standard uncontracted -*ta* and -*te* forms of -*iru* verbs of the second conjugation *(kami ichidan)*. In *kana* the Romaji *i* may be い *(i)*, ひ *(hi)*, or ゐ *(wi)*. E.g.:

> *mochiite (mo-chi-hi-te)* from *mochiiru,* 'use'
> *ite (wi-te* or *i-te)* from *iru* 'be'

(c) Local contractions of *-shita* and *-shite* forms of (S) verbs of the first *(yodan)* conjugation, not often used on the main island. The *kana i* is used for these also. E.g.:

> *mekaita,* contracted from *mekashita (mekasu* 'dress finely')

2. In the colloquial, if these forms are preceded by a consonant they are uncontracted, and may be:

(a) Standard *-ta* and *-te* forms of *-iru* verbs of the second conjugation *(kami ichidan)*. The *kana* for these of course combines the Romaji *i* with the preceding consonant (or consonants). E.g.:

> *mite (mi -te)* from *miru* 'see'
> *omonjite (o-mo-n-ji-te)* from *omonzuru, omonjiru* 'consider important'

(b) Standard *-ta* and *-te* forms of (S) verbs of the first conjugation *(yodan)*. The *kana* for these is *-shi-ta* and *-shi-te*. E.g.:

> *dashita (da-shi-ta)* from *dasu* 'put out'

(c) Standard *-ta* and *-te* forms of *suru* 'do', 'make', either alone or as the final component of a compound. E.g.:

> *benkyō shita (shi-ta)* from *benkyō-suru* 'study'

3. In bungo the *-ta* form does not occur without further suffixes (e.g., *-taru, -taredo,* etc.). As there are no contractions in bungo the Line 2 form *(renyōkei)* of a verb remains when the *-te* (or *-ta*) is removed. The only problem for a student wishing to look up a verb in the dictionary is therefore to find out whether this Line 2 form belongs to a verb of the first conjugation *(yodan)* or the second *(kami ichidan* or *kami nidan)*.

If, however, the bungo is written in Romaji or in "phonetic" *kana,* used in order to approximate the sound, it is quite possible

that the "h" of a *kana* syllable *hi* has been omitted, and it is necessary to look out for this. E.g.:

> *omoite* (*o-mo-hi-te*) from *omo*(*h*)*u* 'think', 'feel'

IWANYA. See under wo YA.

-IYA. (See -YA.) Technically this is not a suffix, but a contraction of the sound *-eba*. It is very common in speech. E.g.:

Kōsan shinakeriya utsu zo   If (you) don't surrender (I)
                                 will fire!

Watashi wa ikanakeriya   I must go.
naranai

Here the *-nakeriya* of course corresponds to *-nakereba* 'if not'.

IYA. In *Kyōgen* there is a *iya* which has the same meaning as
aruiwa 'or', 'perhaps', from which it is probably derived.

JA. Common colloquial contraction, usually written in *kana* as
a sonant *chi* plus *ya* ぢや but also sometimes as a sonant *shi* plus
ya じや. It may be a contraction:
  1. Of *de wa* or *-de wa*. See DE WA. E.g.:

Sō ja nai
Sō de wa nai   It is not that way.

Nonja imasen   (He) is not drinking.

  2. Of *de aru*. E.g.:

Kore wa hon ja
Kore wa hon de aru   This is a book.

JAA. A fairly common, colloquial word. In *kana* it is usually
written as a sonant, *chi* or *shi* plus *ya*, plus *a*, ぢやあ or じやあ.
  As an introductory word, it is a good deal like an English
"We-ell, if that's it." Japanese dictionaries give it as meaning:

> *de wa*
> *sore de wa*
> *saraba*

> *sō nara*
> *shikaraba*
> *sore naraba*

When used within a sentence it seems to be always a substitute for *de wa.*

Hon jaa arimasen	It is not a book.
Iya jaa nee kae	Disagreeable, ain't it? (Vulgar.)

-JAU. A fairly common colloquial contraction of *-de shimau.* There are similar contractions for variant forms. Cf. -CHAU. E.g.:

yonjau *yonde shimau*	finish reading
yonjatta *yonde shimatta*	did finish reading

-JI. A bungo suffix, added to the Line 1 form (*mizenkei*) of verbs. (See also -JIRU and -ZU, -ZURU.)

It indicates negative probability or determination. It corresponds to, but is rather stronger than, the colloquial *-mai.* The idea of determination of course enters in only when one is referring to one's own future actions. (See -MAI.)

Kaze fukaji *Kaze wa fukumai*	It probably won't blow.
Hōshi bakari urayamashi- *karanu mono wa araji*	There are probably none who are envied so little as Buddhist priests.
Yo wa ichi gon mo iwaji	I won't say another word.

-JIRU. A modified form of *-zuru* (*suru*), which is much used in the spoken colloquial. It belongs to the second (*kami ichidan*) conjugation. See -ZURU, and -NZURU. E.g., *meijiru* 'order' (*meisuru, meizuru*).

-JŌ. Suffix, usually added to Chinese compound nouns, occasionally to other nouns also. It forms a new compound noun.

This -*jō* is written with the Chinese character for *ue* 'up', 'above'. Compare with . . . *no ue kara* 'from the point of view of . . . ', and the adverbial use of *-teki* or *-teki ni*.

It means "circumstances surrounding . . . ," or when used adverbially "from the point of view of . . . ," "in the world of . . . ," etc.

Kōkogakujō Anyō no	In the world of archeology the
hakkutsu wa yūmei de aru	excavations of Anyang are **famous.**

KA.   A pronunciation of the particle *ke,* used in counting years, **months,** or weeks, as in *ni ka getsu* 'two months'. See KE.

KA.   A particle indicating doubtfulness.   In many of its uses it corresponds to a verbal question-mark.

It is impossible here to give all the innuendoes of *ka,* but the student should have no great difficulty in understanding the uses of *ka* if he studies the examples given below and remembers that *ka* always expresses a very definite doubt about what precedes it. See also KAMO, KANA, KASHI, KA SHIRA, MONO KA, KA WA.

The functions of *ka* in the colloquial are fairly simple, but the bungo uses present certain difficulties.   It has therefore seemed best to give separate treatment to *ka* in the colloquial and in bungo.

THE COLLOQUIAL

In the colloquial the function of *ka* depends primarily on its position in a sentence', that is, whether it is placed at the end or in the interior.   It depends secondarily on the nature of the word or phrase it follows.   (Cf. MONO KA.)

1. At the end of declarative sentences *ka* turns the statement into a question, either actual or rhetorical.   Note that the verb 'to be" is often omitted where the meaning is obvious without it.

(a)   After positive statements we have a simple question:

Kimi wa mainichi gakkō e ıku ka	Do you go to (the) school every day?
Kore wa kimi no empitsu ka	Is this your pencil?

Koko ni geisha ga oranu to   Do you mean to tell me that
  mōsu no ka   there are no geisha here?
(Q) *Sō desu ka*— (A) *Sō desu* Is it that way?—It is that way.

Note, however, that in ordinary conversation, if the expression *sō desu ka* is used in answer to a positive statement, it is a rhetorical question only, accepting the statement. This usage is very much like the English "Is that the way it is?" which may be used in the sense of "I hadn't heard that before."

(b) After negative statements *ka* often demands a positive answer. This is especially true after forms of *de wa nai*, and exactly parallels English usage.

Kono hana wa kirei de wa nai   These flowers are beautiful,
  ka   aren't they?

Ikō de wa nai ka   Let's go, shan't we?
Ikō ja nai ka

Sō de nai ka   Isn't it so?
Ii kufū wa arumai ka   Mightn't there be a good plan?

(c) After "dubitative" statements (i.e., those in which the verb has the *-u, -yō* ending) the *ka* may question the doubt (or doubt the supposition) and so be equivalent to irony. This also more or less parallels the English usage.

Sō deshō ka   Is that likely?
Boku wa baka de arō ka   I am probably a fool, eh?

It may also be used to question the probability, and so have an effect something like an "I guess."

Mono no nijūdo mo yattarō ka   I probably tried it some
                                 twenty times, I guess.

2. When *ka* is used at the end of sentences that are already interrogatory it sharpens them and rather demands an answer. In such sentences it is practically untranslatable except by vocal inflection:

Dare da   Who is it?
Dare desu ka   Who is it? — ? — ?

Ima kita no wa dare ka   Who's that who's just come?
Doko ni (desu) ka   Where (is it at)?
Shokun, bungaku to wa nan   Gentlemen, what is "litera-
de aru ka   ture"?

3. When *ka* is used in pairs it has the effect of "either . . . or," "whether . . . or." It may sometimes be translated by a single "or."

Kore desu ka   Are desu ka   Is it this or is it that?
Shiroi no desu ka akai no desu   (I) don't know whether it is
ka wakaranai   a red or a white one.
Biiru ka sake ka wo kudasai   Please give me either beer or
                                    sake.
Kinō kimi ga kaeru ka kaera-   He came yesterday just when
nai ka ni ano hito ga kita   you had gone home (when
                                    I was in doubt whether you
                                    had gone home).

4. When *ka* is used in the interior of sentences after interrogative pronouns it causes them to lose their interrogative force and to become indefinite.

When so used *ka* may substitute for *ga* or *wo,* or be followed by them. It may be either preceded or followed by other postpositions such as *ni, to, e,* etc.

Dare ka heya ni orimasu ka   Is there anybody in the room?
Dare ka orimasu   There is somebody there.
Dare ka ga mite orimashita   *Somebody* was looking on.
Koko ni dare ka no bōshi ga   Here's somebody's hat!
aru
Nani ka shiroi mono ga sokoni   There was something white
arimashita   there.
Itsu ka mata aimashō   We may meet again some time.
Dō ka   Somehow.
Dono hon ka ni kimeyō   I will decide on some book.
                                    [Note that this is literally:
                                    I will decide in connection
                                    with (the question) "which
                                    book?"]

Ikutsu ka kaimashō	I will buy a number (of them).
Dochira ka wo anata ni age-masu	I will give you one or the other.
Nani ka de mita yō da	I'm pretty sure I've seen it in something (i.e., in some book or magazine, etc.).
Dare ka ni yarō *Dare ni ka yarō*	I'll give it to somebody.

There is one apparent exception to the above rule, found in such interrogative sentences as:

| *Nani ka tabetai* *Nani ka tabetai no* | There is something you would like to eat? |

It is, however, only an apparent exception, as the interrogative word does have the force of an indefinite. The example given is not equivalent to a bold "What do you want to eat?"

Why such sentences are questions and not simple statements is not wholly clear. However, they all seem to be very short sentences. Possibly they are so short that the influence of the interrogative is not wholly lost.

It should be noted that some gesture or tone of voice is needed to make sure that sentences like these are to be regarded as questions. With another tone of voice, *Aa, nanika tabetai* might be equivalent to "Gosh, I'm hungry!"

5. When *ka* is used in the interior of sentences after nouns, pronouns, or substantive phrases which are not interrogative, it shows some kind of uncertainty about them.

Ōsaka ni ka orimashō	I think he lives in Osaka (but I am not sure).
Yoshida to ka iu hito . . .	Someone named, I think, Yoshida . . .
Iku to iu ga hayai ka ikimashita	Almost before he had said "I will go," he had gone. (More literally: "Was the thus saying earlier?")

(a) In some sentences it is obvious that a second *ka* has been omitted (cf. section 3).

Biiru ka sake (ka) kudasai	Please give me beer or sake.
Ōsaka ka Nagasaki no uchi ni orimasu	He is in either his Osaka or his Nagasaki house.

(b) Note that in examples such as the two given below it is usually a question of nomenclature whether we consider them as each one sentence, or as two sentences of which the first is a question. The sense would be the same, however, in either case.

Ame ga futta no ka michi ga nurete imasu	It has rained, has it? The road is all wet.
Boku ni dekiru ka yatte miyō	I'll try and see whether I can do it (or not).

(c) In some sentences the parsing is difficult, yet the meaning is perfectly obvious. E.g.:

Seifu wa Rokoku ni chūkoku-shita ga, Rokoku wa kore ni ōjinai bakari ka, kaette bobi wo kataku shita	The Government made remonstrances to Russia, but Russia was not only unresponsive to these—on the contrary, she made the defenses stronger.

Here the *bakari ka* has the effect of an interpolated "Was it only that?—No!"

NOTE. In order to appreciate the importance of the position of *ka*, note the difference between:

Doko e iku ka	
Doko e ka	Where (are you) going?

and

Doko ka e iku	
Doko ka e	(I am) going somewhere.

and also such a poem as the following, where it is obvious that the verb *suru* has been omitted:

Kane tsukanu	A village where they ring
Mura wa nani wo ka	No bells!—What do they do at
Haru no kure	Dusk in Spring?

It may be of interest to append the following variations of the question "Where do you live?"

Doko ni iru	Business language (slightly rude in conversation)
Doko ni iru ka	Complete—not polite nor impolite
Doko ni iru no	Slight deference—woman's type of phrase
Doko ni iru no ka	Demands an answer, but is not rude
Doko ni iru no desu	Polite, standard
Doko ni iru no desu ka	Polite, but complete and rather urges answer

There are a countless number of other possible politer variations, which include the use of *dochira* for *doko; oru, irassharu, o-ide-ni-naru* and their *-masu* forms for *iku; de arimasu* and *de gozaimasu* for *desu;* etc.

WARNING. *Ka* is sometimes used, as an abbreviation of *shika,* 'more than'. Cf. KYA.

This usually occurs, in the colloquial, when the *ka* immediately follows *bakari, dake, hodo, kiri,* or *kurai (-gurai)*, and is itself followed by a negative verb. E.g.:

Hyakunin bakari ka ikana-katta	Not more than about one
Hyakunin bakari shika ika-nakatta	hundred people went.

BUNGO

In bungo *ka* has all the functions that it has in the colloquial, and some others besides.

Note that it normally demands the Line 3A form (*rentaikei*)

for the verbs affected by it, and the -*ki* form for the "adjectives,"
i.e., sentence-ending verbs which are "adjective" in form.

1. At the end of sentences it performs the same interrogative
function as in the colloquial (cf. sections 1 and 2). However
after "dubitative" sentences using -*mu* or -*majiki* suffixes, it is
likely to be more strongly rhetorical.

Saru koto iubeki ka	Should such things as that be said?
Umi to yama to izure wo kono-mu ka	Which do you prefer, the sea or the mountains?
Harusame no furu wa namida ka	The fall of spring rain—is it tears?
Makoto ni sono hito ka	Is it truly that person?
Ima ichido dani miru majiki ka	Will I probably not look even once again?
Kore wo tango to mitometaru ka ni tsukite ronzemu	I shall now talk about (the question) "Does one consider these as being words?"
Kare wa ikitaramu ka	Is he likely to be alive? (Suggesting it is not likely.)

There is one case where *ka* comes at the end of a sentence and
is not interrogative. This apparently occurs only in old bungo
and after a previous *mo*. Under these conditions the *ka* may be
a sign of emotion. As an example, take the following from the
Kokinshū:

Shiratsuyu wo	Ah, the spring willows,
Tama ni mo nukeru	Which let white dewdrops
Haru no yanagi ka	Fall like pearls!
Kokoro yowaku mo	My heart is weak, and oh!-
Otsuru namida ka	My falling tears!

But in more recent bungo a previous *mo* still leaves the final
ka interrogative. Take the following *haiku* by Bashō:

Futari mishi	The snow that we two
Yuki wa kotoshi mo	Saw (together) this year also
Furikeru ka	Has it fallen?

(Incidentally, this was sent as an invitation to one of Bashō's fellow-poets.)

2. When *ka* is used in pairs it has the same effect of "either . . . or" as in the colloquial. In some sentences it is obvious that the second *ka* has been omitted.

Kimi ni nashi ka ringo ka wo teisemu	I will give you either pears or apples.
Kare wa yukitaru ka kaeritaru ka	Has he gone or has he come back home?
Hitori ka futari kitaru	One or two people have come.
Sore ka aranu ka koe no kawaranu	Be it that or not, the voice did not change.
Nasubeki koto no aru ka naki ka	Is there or is there not something that ought to be done?

3. Even in the interior of sentences *ka* retains its interrogative force in the older bungo, and makes the whole sentence a question. In later bungo the double *ka* is used to mean "either . . or . . .," and in modern bungo *ka* after an interrogative pronoun makes it an indefinite pronoun, in the same way as in the colloquial (cf. colloquial, section 4).

Strictly, if the sentence is a question the Line 3A form (*rentaikei*) should be used for the final verb; if not, then the Line 3 form (*shūshikei*) or the imperative (*meireikei*). This rule, however, does not seem to be always observed

The question of when *ka* is *kakari* and when it is *musubi* is of great interest for grammarians, but quite complicated. It does not seem of much practical importance to students who are simply learning modern bungo. Others are referred to grammars where the subject is adequately treated. Limitations of space prevent adequate treatment here.

Examples for older bungo:

Kotoshi wa ikutsu ni ka nareru	How old have you become this year?
Hito tare ka fubo nakaramu	Among men who is there without parents?
Ikanaru yue ni ka arikemu	What may have been the reason?

For modern bungo:

Nanji ga konomu tokoro izure   Choose whichever you like.
  ka wo erabe
Nanji ka ware ka yukazaru   Either you or I must go.
  bekarazu

4. There is a special case when *ka* follows a verb in the Line 4 form *(izenkei)*. Normally this presents no difficulties, because the suffix *-ba* is usually added to the verb form. E.g.:

Ikubaku no ta wo tsukureba ka Is it because (you) work so
  hototogisu   many fields, O, cuckoo?

But even when the *-ba* is omitted the feeling of "is it because" remains, though it is not quite so sharp. This use of a Line 4 form with a following *ka* rather suggests that a negative answer is expected.

Ashibe yori   Is it perhaps because my
  Michikuru shio no   thoughts are with the con-
    Iyamashi ni   stant growing of the tide
  Omoe ka kimi ga   that comes in from the reed-
    Wasurekane tsutsu   beds, that I continue unable
                     to forget you?

5. There is one other special case that must be mentioned. When *ka* follows a subordinate clause ending with a verb in the *-mu, -n* "dubitative" form, the idea of supposition is conveyed. Apparently this occurs only in modern bungo, and only when the supposition is not a factual one. E.g.:

Happyaku man no shōgakusei If the eight million primary
  yoretsu ni narite arukan   school children should walk
  ka . . .   four abreast . . .

NOTE. As was said at the beginning of this article, it is impossible to give examples of all the innuendoes of *ka*, but it always shows some kind of doubt about what precedes it.

It is amusing to note that English idiom sometimes expresses such a doubt by the use of the word "doubtless." E.g.:

| *Kare wa kanzuru tokoro arite jishoku seri* | For good reasons he has resigned his position. |
| *Kare wa kanzuru tokoro arite ka jishoku seri* | Doubtless for good reasons, he has resigned his position. |

-KA. A contraction sometimes found as a suffix to adjective roots. It may be derived from the suffix *-ku* plus the particle *ha* (*wa*). For example,

> *Iitaka ie,* "If you wish to speak, speak!"

Note that this corresponds to the normal *-kuba* form which is often written *-kuha*. Its derivation, however, may have been along the lines of *-kereba, -keriya, -kya*.

-KABA, -KADO.   See -BA, -DO, and -SHIKA.

KAMO. A bungo particle expressing emotion. Apparently it originally had both the questioning effect of *ka* and the additive effect of *mo,* but it is often quite untranslatable.

> *. . ideshi tsuki kamo*   . . . the moon that rose! . . .

WARNING. When *ka* and *mo* occur together in the colloquial, they do not form one particle, but remain separate, each particle having its usual function.

KAMOSHIRAN, etc. When *kamo* is immediately followed by negative forms of *shiru* 'know', we get forms like *kamoshiran, kamoshiremasen,* etc., which may be regarded as independent words meaning "maybe," "possibly," "perhaps."

KANA, GANA. In bungo a literary particle, expressing emotion. When the emotion is desire, *kana* is usually preceded by *mo* and pronounced as the sonant *gana*. It is usually untranslatable, and its exact effect will depend on the context. In poetry it always carries on the thought and is sometimes regarded as a more modern form of *kamo*. (See KAMO.)

| *Mukashi wo ima ni nasu yoshi mo gana* | Would that I could make the past into the present. |

Yononaka wa	Oh, the wide world's ways!
Mikka minu ma ni	Cherry blossoms left un-
Sakura kana	watched
	Even for three days!
Ame harete	Clearing after showers;
Shibaraku bara no	And for a little while the
Nioi kana	scent
	Of hawthorn flowers . . .

Note that when it follows a verb or adjective, these are put in the *rentaikei* (attributive) form.

Aa, kanashiki kana	Ah, woe is me!
Ame furikeru kana	The rain has fallen!

THE COLLOQUIAL

In the colloquial *kana* is not one particle, but the two separate particles *ka* and *na*, each of which retains its own force. The *na* is very often pronounced *nā* (long). (Cf. KA, NA, NE.)

This combination is found at the end of sentences. *Ka* puts the sentence in question form, and *na* shows that agreement is expected from the person addressed. An answer in words, however, is not necessarily expected. There are various English forms which give a similar effect.

Mō chiru ka na	Noon already, eh?
Osoku naranai ka na	(I'm) not late, then?
Fushiginaru ka na	Wasn't it strange!
	(Used as an interjection, quoted from bungo.)
Boku no tokei wa chigatte ita no ka na	My watch was wrong after all, wasn't it?
Kyō wa konai no ka na	He won't come today, I'm afraid.

KARA.   A postposition, often used as a conjunction.

In the early language *kara* seems to have been a noun meaning something like "starting-point," "origin," and hence "cause." As a postposition it is used much less in bungo than in the colloquial.

Kara marks what it follows as a limit or base from which action takes place.   (See YORI NI.)   It may follow:

1. Substantives
2. Statements
3. Verbs in the *-te* form.

It will be noted that when *kara* follows statements, these are always definite and particularized enough to be thought of as "limits" (either time-limits or causal bases), from which another action develops.   These statements therefore closely resemble substantives in all essentials except form—in fact, whether or not they are substantives is chiefly a matter of nomenclature.   After such statements, however, *kara* performs functions hardly distinguishable from those of a conjunction, and if one prefers to call it a conjunction there is no harm done, except to nomenclaturists. For special uses see also KARA NI and KARA WA.

The following examples will illustrate the functions of *kara*:

I. After Substantives

After substantives, *kara* usually indicates a limit in space or time.   However, if the substantive is used to describe a state of affairs, it is considered as the beginning, and hence the cause, of subsequent action.

Note that while *kara* performs much the same functions as the English word "from," other locutions are often to be preferred.

Furansu kara kita hikōki . . .	The aeroplane which arrived from France . . .
Nagai ryokō kara kaette kuru	Come back from a long journey.
Goji kara kaien suru	Open the performance at 5 o'clock.
Chichi kara goaisatsu itashimasu	I bring you greetings from my father.
Seigun kara shutsudō wo kaishishita	Started the mobilization with the western troops.

Ame wa kumo kara okoru	Rain comes from clouds.
Kō iu jiken kara shuppatsu wo miawaseta	Owing to these conditions he postponed his departure.
Ojisan kara tebukuro wo morau	Receive (a pair of) gloves from one's uncle.
Saishi kara hanareru	Be separated from wife and child.
Sore kara nochi ni . . .	In the period after that . . .
Niitakayama wa ichiman sanzenjaku kara desu	Mt. Niitaka is more than thirteen thousand feet (high).
Tōkyō kara no tegami da	It is a letter from Tokyo.
Sanshu no jingi wa tsurugi to tama to kagami kara naru	The "three-fold regalia" is composed of (comes-into-being from) sword, jewel, and mirror.
Asa kara ban made hataraku	He works from morning to night-time.
Watakushi kara hajimemashō	Let us start with me.
Hitsuyō kara yatta	He acted from necessity.

2. After Statements

When *kara* follows a statement (i.e., a statement of fact in sentence form) it marks that statement as the basis or origin, and therefore the cause, of subsequent action.

When so used *kara* may be considered a conjunction meaning "hence," or "therefore." Some students prefer to think of it as "from" in the sense of "because." For a comparison with *node*, see under NODE.

Note that technically *kara* follows the *rentaikei* (the attributive form) of verbs and adjectives. In the colloquial there is no difference between this and the *shūshikei* (sentence-ending form). Therefore it is correct to say that in the colloquial it may follow sentence-ending forms.

Kore wa ōkii kara motto chiisai no wo koshiraete ageyō	This is (too) big, so I shall make a smaller one for you.

Torō to omoimashita ga oyadori ga kawaisō da kara yamemashita	I thought I would take them, but the mother bird was so pitiful that I gave up the idea.
Usagi wa itakute tamarimasen kara naite imashita	The rabbit could not stand the pain and so was weeping.
Sō desu kara dō shimashō	Since it is that way what shall we do?
Kō iu jiken ga atta kara shuppatsu wo miawaseta	Because such conditions existed he postponed his departure.

Note that in such a sentence as *ano hito wa miru kara osoroshii hito da* 'from one look, he's a dreadful person', *miru* may be regarded as "a looking," i.e., a substantive even though in verb form.

In Japanese, conjunctions come at the end of clauses; in English, they come at the beginning. Sometimes it is desirable to preserve, even in translation, the Japanese feeling that the whole *kara* clause, including the *kara,* is a unit. This can often be done by translating the *kara* as an initial "because," instead of by an expression like "hence" or "therefore," which in English would have to be attached to the following clause.

Benkyō shita kara desu	It is because he studied.

In this example the subject ("it") must of course have been indicated by some previous sentence, such as "Why did he succeed so well?" For a further discussion of *kara,* acting as a conjunction at the end of a statement, see under TOTE.

3. After -TE Forms

When *kara* follows the *-te* (*-de*) form of a verb it marks the described action as a limit in time. Here the . . . *-te kara* is equivalent to our "after . . . ing."

Some students prefer to think of this *kara* as meaning "from" in the sense of "after." Note that if this *kara* is followed by a phrase like *ato de* or *nochi ni,* the whole phrase has an effect like "some time after."

Asahan wo tabete kara dekaketa	After eating breakfast (he) went out.
Nippon e mairimashite kara taihen kenkō ni narimashita	After I arrived in Japan I became very healthy.
Anata no kozutsumi wo uketotte kara ato de anata no tegami wo itadakimashita	Your package arrived, and then after that I received your letter.
Shigoto ga sunde kara kaetta	(He) went home after the work was done.

WARNING. The above discussion has been confined to the uses of *kara* in the colloquial, because of the fact that *kara* is little used in bungo. See YORI.

When *kara* is used in bungo it should present no difficulties to the student, as it will have the same meaning as in the colloquial. Most grammarians state, however, that it should be used only to mark a limit in space or time, and never to mark the cause of a subsequent action.

This rule does not seem to be always strictly observed by Japanese writers (cf. KARA NI), but it certainly should be followed by any non-Japanese attempting to write in bungo. In fact it would probably be better for him not to try to use *kara* at all.

-KARA. Suffix to adjective roots. It is a contraction of *-ku ara,* that is, the suffix *-ku* and *ara,* the Line 1 form *(mizenkei)* of *aru* 'be'. (See under -KARI and the introductory Note on Adjectives.)

KARA NI. A combination used in bungo after the Line 3A form *(rentaikei)* to mean "because." In English translation the "because" is naturally inserted at the beginning of the clause marked by *kara ni.*

Kaze fuku kara ni . . .	Because the wind blows . . .
Taburu kara ni . . .	Because one eats . . .

This of course corresponds to the ordinary colloquial use of *kara* after the Line 3 form *(shūshikei)* of verbs.

THE COLLOQUIAL

When the combination *kara ni* is used in the colloquial the *ni* simply accentuates the *kara.* E.g.:

Mazu watakushi no kubi wo   Please do it *after* you have first
  hanete kara ni shite kudasai   cut off my head!

In the combination *kara ni wa* the *kara ni* seems to be practically
equivalent to *ijō.* For examples see under NI WA.

KARA WA. A combination used in bungo after the Line 3A
form *(rentaikei)* to mean "in addition" or "furthermore." The
feeling is "with this as a basis." Hence *kara wa* has the force of
no ue wa or *ijō wa* 'on top of (this)'. For example, the following,
from a *kyōgen:*

Mohaya, futari ga mairanu   As it is, on top of the fact that
  kara wa betsu ni mairu   the two won't go, there prob-
  mono mo gozaru mai   ably won't be any others
                                       who'll go either.

-KARE. Suffix, added to adjective roots. It is a contraction of
-ku are. (That is, the suffix *-ku,* and the verb-form *are.*)
  1. For its use in bungo see -KARI.
  2. The colloquial use of this form is apparently confined to a
doubled . . . *kare* . . . *kare* in semi-adverbial disjunctive expressions like:

Yokare ashikare yatte miyō   (Be it) good or bad, let's try.
Osokare hayakare   (Be it) late or early, (I) must
  ikanebanaran   go.
Takakare yasukare sore wo   (Be it) costly or cheap, (I)
  kaimasu   will buy that.

Japanese grammarians tend to consider this a use of the imperative
form *(meireikei)*.

-KARI. A suffix, added to adjective roots, it is a contraction
of the so-called "adverbial" suffix *-ku* and the verb *ari* 'be'.

BUNGO

In bungo this suffix has a full conjugation corresponding to that
of *ari,* to which further suffixes may be added.

Line 1	*Mizenkei*	*-kara*
Line 2	*Renyōkei*	*-kari*

Line 3 *Shūshikei*	-*kari*
Line 3A *Rentaikei*	-*karu*
Line 4 *Izenkei*	-*kare*
Imperative *Meireikei*	-*kare*

Examples:

Yasukarazu	(It) is not cheap.
Wakakarishi koro . . .	When young . . .
Miyako wa tōkari	The capital is far away.
Tōkaru miyako wa . . .	As for the far-away capital . . .
Miyako tōkareba . . .	Since the capital is far away . . .
Takakare	Be high!

THE COLLOQUIAL

In the colloquial there is only a partial conjugation. (Cf. introductory Note on Adjectives.)

Line 1 *Mizenkei*	-*kara*
Line 2 *Renyōkei*	-*kari*
Line 3 *Shūshikei*	-*karu*
Imperative *Meireikei*	-*kare*

The Line 1 form is not used without further suffixes. E.g.:

tōkarau (*tōkarō*)	is probably far

The Line 2 form is usually combined with further suffixes.

1. With -*ta* (and -*tara, -tari*), the form -*karita* is contracted to -*katta*. E.g.:

tōkatta	was far

2. With -*te,* the form -*karite* is usually contracted to (or replaced by) -*kute* or -*kutte,* but is also, especially in Tokyo, sometimes contracted to -*katte.* E.g.:

(Standard) *shirokute*	
(Emphatic) *shirokutte*	being white, or is white and . . .
(Dialect) *shirokatte*	

3. Examples with other suffixes are rather unusual. When they do occur, there are no further contractions.

Yōkarisōna mono   A thing that seems to be good.

The Line 3 form is not used in the standard colloquial.
The imperative form seems to be used only as shown under -KARE.
There is no Line 4 form, as the standard colloquial contraction is *-kere*. (See also the introductory Note on Adjectives.)

-KARŌ.   See -KARI, -KATTA, and introductory Note on Adjectives.

KASHI.   Bungo particle, expressing emphasis. It is found after Line 3 forms (*shūshikei*) or imperatives (*meireikei*). After imperatives it has the effect of emphasizing the speaker's desire.

Nakare kashi	Heaven forbid!
Kake-yo kashi	Do write!
Sate mo kimi wasurekeri kashi	So you have forgotten!
Ureshiki koto zo kashi	What a happy thing!
Shimbutsu mo shōran are kashi	May it be that the gods too are witnesses!

KA SHIRA.   A combination of the particle *ka,* which indicates doubtfulness, and *shira,* which apparently is an abbreviation of *shiranu* 'not know'.

This combination is used at the end of sentences to give an effect like an English "I wonder (whether or not it is so)." It is not, however, always to be translated by this idiom. E.g.:

Itte miyō ka shira	I have half a mind to go (i.e., I will probably try going, but I'm not sure about it).

Most dictionaries give examples of its use under both *shira* and *kashira.*

-KATTA, -KATTARA (-KARŌ).   These forms, when used as suffixes to adjective roots, are colloquial contractions of the *-ku* form of adjectives with forms of the verb *aru* 'be'. E.g.:

shirokarō	*shiroku arō*	probably be white
shirokatta	*shiroku atta*	was white
shirokattara	*shiroku attara*	if (or when) was white

(Cf. the introductory Note on Adjectives.)

-KATA. See -GATA.

KA WA. 1. When found at the end of sentences this combination of particles indicates "irony"—in practice equivalent to a strong assertion of the contrary.

Kawaru wa hito no kokoro	That which changes, is only
nomi ka wa	the hearts of men?
Kakute yamubeki koto ka wa	And so (we) are to stop?
	(We aren't going to!)

This is primarily a literary usage. The colloquial . . . *mono ka* gives much the same effect less politely.

2. Within sentences, especially in the colloquial, there is no ironic suggestion.

Itsu ka wa jibun no	Some time or other there will
kokorozashi ga wakaru toki	come a time when my mo-
ga aru	tives will be understood.
Tōji no kuge ga donna ni	How wretched was the life that
awarenakurashi wo shite ita	the courtiers of those days
ka wa kono hanashi kara	lived, can to a great extent
demo ōkata shiru koto ga	be known from such stories
dekiyō	as these.

KA YA. A bungo expression of emotion, practically equivalent to *kana*. It seems to be especially common in songs and ballads.

Awarenaru ka ya	How pitiful!
Ishidōmaru wa	Ishidōmaru
Chichi wo tazunete	Searching for his father
Kōya no yama i	To Mt. Koya (goes).

KE. A particle, usually written in *katakana*. It may be pronounced either as *ka* or as *ga*, depending on its use.

1. It is to be pronounced as *ka* when it comes between a number and a word for year, month or week.

In such phrases both the number and the noun are to be given their Sino-Japanese pronunciation.

go ka nen	five years
san ka getsu	three months

2. It is to be pronounced as *ga* at all other times. When so used it is equivalent to a bungo *ga* or a colloquial *no*. This use is most frequent in proper names, but is not confined to them.

Amagasaki	The name of a town, literally, "Nun's Promontory"
Hiruga kojima	The name of an island, literally, "Islet of Leeches"
yomogi ga yado	a thatched cottage

-KE. A suffix, usually written as 氣, i.e., with the character for *ki* 'spirit'. It may be added to nouns, adjective roots, and the Line 2 form (*renyōkei*) of verbs. It makes a new noun.

The meaning of the new noun varies to a certain extent depending on the base to which *-ke* is suffixed.

1. When *-ke* is added to a noun, the new noun describes some essential quality.

aburake no nai kami	dry hair (hair without the grease-quality)
mizuke no aru niku	juicy meat (meat which has the water-quality)
shikke	humidity

Words of this sort are really compound nouns. It should be noted that when the base noun is a word of Chinese origin the suffix is often pronounced *-ki,* e.g., *shikki* instead of *shikke.* Actually, *-ke* is a "go-on," particularly used in Buddhist circles; *-ki* is a "to-on." We often hear the sonant form *-gi,* as in *shinsetsu-gi no aru hito* 'a person who has the quality of kindness'. For comparison with *-ge,* note that *shinsetsu-gena hito* means "a person who seems to be kind."

2. When *-ke* is added to an adjective root, the new noun

denotes a positive feeling. Naturally this is a feeling of the
quality described by the adjective. E.g.:

samuke	a cold feeling; chilliness
nemuke	a sleepy feeling; drowsiness

Feelings about which one is positive are usually one's own
feelings, hence: *Samuke ga suru* would normally mean "I feel a
chilliness."

3. When *-ke* is added to the Line 2 form of verbs it may have
either one or both of the meanings described above. E.g.:

nebarike	stickiness; adhering quality
kuike	appetite; the eating feeling
shimerike	dampness, a feeling of dampness

WARNING. Certain words ending in *-ke,* which are usually written
as compounds using the Chinese character *ki* (氣) for the *ke*
sound, seem to be really Line 2 forms (*renyōkei*) of verbs, e.g.,
ojike 'fear', from *ojikeru.*

-KEDO. A contraction of *-keredo* or *-keredomo.* (See -DOMO.)

-KEKU. Suffix, added to adjective roots, making a noun. It is
an archaic bungo form, possibly a contraction of *-ku aru koto.*
(Cf. -AKU.)

. . . *yokeku wo mireba* . . .	. . . as (I) see the good-ness . . .

-KEME, -KEMU, -KEN. A bungo suffix, now obsolescent, with
different uses depending on what it is added to.

1. It may be added to the Line 2 form (*renyōkei*) of verbs or to
a *ni* following such a form. When so added it is a contraction of
-keramu, that is, the *-kera* form of the "past" suffix *-keri,* plus the
"dubitative" suffix *-mu.* It indicates a "probable past."

This form corresponds to the colloquial forms *-tarō, -ta deshō,* etc.
In modern bungo it is usually replaced by *-shi naramu, -shi narubeshi.*

There is a partial conjugation, only the following forms being
known:

Line 3   *Shūshikei*   *-kemu*
Line 3A *Rentaikei*   *-kemu*
Line 4   *Izenkei*   · *-keme*

Note that the *-kemu* form is often written *-ken*.

Sude ni shite haramichi ni *kemu tachi-ide ni keri*	After a while, being probably full of food, he left the place.
Ikutabi ka *Shimo wa okikemu* *Kiku no hana*	How often may hoar-frost have settled on the chrysanthemums?

2. The suffix *-kemu* (*-keme*) may occasionally be found added to adjective roots. When so used it is probably a contraction of *-ku aramu,* and has of course no suggestion of a "past" tense. E.g.:

   takakemu   may be high

and is equivalent to the colloquial *takakarō, takai deshō,* etc.

-KERE. A suffix with two distinct uses.
   1. It may be added to adjective roots. This *-kere* is derived from *-ku are.* It is usually followed by the further suffixes *-ba, -do,* or *-domo.* The *-ku* is the so-called "adverbial" suffix to adjective roots. (See the introductory Note on Adjectives.)
   Its use without further suffixes is confined to bungo. E.g.:

   Kore koso yokere   This, of all, is good.

(See KOSO.)
   2. It may be added to the Line 2 form (*renyōkei*) of verbs. For this use, which is purely bungo, see under -KERI.

-KEREBA. In the colloquial this is the standard contraction of *-ku areba,* meaning "if it be."
   In bungo it is also a contraction of *-ku areba,* but with the meaning "because it is." (See -BA and -KERE.)

-KEREDO (-KEREDOMO). In both bungo and colloquial these suffixes are standard contractions of *-ku aredo* and *-ku aredomo,* meaning "although it is." (See -DO, -DOMO and -KERE.)

The common conjunctions *keredo* and *keredomo*, both of which mean "but," were derived from these suffixes, probably through the form *kaku aredomo* 'although it be this way'.

-KERI. Bungo suffix added to the Line 2 form (*renyōkei*) of verbs, including the Line 2 forms *-te, -ni, -ri, -tari* of the verb-suffixes *-tsu, -nu, -ri, -tari*.

It expresses completion, ending, and is used as marking a past tense—a more definite or remote past than *-tsu, -nu, -ri,* and *-tari,* which see. For comparison with *-ki* see -KI.

A doubly complete past is indicated by combinations with *-te, -ni, -ri,* and *-tari.*

This *-keri* is almost surely a combination of *-ki* plus *ari.* (See -KI.) It is probably this combination of verb-forms—a sort of "it is that it was"—which gives to *-keri* the quality of suggesting some sort of emotion on the part of the speaker or writer who uses it. In poetry the emotional value tends to obscure the idea of tense. (See KERI.)

It has a partial conjugation:

Line 3	*Shūshikei*	*-keri*
Line 3A	*Rentaikei*	*-keru*
Line 4	*Izenkei*	*-kere*

Line 1 *-kera* (*mizenkei*) and Line 2 *-keri* (*renyōkei*) are forms which theoretically exist, but which are very seldom used. We may regard at least the *-kera* as wholly obsolete.

Ame furikeri	The rain fell.
furikeru ame	rain that fell
Ame koso furikere	Rain indeed fell.
Keri wo tsukeru	Add *keri* (i.e., "come to an end," or "bring something to an end" like the English "put a full stop to").

KERI. In poetry or poetical prose, *keri* becomes an auxiliary verb of emotion, often untranslatable, practically equivalent to an interjection. It does not necessarily follow a verb form, but if it does, that form is the Line 2 form (*renyōkei*).

Ama gaeru	The tree-frog
Bashō ni norite	On a banana-leaf riding and
Soyogi keri	Swaying, swaying, . . .
	18th century
Koromo no tate wa	The seams of the garment
Hokorobi ni keri	Are tattered and torn.
	or:
	The Koromo fortress has been
	destroyed. 12th century

-KERU. The Line 3A form (*rentaikei*) of *-keri*. (See **-KERI.**)

-KI. A suffix, primarily bungo, with distinct uses depending on whether it is added to an adjective root or to verb forms.

1. When it is combined with an adjective root, the result is a true adjective form which is used to modify a noun or some other substantive.

It is a literary form, and is not used in the colloquial except in certain particular expressions taken from bungo. (See introductory Note on Adjectives.)

takaki yama	high mountains
Yama takashi	The mountains are high.

There is also a special use of this form, in which the root plus *-ki* is treated as a noun indicating a "state of affairs."

In this special use the *-ki* form may be regarded as an adjective, with the following noun omitted as obvious and hence unnecessary. The omitted noun would of course be *tokoro, koto,* or some equivalent.

Take for example a sentence like:

Kemuri no sukunaki wo miru	(He) sees that the smoke is small in quantity.

This would be equivalent to:

Kemuri no sukunaki koto wo miru

or to the colloquial:

Kemuri no sukunai no wo miru.

Note that if the suffix -*sa* were substituted for -*ki* in the original sentence its meaning would be: "(He) sees the smallness of quantity of the smoke."

2. As a suffix to verb-forms, it expresses completion, ending, and is used as marking a past tense—a more definite completion than -*tsu, -nu, -ri,* or -*tari.* It is more abrupt and more positive than -*keri,* and does not, as -*keri* does, suggest emotion.

It is usually added to the Line 2 form (*renyōkei*) of verbs, but may occasionally be found added to the -*se* (Line 4) form of (S) column verbs of the first (*yodan*) conjugation.

When added to the Line 2 form (*renyōkei*) of another "past" suffix (e.g., -*te, -ni*) it expresses a doubly complete past.

In its use after verb-forms, -*ki* is itself a sentence-ending form It may be regarded as the Line 3 form (*shūshikei*) of a partial conjugation (cf. -SHI and -SHIKA).

Line 3	*Shūshikei*	-*ki*
Line 3A	*Rentaikei*	-*shi*
Line 4	*Izenkei*	-*shika*

Examples:

Shihō wo sōsaku-seshi-mo tsui ni miezariki	Though (I) hunted all round, in the end it didn't turn up.
Yo wa kare wo sūnen yashinaiki	I took care of him for many years.
Kōka wa nakariki	There was no result.
Ame furiki	It rained.
Ame furiteki	
Ame furiniki	It did rain!
Ame fureriki	

KIRI. Particle. It is derived from *kiru* 'to cut'. It is used to indicate a cutting off, break, finish, etc.

Sore kiri kimasen	He has never come since then.
Ikkai itta kiri desu	I went once, and never again.
Shuppatsu shita kiri nan no tayori mo nai	He left, and since then there has been no word.

-KKE. A colloquial suffix, added to the copula *da* or to the *-ta, -da* forms of verbs.

It is used when the speaker has a sudden recollection of some past occurrence, but is not sure of his facts. It may be followed by *ka* without particularly affecting the sense.

Iku no dakke	Is it that I am to go? (I.e.: Was it so decided?)
Iku no dattakke	Was it that I was to go? (I.e.: Ought I to have gone?)

KOSO. A particle with some of the force of an interjection. It singles out whatever it follows with the strongest possible emphasis. It may follow almost any word-form, including postpositions, except *wa, wo,* and the colloquial *ga,* which it may replace.

It has much the value of an English "indeed," "truly," "particularly," etc., and, like the English "indeed" or "certainly," may have a certain concessive effect when used in the first clause of a compound sentence. In colloquial prose such clauses are usually connected by *ga.*

BUNGO

In bungo *koso* calls for the Line 4 form (*izenkei*) of verbs.

Yoku koso kitsure	You are indeed well come!
Kore koso waga uma nare	Certainly *this* is my horse!
Imashimubeki wa iro to sake ni koso (are)	What you must guard against are women and wine in particular.
Yado no haru	At my hut, the Spring.
Nanimo naki koso	Nothing is here, indeed —
Nanimo are	There's Everything!

At the end of a phrase, after the Line 2 form (*renyōkei*) of verbs, it is used to express a wish.

Sake ni ukabe koso	I wish that I floated in sake.
Chirazu ari koso	Oh that (the blossoms) might not fall!

THE COLLOQUIAL

In the pure colloquial *koso* has the same strong emphasis as in bungo, but does not require the use of the Line 4 form of verbs.

Kore koso watakushi no uma yo	Certainly *this* is my horse.
Kimi koso geshunin da	You in particular are a criminal.
Kuchi ni koso dasanu ga wasure wa shinai	In *words,* indeed (he) does not express it, but (he) does not forget!
Miyako ni koso iru ga seken no koto wa shiranu	(He) lives in the capital, certainly, but (he) does not know the world.
O-mae kara koso kikanai ga yoku shitte iru	(I) did not hear it from *you,* indeed, but I know it well.
Yomase koso suru ga kakase wa senu	(He) makes (them) read, certainly, but does not make them write.
Sōshite koso rippana gunjin da	To do that indeed would be (the act of) a splendid soldier.

Note, however, that one not infrequently hears in speech an expression taken direct from bungo, in which *koso* follows a *-ba* suffixed to the Line 4 form (*izenkei*) of verbs.

In this expression the verb-form retains its bungo meaning of "because," and the *-ba koso* has the effect of "it is just because (of this) that . . . ." (Cf. -BA KOSO.)

Aisureba koso . . .	It is just because one loves that . . . (one criticizes, etc.)
Suki nareba koso jōzu ni natta	It is just because (he) likes (it) that he has become skilful (at it).

One may also hear expressions in which *koso* follows a *-ba* suffixed to the Line 1 form (*mizenkei*) of verbs, particularly *naraba.* (See NARABA.)   This may also be regarded as basically a bungo formation.

Suki naraba koso jōzu ni naru   If actually (he) likes it (he) will become skilful at it.

In general statements, where the subject is not particularized, a comparison between subjects is naturally suggested.   For example, taking the above sentence as a general statement, meaning "When one actually likes it, one will become skilful at it," there is an inherent implication that the more anyone likes it, the more skilful that person will become.   In fact at times the best English rendering would be "The more one likes things the more skilful one gets at them."

WARNING.   This *-ba koso* form is a tricky one.   In loose speech, particularly in general statements not specifically referring to the past, the distinction between such forms as *naraba koso* and *nareba koso* tends to disappear.

-KOTO.   In addition to its regular use as a noun meaning "matter," "affair," etc., *koto* has two special uses as a suffix.
  1. As a suffix to a name, when immediately followed by another name, *-koto* indicates that the first name is an alias, and the second the real one.

  Arakuma-koto Arai   Arai, alias Arakuma

  2. At the end of a sentence *-koto* emphasizes the statement and indicates emotion.   When *-koto* is used in this way an introductory emotion-word is likely to be used also.   Whether or not *koto* is a true suffix is a matter of nomenclature.

  Maa, samui koto
  Maa, samui desu koto   Oh, how cold it is!

  Oya, shizuka 'da koto   Goodness, it's quiet!

KOTO ARI, KOTO GA ARU.   These phrases state that a certain given condition does exist.   Thus *kare wa shōbai wo shita koto ga aru* states that it is the case that he has been in trade. Whether once or more is not stated.

If it is desired to show clearly that a condition occurred more than once, and so give the effect of "There are cases when . . ." some additional word or phrase like *katsu, mo,* or *toki to shite* will usually be used.

Examples will be found in the Kenkyusha and other dictionaries under *koto.*

-KU. Suffix, added to adjective roots, to give what is some-times called the "adverbial" form. See introductory Note on Adjectives; also, for special uses, -KARE, -KARI, -KERE, -KU MO, -KUTE, -BA, MO.

For a *-ku* suffix not added to adjective roots, see -AKU, -KEKU.

Words formed by the addition of *-ku* to adjective roots may perform the functions of adverbs, adjectives, verbs, or nouns. These functions are described below. They are usually distinct and do not lead to confusion.

1. This "*-ku* form of adjectives" is the one normally used before verbs and verb-phrases, and when so used it may perform the functions of either an English adverb or an English adjective. (Cf. with -U.) Which function it performs depends entirely on the context. It should be remembered that *-ku* correlates rather than modifies.

"Before verbs" does not necessarily mean only "immediately before verbs." The *-ku* may be separated from its verb or verb-phrase by a particle, such as *wa.* Also, when it precedes a verb-phrase, it may be separated by many words from the actual verb itself. The term "verb-phrase" is here used to mean any combination of words that performs the functions of a simple verb. It might be called a "complex verb."

Bungo:

Sono katachi maruku shite . . .	Its shape being round . . .
Kaze hayaku hageshiku nariki	The wind quickly becomes violent. (Here *hageshiku nariki* is a verb-phrase.)

Colloquial:

Yoku dekita	Well done!
Ie wo shiroku nuru	He paints the house white.
Kono hana wa akaku wa arimasen	These flowers are not red.
Sembei wo usuku koshiraeru	(She) makes the cake light.
Sembei wo usuku yaku	(She) bakes the cake lightly.
Kare wa hidoku sei ga takai	He is terribly tall. (Here *sei-ga-takai* is a verb-phrase.)

An example of what may be considered pure correlation is such a sentence as:

Watakushi wa haha ga koishi-ku omou	I feel a longing for my mother.

Here the *-ku* simply correlates the feeling of *haha ga koishii* 'I long for my mother', with the verb *omou* 'feel'.

From a grammatical point of view it is possible to say that the *-ku* form makes the whole statement *haha ga koishii* adverbial. It seems almost certain, however, that the Japanese themselves do not think of it that way.

2. It may also be used as a verb-form. When so used (without further suffixes) it may be compared to the Line 2 form (*renyōkei*) of verbs, as it has the force of "be . . . and." Hence it may be used at the end of clauses, or to join on to a following adjective. (See also -KUTE.)

The *-ku* gives no suggestion of tense. Any idea of tense must come from the final verb. Note that in certain uses referred to in paragraph 1 (e.g., *akaku wa arimasen*) it is possible to consider the *-ku* as a verb form.

Sono kao wa hi no yō ni akaku ibiki wa kaminari no yō deshita	His face was red like fire and his snoring was like thunder.
Matsu aoku suna shiroshi	The pines are green and the sand is white.
Aoku takaki matsu . . .	Pines that are green and tall . . .

Matsu aoku takakereba . . .	Since the pines are green and tall . . .
Futoku tsuyoi ashi . . .	Legs that are thick and strong . . .

Note that *futoi tsuyoi ashi* 'thick, strong legs' is also a perfectly grammatical form, and that *futokute tsuyoi ashi* is the most common colloquial form.

3. When *-ku* is added to the roots of certain adjectives indicating measure (i.e., measure of time, distance, quality, size, etc.) the resultant word may be treated as if it were a substantive.

Bungo:

Furuku yori . . .	From of old . . .

Colloquial:

Tōku no hō ni . . .	In the distance . . .
Ōku no hana . . .	Many flowers . . .
Sono chikaku ni . . .	In that (its) neighborhood . . .
Yoru osoku made . . .	Up till late at night . . .

It may help the student in his understanding of this usage to point out that in the older language it is not confined to adjectives indicating measure. E.g., from the *Manyoshū*:

Koishiku no ōkare ware wa . . .	I, who have many yearnings . . .

4. Adjective roots plus *-ku* may take further suffixes. Such compounds are treated under the headings of these later suffixes.

The common contractions of *-ku* with various forms of *aru* 'be' are listed in the introductory Note on Adjectives.

Notice, however, that it has been customary in the Japanese army not to employ most of these contractions. Hence in army speech we have such forms as:

Kyō wa samuku aru	Today is cold.

rather than the common colloquial:

Kyō wa samui (n'desu)	

-KU BA, -KU WA. For special uses of these forms see under
-AKU.

-KU MO. This is primarily a bungo form, added to adjective
roots. It is, however, sometimes used in rather flowery colloquial.
   1. In bungo a *mo* used after *-ku* is often equivalent to *tomo,*
especially when the *mo* is not duplicated.

> *Osoku mo yukamu*   Even if I be late, I will go.

For further examples and discussion see under MO 2, (a). Cf. also
TOMO and MO . . . MO.
   2. There is also a special case, where the *-ku* form is separated
from a verb by the particle *mo,* and the *mo* is repeated in the
sentence. It is an academic question here whether or not the *-ku*
form is to be regarded as a substantive. Fortunately it does not
matter, as the meaning is obvious. E.g.:

> *Mitaku mo aru shi kowaku*   (I) both wish to look and
>   *mo aru*   dread to.

   3. There is also another use, in which the *-ku* is used purely
adverbially, and the *mo* strengthens the force of the adverb. This
use of *-ku mo* seems to be the most common one in the colloquial.

> *Nasakenaku mo ōyuki ga futta*   To our great distress a heavy
>   snow fell.
> *Ureshiku mo o-tegami wo*   To my great delight you sent
>   *kudasatta*   me your letter.

It is also found in bungo:

> *Nikuku mo hozakitaru mono*   To my great disgust, you have
>   *kana*   babbled and babbled.

WARNING. The common phrase *osoreōku mo* rather suggests that
an *ari* has been omitted. This phrase does not have the meaning
of "graciously" as given by most dictionaries. It is an interjection
like "say it with awe!" indicating that the speaker or writer is
awestruck at relating the experiences of some very highly exalted
personage.

-KURAI (-GURAI).   Noun and semi-suffix.   As a noun it means "rank," "class," "position," etc.   As a semi-suffix it is often softened to *gurai* and marks the word or phrase preceding it as descriptive of a rank, class, or grade.   This use seems confined to the colloquial.

As a semi-suffix, *-kurai* may be translated in various ways according to the context.   Note, however, that as even numerical phrases are marked by *kurai* as descriptions of a grade, they are to be taken as approximations, and *kurai* may be rendered by "about," "approximately," etc.   For comparison with *bakari,* *hodo,* and *dake,* see DAKE.

Nijippun-oki-gurai ni demasu	It goes at intervals of about twenty minutes.
Sensō-gurai zankokuna mono wa nai	There is nothing so inhuman as war.
A san no suru kurai no koto wa watakushi ni mo dekimasu	The kind of things that Mr. A does I can do too. (I can do as well as A.)
Kono gakkō ni wa nan nin gurai seito ga orimasu ka	About how many pupils are there in this school?
Chūi-gurai shite kuretemo yokari-sōna mono da	I don't think it would do any harm if you gave me a little warning. (Even if you did give something like a warning, it would seem to be all right.)

-KUTE.   A combination of *-ku* and *-te,* probably derived from a contraction of *-ku arite.*   (Cf. -KU and -TE.)

It is a suffix added to adjective roots.   Its main use is as a connective form with the approximate effect of "be . . . and."   It depends on the context whether or not there is any suggestion of causality in the connection.   (But see also -TEMO and -TE WA.)

It differs from the *-te* form of verbs chiefly in that it does not unite with a directly following verb to form a verb complex, and that it can be used as a link with a directly following adjective.   It of course describes a state, not a single act.

Rondon no fuyu wa hi ga mijikakute kiri ga ōkute makoto ni uttōshii n'desu	As for London winters, the days are short and the fogs are many, and it is truly depressing.
Hidari no wa atsukute kuroi hon desu	The one on the left is a thick (heavy) black book.
Kono nawa wa futokute tsuyoi n'deshita	This rope was thick and strong.
Kono nawa wa futokute tsukainikui	This rope is thick and (so) difficult to use.
Jidōsha wa hayakute benrina mono da	Automobiles are rapid and convenient things.
Chotto Toyo ni aitakute mairimashita	I would like to see Toyo for just a moment, please. (Literally: Wanting to . . . I have come.)
Samukute tamaranai	It is cold, and I can't bear it! I can't bear its being so cold!
Kore wo tsukatte itadakitakute itadaite mairimashita	Hoping that you would use it I have gotten this and brought it here.

Note the different uses of the *-te* and *-kute* forms before "verbs of giving and receiving." If one gives or receives a "not doing," the *-naide* form is normally used. E.g.:

Sore wo shinaide kudasai	Please don't do that.

-KUTTE. A colloquial form of *-kute,* particularly common in the Tokyo dialect. It is not yet, however, regarded as standard.

-KYA. A colloquial contraction, usually a contraction of *-keriya.*

ikanakereba	
ikanakeriya	if not go
ikanakya	

KYA, KYĀ. A rather vulgar contraction, equivalent to *kiri shika.*

Jissen kya nai	Ten sen—and there ain't no more!

-M- This letter of course does not appear alone in the Japanese *kana*. In speech, however, an "n" may be replaced by an "m" sound, especially before "b" or another "m" sound, and be so written in Roman letters.

The sound may also be inserted simply for ease of articulation. (Cf. -BA.)

MADA. A word used to indicate the thought that some state of affairs is not yet finished; that is, is still continuing.

It is usually translatable by such expressions as "still," or "as yet," though other forms may be preferable in idiomatic English.

Mada konai	It still has not come. As yet it has not arrived. It has not come yet. It is still to come.
Mada tatakatte imasu	They are still fighting.

Notice that when a negative verb is used the idea is that the negative state is still continuing. Hence the verb itself may refer to either a single action or a continued state.

Mada gakkō e ikanai ka	Does he still not go to school? Doesn't he go to school yet? (Etc.)
Mada gakkō e itte inai	He still is not going to school. He is not yet going to school. (Etc.)
Mada gakkō e ikanakatta	He still had not gone to school. He had as yet not gone to school. (Etc.)
Mada gakkō e itte inakatta ka	Had he not yet been going to school? (Etc.)

However, when a positive verb is used, the idea is that the positive condition is continuing. Hence the verb must refer to a continued action or state.

	Is he still going to school?
Mada gakkō e itte iru ka	Has he not yet finished going
	to school? (Etc.)

	He was still going to school.
Mada gakkō e itte ita	He had not yet finished going
	to school. (Etc.)

The preceding paragraph does not mean that a *-te iru* form is always necessary when *mada* is used with positive verbs. The verb itself may describe continued action or state.

Mada tatakatte iru kara . . .	As they are still fighting . . .
Mada tatakau	They still will fight.
Mada atta ka	Were there still some? (I had
Mada shiroi n'desu ka	thought there were not.)
	Is it still white?

It is not logically possible to have a single instantaneous action "still continuing." Hence *mada* cannot be properly used with a positive verb which describes such an action. It is true that one may hear such expressions as *mada itta ka* used in the sense of "Did he go again?" However, when *mada* is used in this way it is simply a mispronunciation of *mata*. Mispronunciations of this sort are not unusual in certain dialects, especially those of northern Japan, where there is a tendency to confuse the "t" and "d" sounds.

Special Uses

1. When *mada* is used directly before a copula (*de aru, desu,* etc.) or with words indicating a point of time followed by a copula, there is a special usage.

(Q) *Goran ni narimashita ka*	Did you see it?
(Q) *Goran ni narimasen ka*	Haven't you seen it?
(A) *Mada desu*	Not yet. (Literally: It is "as yet.")

This usage is quite as logical as the English idiom, indicating that the previous state of affairs is still unchanged.

| *Mada hachiji desu* | It is still (only) eight o'clock. |

2. Normally a predicate adjective will act like an ordinary verb describing a state.

Arattemo mada kuroi   Though we wash it, it is still black.

There is, however, a special usage, which seems to have developed comparatively recently, probably in the Tokugawa period. Here the idea of continued state is applied to comparisons.

For example, if one gentleman should boast of the length of his mustaches, a friend might reply:

Boku no wa mada nagai   Mine are still longer.

NOTE. *Mada* has come down from an original form *imada,* which was used only with negatives.

MADE. A postposition. It has the force of the English "up to," "down to," or "as far as." That is, it marks what it follows as a limit "up to" (and including) which an action takes place.

Made may or may not be combined with other postpositions.

Jū-ichi-ji made matte imashita   (I) was waiting up to eleven o'clock.

Tōkyō made no kippu wo kau   (He) buys a ticket for (as far as) Tokyo.

Asu no asa made (ni) wa shimau sō desu   (They) will finish by tomorrow morning, I am told. (Here *made ni wa* or *made wa* has the force of "when it gets to be.")

Okaasan made shinjinakatta   Up to the mother (they) did not believe (i.e., the whole household).

Omae made sō suru no ka   Even you will do that? ("Et tu, Brute?") (It goes as far as you, the doing of that?)

Hana ga migoto na no ni mi made kekkō da   The flowers are good to look at, and it's good (all through) up to the fruit.

Sore made   That's the end!

In certain sentences, such as the following, *made* seems to have a rather special derived use.

Ame-kaze ga tsuyoi no ni	The wind and rain were
kaminari made nari-watatta	strong, and in addition
	thunder reverberated.

This use of *made* is sometimes explained as showing "the addition of something to something already existing." I feel that even in its "special" uses *made* marks what precedes it as being a limit.

-MAHOSHI. Obsolescent bungo suffix added to the Line 1 form (*mizenkei*) of verbs. It indicates desire.

It is adjective in form, *-mahoshi* being therefore both the adjective root and the *shūshikei* or sentence-ending form.

According to Yamada it seems to be derived from the adjective of desire, *hoshi,* suffixed to a now obsolete Line 1 form (*mizenkei*) of *-mu.* (See -MU, -MASHI.)

Yukamahoshiki ware wa . . .	I, who desire to go . . .
Ware mo yukamahoshi	I also wish to go.

-MAI. Colloquial suffix, added to the Line 3 form (*shūshikei*) of first conjugation (*yōdan*) verbs, and to the Line 1 form (*mizenkei*) of all other verbs. (*Suru* becomes *shimai* or *semai.*) It is always used for sentence-ending, never attributively, except with *mono* and *koto.*

If the attributive form is required the bungo form *-majiki* may be used in an otherwise colloquial sentence. This, however, is very rarely done. (Cf. -MAJI, -MAJIKI.)

Note that *-mai* has a formal sound except in certain fixed phrases like *arumaishi.* It is now more used in the west and south than in Tokyo and apparently is gradually going out of use.

In use it may be regarded as the negative equivalent of the positive *-u* and *-yō* "dubitative" forms. It usually indicates a negative probability, an unsureness more or less corresponding to an "I think not."

There are, however, extensions of this use. When applied to one's own future actions the *-mai* form is used to express one's intentions. (As in English we may use "I do not think I will . . ." in the sense of "I do not intend to . . .")

Also, when applied to general statements, the *-mai* form may be used to express a feeling of impropriety, an "ought not to." (This use is particularly common after the verb *naru* 'become'.)

Ano hito wa ikite wa imai	As for his being alive, it seems to me unlikely.
Konya wa tsuki wa demai	Tonight the moon will probably not come out (i.e., be visible).
Totemo ma ni aumai	Whatever happens we probably won't be in time.
Mō nasaimasumai	He probably won't do it in the future.
Mada okiraremai .	I'm afraid he can't get up yet.
Akambō ja arumaishi sonna koto wa shitteru darō	You don't seem a babe in arms, so it is expected that you know that sort of thing.
Ikumai mono demo nai	It is not that he may not go, or that sort of thing. (I. e., One can't say that he probably won't go.)

It may help to illustrate the force of *-mai* to compare the example just given with a similar sentence in which *-nai* is used.

Ikanai mono demo nai	It is not that he won't go, or that sort of thing! (I.e., The chances are that he will go.)

Referring to one's own intentions:

Moshi kore wo isokonattara ikite wa imai	If I miss this (target) I do not intend to live!
Watakushi wa ichigon mo iumai	I won't say even a single word.
Ikō ga ikumai ga ore no katte da	Whether I go or not is my own business.
Odoroki wa semai (shimai)	I do not intend to be frightened

Indicating "ought not to":

Benkyō to iu koto wa gakusei ni totte wa tsune ni wasurete wa narumai to omoimasu	It seems to me that study (is a thing that) ought not to be habitually neglected by students.

-MAJI. Bungo suffix, replaced by *-mai* in the colloquial. Like *-mai* it is used to suggest negative probability, personal intention, etc. (See -MAI.)

It is added to the Line 3 form (*shūshikei*) of all verbs, except those of the irregular *-ru* conjugation, with which it is added to the Line 3A form (*rentaikei*), that is, to the forms *aru* (*naru*), *oru,* and *haberu.*

It is an adjective base, and like all bungo adjective bases ending in *-shi* or *-ji,* is also a sentence-ending (*shūshikei*) form.

Being an adjective base, it may take further suffixes, so that we have the forms *-majiku, -majiki,* etc.

This form is apparently composed of a "lost" Line 1 form (*mizenkei*) *-ma* of the "dubitative" suffix *-mu,* plus the negative suffix *-ji.* Originally *-maji* seems to have been used as the opposite of *-beshi,* with the general meaning "is not to be." It is still sometimes so used.

Uma ni norumaji	He will (probably) not mount a horse.
Arumajiki koto	An unlikely thing (a thing that should not happen).
Hito ni katarumajikuba misen	If you will not tell anyone, I will show you.
Yukumajikereba sasowazu	Since he (probably) would not go, I will not invite him.
Koyoi wa tsuki izumaji	Tonight the moon will probably not come out (i.e., be visible).
Kono ichigon wa tanin ni wa hanasumaji	I will not say one word of this to others.
Benkyō no ichiji wa gakusei ni totte tsune ni wasurumajiki koto nari	Study (is a thing that) ought not to be habitually neglected by students.

It is sometimes used in the colloquial, particularly in the
-*majiki* form. When so used it conveys a sense of "ought not to."

Sore wa shōnen no *nasumajiki koto da*	That is a thing a boy ought not to do.

-MAJIKARI. Contraction of -*majiku* plus *ari*.

-MAJIKI, -MAJIKU. Literary forms, treated under -MAJI.
Note, however, that the -*majiki* suffix may be used in the colloquial as an adjective. (Cf. -MAI.) E.g.:

Kyōshi to shite arumajiki *okonai desu*	Considering that (he) is a teacher it is an unbecoming act.

-MARE, -MARU, etc. Contractions of "m" syllables with forms
of *aru* 'be'. For example, *mo are* may contract to *mare,* as:

Tomare kakumare	Be it that or be it this (or whatever way it be).

It is also possible that many verbs ending in -*maru* are contractions of -*mi aru*. For example, the verb *hiromaru* 'to spread' is
quite possibly derived from *hiromi* 'wideness' plus *aru*.

-MASEN. See under -MASU.

-MASHI. Bungo suffix, added to the Line 1 form (*mizenkei*) of
verbs.
It means either "would" or "would like to" do or be something.
It is sometimes used as an expression of determination, and sometimes in ironical sentences.
Yamada calls it "hypothetical" (*kasō*), and indicates a partial
conjugation:

Line 1	*Mizenkei*	-*mase*
Line 3	*Shūshikei*	-*mashi*
Line 3A	*Rentaikei*	-*mashi*
Line 4	*Kizenkei*	-*mashika*

He adds that this suffix was always rare and is now practically
obsolete. E.g.:

Itoma araba yukamashi   If I had time I would (like to) go.

-MASU. A suffix, added to the Line 2 form (*renyōkei*) of verbs.

It has no meaning, and serves only to make a sentence less abrupt, and hence more polite toward the hearer or reader.

For the conjugation of *-masu,* which is irregular, see the introductory Note on Verbs.

The formation of the negative of *-masu* may be regarded as irregular in that the ordinary negative suffix *-nai* is not used. Instead of *-nai* the negative suffix *-nu* is used, and this is usually shortened to *-n,* to give the form *-masen.*

The negative *-te, -de* form is *masenude,* normally both pronounced and written *-masende.*

The conjugation of the negative is carried out by adding various forms of *desu,* or their equivalents. E.g.:

-masen deshita	did not
-masen deshō	probably does not

Note that there is still in use what might be called a "fossilized" form of *masu* in its original meaning of "to be."

Ten ni mashimasu waga chichi . . .	Our Father Who art in Heaven . . .

-MASURU. An old and very formal form of -MASU.

-ME. A suffix with various functions.

1. When it is added to numerals or to words containing a numerical idea, it forms a new substantive indicating order.

hitotsu-me	first
ikutsu-me	the "which"th?
ichido-me	the first time
ni-ken-me (no uchi)	the second (house)
go-nen-me	the fifth year
dai-ichi-ban-me	the first (very exact)

2. When it is added to substantives referring to people, it forms a new substantive suggesting contempt or self-depreciation.

koitsu-me	I (very humble), or a contemptuous term if applied to another
hyakusho-me	wretched peasants
Tarō-me	that fool of a Tarō
watakushi-me	I (humble)

3. When it is added to the roots of adjectives or the Line 2 form (*renyōkei*) of verbs, it forms a new noun, in which the *-me* has a function much like that of the English "-ishness."

hosome	narrowishness (from *hosoi*, narrow)
hikeme	drawback, or difficulty (from *hikeru*, to close down)
hikaeme	moderation (from *hikaeru*, to hold within bounds)

4. In bungo, when it is added to the Line 1 form (*mizenkei*) of verbs, it makes a new verb form. This *-me* is the Line 4 form (*izenkei*) of the "dubitative" or "future" suffix *-mu*. (See -MU.)

Kono otoko wa chikushō nite mo arame	This man may well be a beast!

-MEKASU, -MEKU. Suffixes added to nouns to make a verb of the first (*yodan*) conjugation.

1. *-Meku* means to to "have or take on an appearance of."

ima-meku	to modernize
toki-meku	to flourish

2. The suffix *-mekasu* indicates that a subject intentionally shows himself of the quality indicated.

ima-mekasu	make oneself seem up to date

-MERI, -MERU, -MERE. A bungo suffix, added to the Line 3 forms (*shūshikei*) of all verbs except *ari* (*nari*), *ori*, and *haberi*. With these verbs it is added to the Line 3A forms (*rentaikei*) *aru* (*naru*), *oru*, and *haberu*.

This suffix is a contraction of *mie-ari* 'seems to be' and retains this meaning. It is practically an equivalent of the colloquial *-rashii* or *to mieru*.

There is a partial conjugation, the following forms being known:

Line 2	*Renyōkei*	*-meri*
Line 3	*Shūshikei*	*-meri*
Line 3A	*Rentaikei*	*-meru*
Line 4	*Izenkei*	*-mere*

Examples:

Aki-hagi chirinu-meri	The (blossoms of the) autumn lespedeza have fallen and scattered, it seems.
Kono yō ni umarete wa negawashikarubeki koto koso ōkaru-mere	For those who are born in this world, indeed the things that are to be desired seem to be many.

WARNING. Note that a *-ru* coming before the "m" sound was often dropped, especially in early bungo, so that one finds forms like *omoitarazameru* for *omoitarazarumeru* 'seems not to have thought', etc.

-MI. A suffix with two uses. It may be:

1. A suffix added to the root of Japanese adjectives and forming a new substantive therefrom.

It indicates simply the existence of an observed quality, without stipulating the degree.

aka-mi	redness or reddishness
taka-mi	highness or highishness

Note that *-mi* words do not indicate degree. Even if one object be scarlet and another only tinged with pink, they can both possess *aka-mi* completely. (Cf. -SA.) Note also that words like *kanashi-mi* sadness' may also be regarded as formed regularly from the verb *kanashimu* 'to be sad'.

2. A suffix indicating alternation.

It is added to the Line 2 form *(renyōkei)* of verbs. It is usually, though not always, found in pairs.

Nakimi waraimi	Alternate weeping and laughing.
Furimi furazumi *Sadamenaki shigure*	Alternately falling and not falling The inconstant autumn rain.
Yama no miemi mienu wa . . .	The alternate appearance and disappearance of the hills . . .

-MM-. A doubled or long "m" sound is not infrequently used in speech in place of a single "m." Sometimes this "-mm-" sound is put down in writing.

For example, *amari* 'excessively' may become *ammari,* with an effect of additional emphasis. In *kana* it would then be written *a-n-ma-ri* (あんまり).

MO. A postposition. It is used to indicate that whatever it follows is an addition to other things. (See also Mō.)

These "other things" may be concrete or abstract. If they have been previously referred to, the additive force of *mo* is usually much like that of the English word "also." If these "other things" have not been previously referred to, *mo* normally suggests an addition to "other things of the same general kind," and emphasizes a comparison with them. Under such circumstances *mo* usually has much the force of the English word "even." The meaning of *mo* is therefore greatly influenced by the context.

Note that while *mo* is much like the English "also" or "even," it cannot always be translated by these words. Its exact force depends primarily on what it follows. It is therefore convenient to treat *mo* in its uses

1. After substantives
2. After verbs and adjectives
3. After adverbs.

Note that the discussion under these headings applies to both bungo and the colloquial unless a specific statement is made to the contrary.

For particular uses of *mo* not discussed below see under DEMO, -TEMO, -DOMO, -TOMO, TOMO, MO GANA, MO . . . MO, YORI MO, MONO NO, KA MO.

Note that in the examples given below *mo* is used only once in each sentence. For examples where *mo* is used more than once, see under MO . . . MO. Note also that as these examples are out of context, it has sometimes been necessary, in translating, to assume a context.

1. After Substantives or Substantive Phrases-

When *mo* is so used it takes the place of *wa* and *ga* in marking a subject. It may take the place of *wo* in marking an object, or it may be added to it (*wo mo*) to give a certain increase of emphasis. It cannot take the place of other postpositions, but may be added to them, e.g., *ni mo, de mo, kara mo,* etc.

(a) After most nouns, pronouns, or substantive phrases, *mo* has the effect of "even" or "also."

In general "even" seems to be the best translation in negative sentences.

Pen ga aru Empitsu ga aru Fude mo aru	There are pens. There are pencils. There are also writing brushes.
Boku no hoka ni mo okyaku ga atta	There was another visitor besides me.
Ryōshin yori mo yoroshiku	Greetings from my parents too (i.e., as well as from myself).
Shoku wo koubeki jinka mo nai	There was not even a human dwelling at which (they) could beg for food.
Hito mo arō ni kimi ga sonna koto wo iu to wa	Of all possible people, that you should say such a thing! (Literally: In connection with (the fact that) other people also may exist.)

Kore mo wasurecha ikemasen	And you mustn't forget this either.
Ii mo owarazu . . .	Not even finishing what he was saying . . . (More literally: not-finishing even.)

There are, however, times when *mo* follows a description of something in some way "small," where the effect of "even a little" is best rendered by "at least." E.g.:

Yōi dake mo shite okō	I will at least make preparations.

(b) After words or phrases expressing number *mo* has its normal effect of "even" or "also," except that if there has been no mention of other things to which the number-phrase is to be added, the feeling is that it is an addition to all smaller numbers. Consequently, if the context shows that the number is obviously thought of as large, *mo* has the effect of "as many as" or "no less than." (But cf. MONO NO.)

Kare wa ichinichi mo gakkō ni konai	He has not come to school for (even) one day.
Watakushi wa kare wo sando mo yonda	I have called him (as many as) three times (i.e., not just once or twice).
Ano hito wa jūnin mo kyōdai ga aru	He has no less than ten brothers.

(c) After interrogative words or phrases *mo* has the effect of "all," that is, it suggests that the unknown is added to all known "other things of the same kind." Except that after interrogatives of quantity or of number the effect of *mo* usually is simply to make the phrase mean "very much" or "very many." (Cf. also TOMO, DEMO, KA.)

Dare mo imasen	All the "whos" are not there (i.e., nobody is there).
Doko ni mo arimasen	At all places it is not (i.e., it is not anywhere).
Dono ie ni mo . . .	At every house . . .

Doko mo hito de ippai	Everywhere it is full of people.
Ikura mo kakarimasen	It does not cost very much.
Nan gen mo arimasuka	Are there many houses?
Ikunichi mo . . .	For many a day . . .
Mise wa ikutsu mo dentō	At very many of the shops they
wo tsukemashita	have put in electric light.
	(Here *ikutsu mo* is like
	"more than one can count.")
Yado no haru	At my hut, the Spring!
Nanimo naki koso	(In it) truly there is
Nanimo are	nothing
	There is the Everything.

Note the effect of *nanimo* used with a positive verb.

WARNING. There are naturally a good many instances where English idiom does not easily allow any direct translation of *mo*. E.g.:

Kore zo to iu hodo no koto	There is nothing very special
mo nai	to be said (about her, it,
	them, etc.) .

Here the force of *mo* is to suggest "in addition to the normal things one normally would say." An attempt at a translation made as literally as possible would be something like: "There is no added matter describable as such that one says 'This in particular'."

2. After Verbs and Adjectives

The examples given below refer to cases in which verb and adjective forms are obviously not used as substantives. For the use of *mo* after the *-te* (*-de*) form of verbs see under -TEMO (-DEMO).

(a) After the *-ku* form of adjectives and the Line 3A form (*rentaikei*) of verbs the *mo* is usually equivalent to *tomo*, or to *-domo, -do* (i.e., *-domo* added to the Line 4 form), and has the same effect of an initial "although" or "even if." (See -TEMO. TOMO, -DOMO, and cf. -KU MO.)

Osokumo yukamu *Osokutomo yukamu*	Even if (I be) late, (I) will go.

Sen-man-nin aru mo ware
    yukamu
Sen man nin aritomo ware
    yukamu
	Though there were 10,000,000 men, I'd go!

. . . (*to*) *narishi mo* . . . . . . (*to*) *narishikado* . . .	Even though it happened (that) . . .
Yobumo kotaezu *Yobedomo kotaezu*	Though (I) call, (he) does not answer.

This is primarily a bungo use. It may, however, occasionally be found in the colloquial, particularly in such flowery sentences as:

Hyakuman no tomi wo motte
    suru mo waga kesshin wo
    hirugaesu koto wa dekinai
	Though (they) try using any amount of money, it is impossible to make my resolution falter.

(b) There is a special construction in which *mo* is used between duplicated forms of a verb or an adjective. This use seems to be confined to the colloquial, and gives an effect of piling up the idea.

Karai mo karai, namida no *deru hodo karakatta*	It was sharp, sharp, so sharp that the tears came.
Kui mo kuttari, jippai *mo kutta*	Eating and eating, he ate all of ten bowlfuls. (The second *mo* is that of paragraph 1, b.)

(c) There is a special use of *mo* at the end of sentences. When so used it has a strong emphasizing force. This usage is primarily literary.

Yukue shirazu mo	Where he went I do not know at all!

3. After Adverbs or Adverbial Phrases

When so used the *mo* has the intensifying effect of "even." Good English translation, however, does not always require the use of the word "even."

Tōtei okiraresō ni mo nai	It does not even seem at all possible for him to get up.
Shi yori mo tsuyoi	It is stronger even than death.

MŌ. A particle, not a postposition. Distinguish from the postposition *mo* (short).

Mō has two very different uses, apparently with different origins. The *mō* treated in part 1 is often pronounced *mo* (short). The *mō* treated in part 2 is equivalent in use to the bungo particle *mohaya,* from which it is derived.

1. When *mō* introduces a word indicating number, it has the effect of "in addition," and becomes practically a prefix.

Mō futatsu kudasai	Two more, please.
Mō ichido . . .	Once again . . .
Mō sukoshi . . .	A little more . . .

(By convention, *sukoshi* is used with *mō* as a number word.)

Note that in clauses of the form "numeral . . . *mō* numeral," the *mō*, while retaining its usual effect, is often best translated into smooth English by using the word "other."

Hitori wa otoko-no-ko de mō hitori wa onna-no-ko desu	(The) one is a boy, and the other one a girl.

2. When not introducing a number word *mō* introduces some predication. It indicates that this predication did or will take place at or before some particular point of time.

When this point of time is indicated by context as in the past, *mō* is usually best translated as "already" or "by then." When the present is specified, or when there is no particular specification, *mō* gives the effect of "now," "by now," "from now on," "soon," etc. When a future or hypothetical time is specified, *mō* gives the effect of "by then," and may or may not be translated as "already." *Mō* with a negative may usually be translated as "no longer."

Mō takusan (desu)	(I have) a great deal as it is. (Used for: No more, thank you, etc.)
Asa Tōkyō wo shuttatsu sureba ban ni wa mō Kyōto ni tsuku	If we leave Tokyo in the morning, already by evening we arrive in Kyoto.
Mō kuru deshō	(He) will (probably) arrive soon.
Yokushū ittara kare wa mō soko ni sunde inakatta	When I went the next week he was no longer living there.
Kono haru dote wo takakushite jōbu ni naoshita kara mō suigai no shimpai wa aru mai	This spring they heightened the dykes and rebuilt them strongly and from now on there probably will not be any worry about damage from floods.

MOGANA. Bungo particle, occasionally used in the colloquial. (See KANA, GANA.)

It expresses desire, and usually suggests that the desire cannot be fulfilled.

Mukashi wa ima ni nasu yoshi mogana	Would that I could make the past into the present!
Sake wo nomu aite mogana	I wish I had someone to drink with.

As a colloquial example:

Gorufu no aite mogana	I wish I had someone to play golf with.

MOHAYA. See under MŌ.

MO . . . MO. When *mo* is used in parallel sequence after similar forms, the additive force is very strong.

The meaning is not only "both . . . and . . ." or, with negatives, "neither . . . nor . . .," but there is also a suggestion of "other things of the same kind."

For *mo* repeated after *-ku* or *-te* (*-de*), see -KU MO, -TEMO (-DEMO).

Dō ni mo kō ni mo . . .	In any way whatever . . .
Eigo mo Furansugo mo wakaru	(He) understands both English and French (and at least one other language, such as his own).
Eigo mo Furansugo mo wakaranai	(He) understands neither English nor French (and presumably is lacking in other languages also).
Kane mo kureta shi, kimono mo kureta	(He) gave me both money and clothes (and was kind in general).
Sono shūkan wa mukashi mo ima mo kaerarenai	That custom has remained unaltered down to this day.
Kimi mo kimi da shi shinpu mo shinpu da	You are you and your father is your father. (I.e., Each person is himself, and has his own responsibilities.)
Ashi ni mo migihidari ga ari me ni mo mimi ni mo migihidari ga arimasu	There is a right and a left for feet, and also for eyes and for ears (as well as other parts of the body).
Oya mo nashi ko mo nashi tomo mo nashi	He has no parents, no children, no friends. (The English idiom uses one sen tence to get the effect.)
Tachi mo hikareba me mo hikaru	Both the sword and the eyes glittered. (For this use of *-ba* see under -BA.)
Furusato ya *Yoru mo sawaru mo* *Bara no hana*	The place where I was born! All I come to, all I touch— Blossoms of the thorn!

MONO. *Mono* has of course many uses as a noun, and these cannot be treated here. However, there are certain uses, mostly arising from its use (as a noun) to make a statement very concrete, in which it takes on some of the attributes of a particle.

When *mono* occurs at the end of a sentence, it makes the statement very concrete and has the effect of "definitely," "positively," "of course," and the like, and becomes practically a particle.

Sō desu mono	Of course it's that way!
Mada kodomo da mono	He is still a child—no question about it.

See also MONO KA, MONO NO, MONO TO SU, and MONO WO.

MONO KA. Particle, usually written in *kana* and pronounced *mon'ka*. It is used at the end of sentences, and is very colloquial.

"At the end of sentences" means that a complete sentence is implied, though not necessarily expressed. *Mono ka* is often found after a *-na*, and in such cases the *na* usually is grammatically equivalent to *de aru*.

It means "that state of affairs is to be doubted" and hence "it is not so." Its use is comparable to the English "anything but."

Kare ga gakusha-na mon'ka	He is anything but a scholar.
Sonna koto ga aru mon'ka	I can't believe that's so.
Boku ga dōshite sonna muchana koto wo iu mon'ka	Certainly I did not say anything as wild as that!
Misezuni oku mon'ka	I won't rest until I show it!

MONO NO. 1. When this combination is used at the end of a clause it shows that the statement is true, but subordinate to the following statement. It has the effect of "nevertheless" or "notwithstanding." It is stronger than a *-temo* form.

Mono may be thought of as making the statement concrete, and *no* as making it attributive. Technically in bungo the word before *mono* should be a verb or adjective in the Line 3A form (*rentaikei*). In the colloquial there is of course no difference between this and the Line 3 form (*shūshikei*).

Kuchi de wa ayamaru mono no seii ga tarinai	In words he apologizes, but sincerity is lacking.
Shōdaku wa shita mono no jikkō wa fukanō datta	It is true that I consented, but to actually do it proved impossible.

To wa iu mono no kawai	In spite of what (I) said, I love him.
Sekkaku kita mono no kore de wa shiyō-ga-nai	In spite of the fact that he came with such trouble, there is nothing one can do about it.

2. At the start of a numerical phrase, *mono no* corresponds to the English "as a matter of" in the sense of "approximately." It is apparently always used with *mo* after the phrase.

Mono no niri mo itta koro . . .	When I had gone some two miles . . .
Mono no nijūdo mo yattarō ka	I guess I probably tried it a matter of twenty times.

MONO TO SU.   A phrase often found in laws and formal rules and regulations. When so used it indicates concretely that something "shall be." See also TO SU.

MONO WO.   This combination, coming at the end of a sentence or clause in sentence-form, presents a concrete situation to be acted on.   (Cf. MONO and WO.)

Notice that this *mono wo* acts like a conjunction.   For good English translation we may use a conjunction like "and," or we may start a new sentence, or we may use a phrase like "when the fact is that . . ." at the beginning of the clause which modifies *mono*.   If the context is such that the following clause is highly "adversative," good English may call for a phrase like "in spite of the fact that . . ."

Are hodo ayamatte iru mono wo naze yurusanu no darō	Here he is apologizing so much . . . why don't you forgive him?
Nete ite mo kurushii mono wo tote no okiraresō ni mo nai	Even when he is lying down he is in pain— (so) it does not seem at all possible for him to get up.
Hito ga shinsetsu de suru mono wo arigatai to omowanu	In spite of the fact that people treat him with kindness, he is not grateful.

Isha de sae naosenu mono wo   We can't get him well even
  shiyō ga aru mon'ka   with (the help of) a doctor,
                       and there *isn't* anything to
                       do.

Hito goto ni   Every man
  hitotsu no kuse wa   has one foible.
    aru mono wo   Well, then . . .
      ware ni wa yuruse   May mine be
        Shikishima no michi   The "Way of Japan."
                       (I.e., the composition of
                       poetry.)

MOTE. A special contraction of *motte,* now found particularly in religious works, such as translations of the Bible.

MOTTE. A particle with various uses.

This particle has been used since very early times as a translation of the Chinese word "i" (以). The feel of this Chinese word has never been thoroughly assimilated by most Japanese. Probably in consequence of this, *motte* is used rather vaguely, and gives a rather stiff, un-Japanese effect.

1. It is most commonly found in the combination *wo motte.* This combination is found in both bungo and colloquial Japanese, where it is used with very similar meanings.

In bungo the basic feel is rather "because of (this)"; in the colloquial the sense seems to be more "using (this)."

Both seem to be related to a common idea of "by means of (this)," and the colloquial idiom seems affected by a supposed (and possibly real) connection with the verb *motsu* 'have', 'hold', 'possess'. There is also, however, an underlying connective force, something like that of the English "with."

Bungo examples are:

Nikkō wa momiji wo motte   Nikko is famed for its autumn
  na ari   colors.
Yama takaki wo motte   A mountain is not valued be-
  tōtokarazu   cause it is high.
Yoku benkyō suru wo motte   He studies diligently and be-
  shiken no seiseki yoshi   cause of this the results of his examinations are good.

From formal speech:

Kore wo motte kaikai no ji to itashimasu	This much I say by way of an opening address.

Colloquial examples are:

Teki wo kogatana wo motte korosu	He kills his enemy with a knife.
Hito wo motte tanomu	He makes a request through another person.
Hakarigoto wo motte shiro wo toru	They capture a castle by stratagem.
Kore wo motte mireba . . .	In view of this fact . . .
Kare wa kare no seiryoku wo motte shite mo . . .	Though he make use of all his influence . . .

2. *Motte* may be used, especially after verbs in the Line 2 form (*renyōkei*) but also with other words, as a sort of conjunction, with a feel somewhat like "and with this" or "furthermore."

As a bungo example:

Kono uchi no "ni shite" wa sara ni ryaku-serarete "nite" to nari motte jūbun no jōku wo katachi-zukuru koto ari	The "ni shite" in these (sentences) is again shortened and becomes "nite"; also there are cases when it forms the first clause of a compound sentence.
Gundan wo mōke motte kogo wo hogo su	We raise troops, and with this protect our native land.

As a colloquial example:

Rikō de motte kimben da	He is clever and, furthermore, he is diligent.

3. *Motte* may be used as an emphatic particle, indicating that what it follows is to be noted. It does not in this usage seem to have much force, and may be used almost as much for euphony as for emphasis.

A bungo example:

Hyakume mo senmanme mo dōri wa motte onaji koto da	A single grain or ten million grains—as for the nature, it is just the same.

Colloquial examples:

*Kare wa rikō de **motte** kesshite shissaku senu*	He is clever, and never makes a mistake.
Ginza de motte are ni atta kara . . .	Since it was the Ginza on which I met him . . .

4. In certain dialects (such as that of Tamba), *motte* may be used as an equivalent of *nagara*. E. g.:

Aruki-motte taberu	While walking he eats.

This usage is apparently related to the feeling of "with" that seems to be connected with the verb *motte* (? *mo tote* ?).

-MU. This suffix may be:

1. A bungo suffix, added to the Line 1 form (*mizenkei*) of verbs. It is sometimes both written and read *-n*. It has a partial conjugation:

Line 3	*Shūshikei*	*-mu*
Line 3A	*Rentaikei*	*-mu*
Line 4	*Izenkei*	*-me*

It is equivalent to the colloquial *-u* or *-yō*, which see.

Note that *suru* becomes *semu*. At one time this suffix was also added to the Line 2 form of verbs (*renyōkei*).

Yo wo wabimu	(I) may mourn the world.
Hana sakamu	The flowers will (perhaps) bloom.
Mare ni koso mime	Rarely indeed will I see it!
Ware wasureme ya	I will forget? (Never!)
Saru koto aramu ya	Such things may be, you think? (I don't!)

Yoshi saraba yo wa kimi ga	If (you think) it be well, I
hogosha taramu	will be your protector.
Sakura-iro ni koromo wa	A dress to cherry-color deeply
fukaku somete kimu	dyed I'll wear.
Taemu no kokoro . . .	A heart that may fail (. . .
	Feelings that may come to
	an end . . .)
Hana no ko ni arazaramedomo	Though they may not be
saki ni keri	flowering trees, they have
	bloomed.

2. A suffix added to adjective roots. It makes a verb. E.g.:

hiro-mu	widen (colloquial *hiro-maru,*
	hiro-meru)
kanashimu	grieve

It is added only to certain special adjective roots, and verbs of this form can all, I think, be found in the dictionaries.

N (-N). This may be a contraction of the syllables *mu, no, nu,* or *ru,* etc. (In early times also for *mi, ni,* and *ri.*) [See also -NJIRU (-NZURU).]

1. In the colloquial it may be a contraction of:

(a) A negative *-nu (-nai)*. E.g.:

| *naran (u) - (naranai)* | does not become |
| *sen (u) - (senai)* | does not do |

(b) The substantivizing *no* at the end of a phrase. E.g.,

Takai n'desu	It is high (for *Takai no desu*).
Ame ga furu n'nara . . .	If it rains . . . (for *Ame ga*
	furu no nara . . .)

(c) In informal speech, the postposition *no,* and' also the syllables *ra, ri,* and *ru* before "n" sounds. E.g.

| *boku n bōshi* | my hat |
| *wakannai* | not be clear |

Note also that *-neba* is a common colloquial form equal to dialect contractions. Those instanced in paragraphs (a) and (b), however, may be taken as standard.

2. In bungo it may be a contraction of:

(a) A "dubitative" -*mu* (Line 3 or 3A form). For example:

yukan from *yukamu* 'may go', colloquial *ikō*.

mochiin from *mochiimu* 'may use', colloquial *mochiiyō*

(b) A *ru* before an "m" or "n" sound. For example:

ōkanmere, for *ōkarumere* 'seem to be many'

WARNING. Always remember that bungo forms are sometimes used in colloquial speech. Therefore even in the colloquial an "n" may represent a bungo contraction.

Ie wo taten tote zaimoku wo kau	(He) buys timber in order to build a house.

Here *taten* represents the bungo form *tatemu*, equivalent to the standard colloquial *tateyō*.

NA. A particle with a large number of different uses. Fortunately, in spite of their large number, these uses are not easily confused.

There is a certain overlapping of the colloquial and bungo uses, but for the sake of simplicity they are treated separately here.

For *na* used clearly as a suffix, see under -NA.

For special uses in combination with other particles see also under NA NO, NA NODE, etc.

THE COLLOQUIAL

1. *Na* may be used as the negative imperative. When so used it follows the Line 3, 3A form (*shūshikei*).

In speech this *na* is usually pronounced very sharply and shortly.

Kono hon wo yomu na	Do not read this book!
Rakudai suru na	Do not fail (in this examination)!
Taberu na	Don't eat!

2. *Na* may be used as a positive imperative. When so used it follows either the Line 2 form (*renyōkei*) of verbs, or certain "Chinese" expressions like *goran* and *chōdai*.

This *na* is equivalent to a contracted form of *nasai,* but is less polite and more familiar in feeling.

Tabe na	Do eat it!
Kono hon wo yomi na	Do read this book!
Goji ni nattara okoshite	Do please wake me at five!
chōdai na	
Watakushi to isshōni o-ide na	Do come with me!

3. *Na* may be used as an interjection. When so used it is practically equivalent to the interjection *ne* (see NE), though it seems generally to have a somewhat softer effect. This use is a development of the bungo use.

Like *ne,* it indicates that agreement is expected, and is usually pronounced with a rising, interrogative inflection (almost like *na-a*) if the hearer's agreement is called for. It seldom comes after an imperative, and when it does it is usually followed by *yo* or some equivalent.

Like the bungo *na,* which is used to express emotion, it may be used in a question addressed to oneself.

The following examples show the use of this *na* at the end of sentences. When used otherwise it seems exactly equivalent to *ne.*

Tabe na yo	Do eat it!
Kono hon wo yome, na	Do read this book, won't you?
Ōkii hon wo yonderu na	You are reading a big book, aren't you?
Sō desu na	That's right, isn't it?

The above sentence, in Japanese as in English, may be addressed either to another person or to oneself. Which it is can be determined from the tone in which it is spoken.

4. *Na* may be used as the equivalent of the attributive *de aru.* When so used it is a contraction of the bungo *naru* (*ni aru*).

In the formation of adjectives from Chinese words, etc., *na* is used as a suffix. This use is treated under -NA.

In practice this *na* is usually followed by the substantival *no.* (See NA NO, NA NODE, NA NO DESU.)

Koe wa tsuma no koe da ga	The voice was the voice of his
kao wo miru to yume ni mo	wife, but when he looked at
shiranai onna na node	her face she was an utterly
Ryūzen wa akke ni torareta	unknown woman, and consequently Ryūzen was stupefied with amazement.
Ikusa ga jōzu na bakari	Being not only good at war-
de naku . . .	fare but . . .

5. *Na* may be used as the equivalent of the sentence-ending forms *de aru* or *da*.

When so used it may be regarded as a contraction of the bungo *nari* (*ni ari*). Its historical development, however, is uncertain. (Cf. NA NO.)

This *na* does not seem to be actually used at the end of sentences at the present time, except in the expression *sō na*, added to a verb in the Line 3 form (*shūshikei*). This *sō na* has practically the same effect as *sō da*, i.e., that of "so I am told." It is very commonly used in telling stories, especially children's stories. E.g.:

| *Mukashi, mukashi obaasan ga* | Once upon a time there was |
| *atta sō na* | an old woman, so I am told. |

BUNGO

1. *Na* may be used as the negative imperative. When so used it usually follows the Line 3 form (*shūshikei*) of verbs.

Kono koto tare ni mo	Do not let anyone hear about
kikoesasu na	this matter!
Hito ni warawaru na	Do not be laughed at by people!
Kono hon wo yomu na	Do not read this book!
Tabu na	Do not eat!

However, by custom, which has now become a rule, it is properly used as a negative imperative after the Line 3A form (*rentaikei*) of the verbs "to be," i.e., *aru* (*naru*), *oru*, and *haberu*.

Also, not infrequently it will be found used after the *rentaikei* of other verbs, as in:

> *Kinshi suru na*   Don't stop drinking!

instead of after the *shūshikei*. (*Kinshi su na.*)

When it is so used the *na* may be thought of as a contraction of the negative imperative *nakare,* which properly does follow the *rentaikei.* (*Kinshi suru nakare.*)

There is a now obsolete use of *na . . . so* to express "negative imperative."

The Line 2 form (*renyōkei*) of most verbs is used between *na* and *so*. The exceptions are *ku* and *su,* of which the Line 1 forms (*mizenkei*) are used, i.e., *na ko so* and *na se so.* For example:

> *Ie no atari dani ima wa*   (I) will not now pass through
> *tōraji Onokodomo mo na*   even the neighborhood of
> *ariki so*   her house. (You) men, too, I forbid to go there. (From the *Taketori Monogatari.*)

2. *Na* may be used as an expression of emotion. When so used it does not follow the simple Line 3 "dictionary" form (*shūshikei*).

It has to some extent the effect of a question addressed to oneself, and may be regarded as approximately equal to *kana* or *namo.* It is certainly weaker than *ka* or *ya,* in its interrogative effect.

> *Hana wa chiramu na*   The flowers may fall? (Yes, they will!)
>
> *Oriori no waka koso medetaku*   Certain of the poems indeed,
> *habere na*   how worthy of praise are they!
>
> *Misebaya na*   How I would like to show it!
> *Semi no koe kikeba kanashi na*   When I hear the sound of the cicadas, how mournful! (Is it not?)

3. *Na* may be the equivalent of the modern *no*. This is a definitely archaic use of *na* and at present usually occurs only in

names, and in a few compounds which are now regarded as single words.

minamoto	water source (a clan or family name).
onominato	Literally: the male water door (a place name).
tanagokoro	the palm (of the hand). (Literally: the hand's heart.)

4. *Na* may be used as a personal pronoun, in the sense of "thou" (archaic).

na ga na . . .   thy name . . .

Na and *nare,* which now may be regarded as obsolete, corresponded to the *wa* and *ware* which are still used in referring to oneself.

-NA. A suffix, with different uses in bungo and in the colloquial. (See also NA.)

1. When it is added to the Line 1 form (*mizenkei*) of verbs it is the "root" of the negatives *-nai, -naku, -nashi,* etc., and so corresponds to an adjective "root."

This use is found in both bungo and the colloquial, but not without further suffixes to the *-na.* (Cf. -NAI.) E.g.:

Hana sakanashi	The flowers do not bloom.
Hana ga sakanai	

2. When it is added to the Line 2 form (*renyōkei*) of verbs it is the Line 1 form (*mizenkei*) of the "perfect" tense suffix *-nu.* (See -NU.) This is a purely bungo use, and does not occur without further suffixes to the *-na.* E.g.:

Hana sakinaba . . .	If the flowers have bloomed . . . If the flowers should bloom . . .

A *-naba* form, like the colloquial *-tara* and *-taraba* forms, may be used in referring to the future.

3. When -*na* is added to foreign words and to certain Japanese nouns, adverbs, and adjective roots, it forms adjectives. This is a purely colloquial use.

It is used primarily for the purpose of bringing Chinese and other foreign words into the language. Thus: *shōjiki*, which in the original Chinese could mean "honesty," "honest," "honestly," "be honest," etc., by the addition of -*na* is definitely marked as an adjective meaning "honest," "simple," "straightforward," etc.

It should be noted that there seems to be a growing tendency to replace the -*i* suffix in many pure Japanese adjectives by -*na*.

kireina hana	beautiful flowers
shinsetsu na hito	a kind-hearted person
taisetsu-na mondai	an important question
chiisana neko	small cats
chiisai neko	
to iu yōna koto	that sort of thing
shiku-na	"chic"
okashina (*okashii*)	odd

In Romanizing Japanese this -*na* is usually written as part of the word to which it is suffixed. It is, however, sometimes written with a hyphen, and occasionally even as a separate word. All three forms are therefore used in the examples given above.

This -*na* is derived from the bungo -*naru*, which itself is a contraction of *ni aru*. These bungo forms are attributive or Line 3A forms (*rentaikei*), and this colloquial -*na* is consequently an attributive form also. It cannot be used with predicate adjectives. For these some form of *de aru* substitutes for -*na*. E.g.:

Kireina hana desu	They are beautiful flowers.
Kono hana wa kirei desu ne	These flowers are beautiful, aren't they?

This *desu* of course corresponds to the bungo *shūshikei* form *nari* (*ni ari*).

For further discussion see the introductory Notes on Quasi-Adjectives and on Foreign Words.

NAA. An expression, usually used at the end of sentences or phrases, to indicate a certain intensity of emotion. It is also occasionally used in various positions in order to draw the attention of the person addressed. (Cf. with NA.)

It is a very colloquial expression, and it is recommended that foreigners learn to recognize it, but not to try to use it until they are very much at home in the language.

NADO. A particle used as a suffix, meaning "such as."

It follows nouns or pronouns, and usually has a plural suggestion. When *nado* is used with direct subjects or objects the postpositions *wa, ga,* or *wo* may be omitted, or may follow it. When *nado* is used in other circumstances it may either precede or follow a postposition.

It might be useful here to point out that Japanese, being poor in forms to denote number, occasionally has to resort to special devices to suggest number or ideas in which number is an element. Consequently, though the English "etc." is in some contexts adequate to convey the idea intended, *nado* should not be thought of as meaning "etc."

Ringo ya nashi nado wo katta	(I) bought such things as apples and pears.
Boku nado wa nani mo fuhei wa nai	In my position there is nothing to complain of. (Cf. "The likes of me . . .")
Kodomo nado to iu mono wa . . .	Such persons as children . . .
Kenka nado shinai	(I) never do such a thing as quarrel.
Asoko e nado . . .	To such places as that . . .
Watakushi domo nado . . .	Such people as we . . .
Baiu no kisetsu ni wa nomimono ya tabemono nado ni chūi wo yosu	In the rainy season we need to take care about such things as food and drink.
Ore nado wa saru koto nashi	Such (men) as I will not go away.

Nado is written with the same character 等 as *-ra* and *-tō*. For a comparison of the three see under -TŌ.

-NAGARA. Suffix, added to substantives or to the Line 2 form (*renyōkei*) of verbs or to adjectives in the colloquial -*i* and bungo -*ki* forms. It has several uses, which depend on what it follows.

As a matter of nomenclature it might be better to consider *nagara* a "connective" rather than a "suffix" when it follows the -*i* form of adjectives.

1. Its primary use is after words referring to some state which may be either passive being or active doing. Here it indicates that for the same subject at least two states are going on during same time. It has also developed a concessive meaning, and so in certain ways is like the English word "while."

Tabe-nagara hon wo yonda	He read a book while he ate.
Utai-nagara shigoto wo suru	Sing over one's work. (Do one's work while singing.)
Bimbō-nagara . . .	Poor as I am . . .; while I am poor . . .
Zannen-nagara . . .	To my regret . . .; although I regret it . . .; while I am sorry . . .
Kurushii-nagara gamanshite imasu	Although it pains him, he endures it.
Warui to shiri-nagara kinshu shinai	While he knows it is bad (for him) he does not stop drinking.
Henji wo shi-nagara konai	While he answers, he doesn't come.
Tsuyu wo eda-nagara miyo	Look at the dew while it is on the branches!
Kudamono wa kawa-nagara taberu hō ga ii	It is better to eat fruit while it has the skin on.
Kami-nagara no michi . . .	The road one takes while one is with the gods . . .
Wareware no itasubeki shigoto de ari-nagara . . .	While (although) it is work that we ought to do . . .
Uki-nagara nao oshimaruru inochi kana	Oh, this life which one still wishes to keep although one is sad . . . Well . . .

The last example is bungo, the one above it is part of an oration.

2. If *nagara* follows a word having to do with time, it indicates the existence of at least two times for the same state of affairs. If the second time is obviously "now" or "then" the specific statement of the fact may be omitted.

Mukashi-nagara no kechimbō da	He is (still) the miser he used to be.
Umare-nagara no shijin desu	He is a born poet.
Itsumo-nagara . . .	The usual state continuing (to now) . . . (Now) as always . . .
Imasara nagara hazukashii	I am still ashamed (as I was then).
Umare-nagara ni shite no sabetsu ga . . .	A discrimination starting at birth (and continuing through life) . . .

3. There is a special use when *nagara* follows the enumeration of two or more substantives. When so used it means "both," or "all" (at once).

Fūfu nagara usotsuki da	Both man and wife are liars.
Kodomo wa gonin nagara kimashita	All five children have arrived.
Keiken to gakumon to futatsu nagara motte iru	He has at the same time both experience and scholarship.

4. There is a special use of *-nagara* after equivalents of the pronoun "I." Here the idea of "while it is I" is extended to mean "while it is I that I am talking about."

In the following examples the English is an equivalent rather than a strict translation.

Dōshite ii ka ware-nagara wakaranu	I don't know what to do myself!
Aa ware-nagara oroka datta	I *was* an ass! (There's no getting away from it.)
Jibun nagara yoku dekita	Though I say it myself, it was well done (by me).

NAI. This may have two meanings.

1. In the standard colloquial it may be regarded as a verb, the negative of *aru* 'to be'.

This *nai*, however, is an adjective in form, and is conjugated like any regular adjective, i.e., as *naku* plus forms of *aru,* with all the contractions shown in the introductory Note on Adjectives.

It has in addition certain special forms. These are:

    (a) An imperative, *na.* (See NA.)
    (b) A special *-te* form, *naide.* (See NAIDE.)
    (c) A form *nashi* (*ni*), borrowed from bungo. (See NASHI.)

Hana ga nai	There aren't any blossoms.
Nakute yokatta	It is a good thing there weren't any. (Literally: Not be, and good-was.)
Okaasan wa megane ga nakute wa mō nanimo yomu koto ga dekinai	Mother can't read anything any more without spectacles.

2. In certain non-standard dialects, especially that of Kyushu, *nai* is apparently a local form of the bungo *nari* 'it is', which has been retained in speech.

It is used as an equivalent of *hai* 'yes'.

      Nai, sō desu   Yes, it's that way.

-NAI. Colloquial suffix, added to the Line 1 form (*mizenkei*) of verbs. *Suru* becomes *shinai.* The form *senai* is called wrong by some grammarians, but apparently is used by good speakers.

As a suffix, *-nai* gives a negative meaning to the verb it follows. It may be regarded as an auxiliary verb whose function is to form a negative voice.

Although it has much the force of a verb, it has the form of an adjective, with the "root" *-na.* It is therefore conjugated exactly like an ordinary adjective, by adding forms of *aru* 'be' to the *-ku* form *-naku.*

For the usual contraction of the *-ku aru* forms see the introductory Note on Adjectives. For special forms of *-nai,* see -NAIDE and -NANDA.

Yania ga mienai	The mountains are not visible.
Shiranai koto wo shitta fū	It is better not to act as if you
shinai ga yoi	knew things you don't know.
Ikanakarō	He probably won't go.
Tegami wo okuranakereba	(I) must send a letter.
naranai	

-NAIDE. Colloquial suffix added to the Line 1 form (*mizenkei*) of verbs. It may be regarded as an irregular form.

It has a negative meaning, and under most conditions is equivalent to the form *-nakute,* which is derived regularly from the negative suffix *-nai.*

The difference between them is not easy to state. For one thing, *-naide* sounds softer and less formal than *-nakute.* It also has more of an adverbial feeling.

> The distinction between *-naide* and *-nakute* is rather a fine one, and does not seem to be invariably observed. It is primarily a difference of emphasis and usually does not involve any difficulty in understanding Japanese sentences in which either is used. It is mentioned here to warn the student that if he wishes to speak perfect Japanese he should not regard the two forms as absolutely interchangeable when he comes to use them himself.

NAKARE. A literary form, very seldom heard in conversation. It is added to the Line 3A form (*rentaikei*) of verbs.

It is a negative imperative, meaning "do not do!"

Sake wo nomu nakare	Do not drink (alcohol).
Inshu suru nakare	

NAMU. A bungo particle, used for emphasis. It follows unconjugated words (nouns, etc.) and is followed by attributive forms of verbs and adjectives. It is often written and pronounced *nan.*

> It has been suggested that the modern interjections *na* and *ne* are descendants of this *namu.* Whether this be true or not, there is undoubtedly some relationship. Realization of this fact may help students to understand the various uses of *namu,* only a few of which can be shown here. Do not confuse with the Buddhist expression *namu* which is derived from Sanskrit.

Natsu namu atsuki	The summer! It's hot!

Mukashi wa oni to namu yobu mono arikeri	In ancient times there were things called "devils."
Hana wo namu mezuru	(He) admires flowers.
Sono hito bakari namu kurai nado ima sukoshi monomekashiki hodo ni narinaba . . .	Just that man, if in rank or something of the sort he gets to amount to a little more than he does now . . .

-NAMU. Bungo suffix, now apparently obsolete. It had two uses, depending on the line form to which it was added.

1. When added to the Line 1 form (*mizenkei*) of verbs, it expressed desire. It seems to have been always a sentence-ending form.

| *Tori mo nakanamu* | I should like the birds too to sing. |
| *Kimi no na wo tokoshie ni nokoshi-tamawanamu* | I want you to leave a name that will endure forever. |

2. When added to the Line 2 form of verbs it indicated a "dubitative" like the modern bungo *-mu* or the colloquial *-u, -yō* suffixes.

This is a very old form. It is possible that the *-na* is a Line 1 form (*mizenkei*) of a lost verb *nu* 'be'.

| *Fune ni norinamu to su* | We made to get on board. (From the *Tosa Nikki*) |

NAN. A particle with different uses in bungo and the colloquial. For its use in bungo see under NAMU.

In the colloquial it is a contraction of *na no,* grammatically equivalent to *de aru no.* E.g.:

Nan to iu ii tenki nan deshō   What splendid weather!

This is grammatically equivalent to *Nan to iu ii tenki de aru no deshō,* but is shorter and more exclamatory in feeling.

Do not confuse with the first *nan,* which is the interrogative pronoun *nani.*

-NANDA, etc. A provincial suffix, equivalent in meaning to *-nakatta* 'did not'. It is always added to the Line 1 form (*mizenkei*) of verbs. E.g.:

ikananda
ikanakatta   did not go

Kembutsu wa senanda   (We) did not do sightseeing.

The following is a list of *-nanda-* forms with their standard equivalents. They are provincial forms, and seem to be going out of use rather rapidly. Nevertheless they may still occasionally be heard.

-nandara	*-nakattara*
-nandaraba	*-nakattaraba*
-nandarō	*-nakattarō*
-nandari	*-nakattari*
-nandaredo	*-nakatta keredo*
-nandaredomo	*-nakatta keredomo*

-NANKA. A colloquial suffix with a sort of plural feeling. It is sometimes used as practically an equivalent of *-nado,* but has more the effect of "and what not." E.g.:

Tabemono ya nomimono   Such things as food and
nado . . .   drink . . .

Tabemono ya nomimono   Food and drink and what
nanka . . .   not . . .

NA NO. A colloquial combination of the particle *na* (usually equivalent to *de aru*) and the substantival *no.* (See NA, NO, and for special uses NA NO DE, NA NO DESU, and NA NO NI.)

When this combination is found at the end of a sentence, it is usually in woman's speech. It has rather the effect of a very gentle form of . . . *de aru no de aru.*

Kuroda san wa itoko na no   Mr. Kuroda is my cousin.

It may be considered equivalent to *na no desu* or *na no da* in such sentences as:

Soko ga komaru tokoro na no   That's where the trouble is!

NA-NO-DE. A combination with various uses.

The most common use is as an equivalent of *de aru kara*. In this usage the *no de* may be regarded as a conjunction meaning "and consequently." The *na-no-de* will be pronounced almost as if it were one word, with the accent on the *na*. (Cf. NODE.)

Bakemono na-no-de	(She) was an evil spirit, and
uchikoroshita	consequently I killed her.
Kiyomasa wa hitozukiai	Kiyomasa was unskilful in the
wa heta na-no-de . . .	art of meeting people, and
	consequently . . .

The other uses of *na-no-de* should not present difficulties to any student who understands the separate uses of *na, no,* and *de*. The context will usually make the meaning clear.

The main difficulty is usually in deciding whether or not the *na* is to be taken as a suffix *-na*.

Thus without context it is impossible to tell the exact meaning of such a phrase as: *A san wa rikō na no de* . . .

In practice, however, it usually makes comparatively little difference. The phrase means, at any rate, "Mr. A is clever and . . ." or "Mr. A is the clever one and . . ." The context will bring out whether or not the idea of "and so . . ." or "and consequently . . ." is or is not intended. It is recommended that if the student has any doubts on the point, he try finishing out the phrase for himself.

It may be added that the most common meaning for the above phrase would undoubtedly be "Mr. A is clever, and consequently . . ."

NA NO DESU. See also NA, NA NO, and NO DESU. When *na* is followed by a final *no desu*, there is sometimes a possibility of two meanings. These meanings do not differ greatly, and the context will usually make it clear which is intended. Nevertheless, it is important to differentiate them.

Take for example the following sentence: *Honda san wa tsūjin na no desu.* If *tsūjin na* is taken as one word, an adjective modifying *no*, the sentence would mean approximately, "Mr.

Honda is one (or the one) who knows his way about"; or "Mr. Honda is the fashionable one."

On the other hand, if *no desu* is taken as a sentence-ending phrase, *na* becomes very nearly an equivalent of *de aru,* and the sentence would mean approximately, "Mr. Honda is a man of the world."

Unless the context obviously called for the first interpretation, the second would be the more natural one.

It is of interest to compare the above sentence with the simple statement: *Honda san wa tsūjin desu.* This is felt as rather brusque, and implying that it is news to the hearer.

The form *Honda san wa tsūjin de aru no desu* is felt as rather pompous, as if one were addressing a public meeting.

The perfect compromise is *Honda san wa tsūjin na no desu.* It is neither brusque nor pompous, and suggests that the statement is not only one's own, but is a matter of general knowledge, and hence, if directly addressed to another person, quite probably known by him also.

It may be added that in such a sentence the *na no desu* is pronounced almost as if it were one word, with the accent on the *na.*

Of course there are many sentences using this form which have only one possible meaning:

Soko ga komaru tokoro na no da	That is where the trouble is.
Kono hon na no desu	It is this book.
Hanahada taisetsuna koto na no de arimasu	It is a very important matter.

These three examples respectively illustrate the form as used in familiar speech, ordinary speech, and formal public speaking.

NA NO NI. A combination with various uses. See also NA, NO, NO NI, and NONI.

1. The most common use is as an equivalent of *de aru ga,* or *de aru noni.* In this usage the *no ni* may be regarded as a conjunction meaning "and yet" or "but." The *na-no-ni* will be

pronounced almost as if it were one word, with the accent on the *na*.

Musume wa jūhassai gurai na no ni baasan wa hachijū wo koshite iru—Oya ko deshō ka	The girl is about eighteen, but the old woman[1] is over eighty. Would they be mother and daughter?

2. In the other uses of *na no ni*, the *no* is of course the substantival *no*.

If the student understands the separate uses of *na, no,* and *ni,* the context will usually make the meaning clear. See also the discussion under NA NO DE.

Adjectival *-na*:

Ishi no ōkina no ni odoroita	I was startled at the bigness of the stones.

When *na* is like *de aru*:

Hana ga migoto na no ni mi made kekkō da	In addition to the fact that the flowers are good to look at, it's good (all through) up to the fruit.

NANTE. A very informal expression with several uses.
1. It may be used as an equivalent of *nado* 'such as'.

Tabemono ya nomimono nante . . .	Such things as food and drink . . .

2. It may be used as an equivalent of *nan to*.

Nante iu namae	What name (is it)?

3. It may be used as an equivalent of *nan to iu.*

Nante namae	What name (is it)?

NANZO. A colloquial form with several uses.
1. It may be used as an equivalent of *-nado* 'such as'.
2. It may be used as an equivalent of *nanika* 'something'.

NARA. This may be considered as a contracted form of *naraba* (See NARABA.)

It is used in the colloquial as meaning "if be" or "when be," and sounds less formal than *naraba*.

As it is derived from the bungo *nari* 'be', it retains a certain bungo flavor even when it is used in the colloquial. One example of this is a tendency to drop a substantivizing *no* after clauses which are to be followed by *nara,* the reason being that this use of *no* does not occur in bungo. E.g.:

Kippu wo kau no nara . . .	If it is (a question of) buying
Kippu wo kau nara . . .	the tickets . . .

The form with *no* is the full colloquial form, the form without it is the more common one.

Myōnichi Tōkyō e irasshaimasu nara . . .	If you go to Tokyo tomorrow . . .
Myōnichi Tōkyō e irasshaimashita nara . . .	
Nagai aida o mochi nara . . .	If you have had it a long time . . .

NARABA. A form derived from the bungo verb *nari* (*ni ari*) 'to be'. In the colloquial it is used either at the beginning of sentences or after substantives or verbs in the Line 3 (*shūshi*), "dubitative" *-u, -yō,* or "perfect" *-ta* forms.

It is at present a good colloquial form but has a certain tinge of formality. (Cf. NARA.)

The bungo *naraba* includes the ideas of both "if" and "when," and this usage may be occasionally heard in the colloquial. It cannot, however, include the sense of "since" or "because." (See -BA, NARA, -TARA, and KOSO.)

At the beginning of sentences it may mean either "if possible" or "if a question arise."

Naraba hayaku o-ide nasai	If possible, come early.
Naraba kochira ga hoshii	If I had to choose, I would want this one.

After substantives in the colloquial *naraba* may be taken as equivalent to *de areba*. E.g.:

Arita san naraba . . .	If it be Mr. Arita . . .
Arita san de areba . . .	

After verbs in the Line 3 form (*shūshikei*), including of course the -*i* (verb) form of adjectives, or verbs in the dubitative -*u*, *yō* form, it may be taken as equivalent to *no de areba* or *koto de areba*.

Iku naraba . . .	If it be (a question of) going . . .
Iku no de areba . . .	
Iku koto de areba . . .	When it is (a question of) going . . .
Sō de nai naraba . . .	If it be not that way . . .

After a verb in the -*ta* form, it may be taken as equivalent to a -*taraba* suffix, meaning "if or when completed."

Sō shita naraba . . .	If (I) had done so . .
Sō shitaraba . . .	If (I) do so . . .

Some Japanese commentators say that when the reference is to past conditions, the -*taraba* and -*ta naraba* forms should be used for suppositions contrary to fact (i.e., with the meaning of "if"). They also say that the -*tara* and -*ta nara* forms should be used for statements of true "conditions precedent." These commentators may be correct, but their rule does not seem to be carried out in practice. See examples under -TARA.

NARE. See NARU, and under YA, p. 343.

NARI. A colloquial particle derived from the bungo verb-form *nari* (*ni ari*). For its bungo use, see NARU, and under NI, p. 203.

Distinguish this from the noun *nari* 'form', 'appearance', etc. The two are now quite distinct, though they may have had a common origin.

It has several uses, in all of which it acts as a semi-suffix and retains a recognizable connection with the idea of "be."

1. When it is used in parallel sequence it has the effect of "either . . . or . . .," "whether . . . or . . .," with the further suggestion of "or something similar."

It is much like the English "be it (this) or be it (that)."

Saru nari todomaru nari katte ni shi tamae	Whether it be going or staying, do as you please.
Shomen de nari kōtō de nari mōshikomi nasai	Please make your application, either in writing or by a personal interview.
Iwa nari ishi nari e kuttsuku	(They) fasten onto rocks or stones, and the like.
Shigoto ni wa nesshin nari kokoro wa shōjiki nari kanshinna otoko da	Be it that he is assiduous in business, or be it that his heart is honest, he is a man to be admired.
Mita nari kiita nari hakkiri-to ie	Be it what you saw or what you heard, tell it clearly.

2. When it is not in parallel sequence it usually follows a verb, and then conveys an idea of immediacy.

Asa okiru nari mizu wo kaburu	As soon as he gets up in the morning, he pours water over himself.

After a *-ta* form, and followed by *de,* it is usually best translated as "just."

Asa okita nari de mada kao wo arawanu	He has just gotten up and has not yet washed his face.

3. There are very few occasions in the colloquial when *nari* has other uses than those already described. The special instances when it does so will usually be found in the dictionaries (*arenari, iinari,* etc.). E.g.:

Ano koto wa arenari ni natte iru	That matter remains as it was.

NARI-TO, NARI-TOMO. In bungo this is the Line 3 form (*shūshikei*) of the copula *nari* (*ni ari*), plus the particle *to,* usually used as equivalent to *tomo.* The usual meaning of *nari to* is therefore much that of "although it be" or "even if it be." It may be considered as one word, or as two. (See NARI, TO, and TOMO.)

In the colloquial it has developed certain special uses. These naturally are like certain uses of the colloquial *de attemo* or *demo* (which also can mean "although it be").

1. After interrogatives the effect of *narito* is much the same as that of *de attemo*.

Doko nari to sukina tokoro e yukitamae	Whatever place it may be, go to the place you want to.
Nan narito sukina mono wo tabe nasai	Please eat whatever you like.

2. Normally *narito* has the effect of suggesting some other idea in addition to the one it follows. (Cf. under DEMO.)

Its effect is therefore very often like that of the interjection "say" in English. Sometimes, especially in subjunctive clauses, the effect can be best given by "even."

Examples in a subjunctive "if" clause:

Semete karada narito jōbu nara ii no da ga	If only his body, say, were strong it would be all right. (Something else—for example, his brain—is weak also.)
Hanashi narito shite minakereba wakaranai	If you don't try even talking about it, it won't be clear. (Something else—a consultation or an exchange of letters—might make it clear also.)
Dainin narito (mo) yokoseba ii	If you sent, say, a representative it would be all right. (It would probably be better if you could go yourself.)

Examples not in an "if" clause:

Katsudō shashin narito mi ni ikō	Let's go, say, to the movies! (Let's go to the movies, or something.)

| *Ichido atte narito miyō* | Let's try, say, meeting once. (Let's try at least to meet once.) |

3. When the *narito* is used in parallel sequence it gives the effect of "whether . . . or . . ." (Cf. MO . . . MO.)

| *Iku narito kaeru narito kimi no katte desu* | Whether you go or return home is entirely up to you. |
| *Yobu narito yobanu naritomo shikkari kimero* | Whether it is "call" or "not call," make a fixed decision! |

-NARU. Suffix, derived from the bungo verb *naru* (*ni aru*). In bungo its main use is to bring Chinese and other foreign words into the Japanese language when such words are to be used as adjectives. It may be used with all such words when their original meaning is considered as itself adjectival.

In the colloquial it is usually contracted to -*na,* and normally retains its full form only when suffixed to monosyllables.

For examples and further discussion see the introductory Note on Foreign Words, and also the text under -NA.

NARU. In bungo the verb *naru* is the Line 3A form (*rentaikei*) of the copula *nari* (*ni ari*). Both this *naru* (*ni aru*) and the colloquial *de aru* appear to be derived from the copula *nite aru,* and therefore to have practically equivalent uses.

WARNING. Elementary students sometimes confuse the verb *naru* (*ni aru* 'be' in the sense of "be the same as") with another verb *naru,* which means "become" or "get to be." It is usually simple to distinguish them by remembering that the contracted form *naru,* which comes from *ni aru,* is not a pure verb, but consists of a particle *ni* plus a verb, just as the colloquial *desu* may be considered a contraction of *de* plus *arimasu.*

The differences in conjugation of the two verbs *naru* are as follows:

Line		*Naru* 'become'	*Naru* 'be'
1	*Mizenkei*	*nara*	*nara*
2	*Renyōkei*	*nari*	*nari*
3	*Shūshikei*	*naru*	*nari*
3A	*Rentaikei*	*naru*	*naru*
4	*Izenkei*	*nare*	*nare*
5	*Meireikei*	*nare*	*nare*

NASHI. A standard bungo form meaning "is not."

It is a verb in meaning, but an adjective in form. It is made up of the negative "root" *na* plus the suffix *-shi* (the bungo sentence-ending form). See -SHI.

It is also used in the colloquial, especially in the combinations *nashi ni* and *nashi de* which may be translated as "without." E.g.:

Kono matchi wa nioi nashi ni moeru	These matches burn without any smell.
norikae nashi de . . .	without transferring . . .
Sensei to iwareru hodo no baka de nashi	I am not enough of a fool to be called a Teacher.

Note that the subject of the verb *nashi* is usually not marked by a postposition. This is because in bungo it is not necessary to so mark a grammatical subject (cf. under GA), and expressions derived from bungo, even when used in the colloquial, usually follow bungo rather than colloquial customs.

NA TO. A contraction of *nari to*. It is found in several dialects, and may be heard even in Tokyo, though not strictly Tokyo "standard" usage.

-NAZO. A colloquial equivalent of the suffix *-nado*.

-NDA, -NDE. Standard colloquial abbreviations for the *-ta* (*-mita, -bita*) and *-te* (*-mite, -bite*) forms of verbs in *-mu* and *-bu*. E.g.:

> *yonda* and *yonde* from either *yomu* 'read' or *yobu* 'call'
> *tonda* and *tonde* from *tobu* 'fly'

Note that the forms *shinda* and *shinde* occur also as standard contractions of the forms *shinita* and *shinite,* from the verb *shinu* 'to die'. But as this is the only verb in *-nu,* students wishing to consult the dictionary need to look only for *-mu* and *-bu* verbs.

For uses see -TA and -TE. Cf. also the introductory Note on Verbs.

WARNING. Do not confuse these with the negative suffixes *-nanda,* a provincial equivalent of *-nakatta* 'did not', or *-nde,* a contraction of *-nude.* Both of these suffixes are added to Line 1 forms (*mizenkei*). See -NANDA and -NUDE.

Differentiate also from the *n'da* and *n'desu,* which are equivalent to *no da* and *no desu* respectively.

-NE, -NEBA. See -NU. Suffixes which may be found added to either the Line 1 form (*mizenkei*) or the Line 2 form (*renyōkei*) of verbs.

For a general discussion of their use and meaning see under -NU.

Note also that *-neba* is a common colloquial form equal to *-nakereba.* E.g.:

> *Ikaneba naranu*   Must go.

This is equivalent in meaning to the form *Ikanakereba naranai.*

NE, NĒ, NEE, NEI. Each of these may be either an interjection equivalent to *na* or *naa,* or a mispronunciation of the negative *nai.* Which it is will have to be told from the context. E.g.:

> *Sore wo tabe nē (yo)*   Go ahead and eat it.
> *Sore wo tabene- (e)*   I won't eat that!

Both of these sentences may be considered examples of rather low-class Tokyo colloquial speech.

As an interjection the force of *ne* is that of indicating that agreement is expected from the hearer. This is the standard "correct" use of *ne.*

When it is used at the end of a sentence it may turn the sentence into either an actual or a rhetorical question. E.g.:

> *Ii otenki desu ne*   Fine weather, isn't it?
>   (Usually an answer is expected)

Sō desu ne   It is that way, isn't it?
                            (Answer may or may not be
                            expected.)

It should be noted that an expression like *sō desu ne* may be used,
and in fact often is used, in answer to a previous remark or question,
in order to give oneself time to think.

When *ne* is used within a sentence the effect is "You follow me
so far, don't you?" It is constantly so used, and is particularly
prevalent in telephone conversations. E.g.:

Tanaka san no (ne) denwa   Mr. Tanaka's telephone num-
bango wa (ne) Aoyama   ber is Aoyama 1861.
(ne) sen happyaku rokujū
ichi desu

It does not exactly require an answer, but is usually countered
with *he, e, naruhodo,* and the like, to whatever extent the listener
regards as necessary.

NI. A particle (postposition) which is used to connect two
concepts.

The first concept, whatever its form, is always thought of as a
substantive. The second concept may be in the form of a noun,
a verb, or even an entire sentence.

The function of *ni* in any particular sentence depends on the
nature of the concepts connected, and therefore cannot be determined until both concepts are known.

Its use has, however, definite limits. For example, it cannot
mark the first concept as being either the direct subject or the
direct object of a verb. It can, however, mark it as being an
indirect subject or object. It has a sort of static feeling, and
though it may mark the purpose, end, or manner of an action,
whenever it does mark connection with a dynamic concept, such
connection will be at least comparatively indirect.

See also the introductory Note on Foreign Words, and the
special combinations given in the text. (E.g., NO NI, NI SHITE, etc.)

Dictionaries often translate *ni* as meaning "at," "on," "in," "to,"
"into," "for," "of," "with," "from," "as," "by," etc. Most students find
it easier to think of it as meaning simply "in-connection-with." This

seems satisfactory for most uses of *ni*, but of course is not a proper translation. It is possible that *ni* was originally the Line 2 form (*renyōkei*) of a now obsolete verb *nu*, meaning "be."

It is not possible here to give examples of all the conceivable uses of *ni*. It has therefore seemed best to particularize a few of the important uses, and then give a sufficiently large number of examples of other uses for students to get the feel of *ni*. See also the following text headings NI NARU, NI OITE, NI SHITE, etc.

As the colloquial and bungo uses of *ni* are not absolutely the same, they are treated separately.

THE COLLOQUIAL

In the colloquial *ni* has the following uses:

1. Use to mark adverbs
2. Use to mark an indirect object
3. Use to mark an indirect subject
4. Use after words indicating places
5. Use connecting Line 2 verb forms with verbs of going or coming
6. Use connecting forms of the same verb
7. Use connecting nouns
8. Other uses

1. Use to Mark Adverbs

In Japanese, adverbs are not necessarily marked as such. However, single words of which the function is solely adverbial are very rare. Many words can function both as substantives and as adverbs, and when they are to be used as adverbs it may be necessary to point out the fact. One way of doing so, the most common way, is by the use of *ni*. (See also TO and the introductory Note on Foreign Words.)

Many expressions can function adverbially either with or without *ni*, and for most of these the presence of *ni* simply makes the phrase more emphatic. There are, however, exceptions to this rule, in which the actual basic meaning is affected.

Sono toki . . .

Sono toki ni . . .   At that time . . .

Ichido . . .   Once, on one occasion . . .
Ichido ni . . .   All at once (at the same
                                    time) . . .

2. Use to Mark an Indirect Object

The term "indirect object" cannot be taken with all its Western
connotations when applied to Japanese. However, some uses of
ni have not unreasonably been called "marking an indirect
object," though often they are more properly "locatives."

Kore wo anata ni agemasu   I present this to you.
Kaban wo engawa ni   He threw down the bag on the
nagedashimashita   floor.

Perhaps under this heading should also come such uses of *ni*
as in:

oya ni niru   resemble one's parents
otona ni naru   become an adult

3. Use as an Indirect Subject

This use is found only in sentences in which the main or direct
subject causes, undergoes, gives, or receives an action described
by a transitive verb. In such sentences *ni* marks the subject of
the action which is caused, undergone, given, or received. Notice
that "causing" may itself be an action which is "undergone," etc.

If the action is described by a "reflexive" verb, the "indirect subject"
is marked by *wo*. For further examples see under -SERU, -SASERU,
-RERU, and -TE.

Haha ga ko ni kusuri wo   The mother caused the child
nomaseta   to drink medicine. (Here
                                      the child does the drinking.)

Haha ga ko ni kusuri wo   The mother was caused by the
nomaserareta   child to drink medicine.
                                      (Here the child does the
                                      causing.)

Hito ni tansho wo mirareru   One has one's faults seen by
                                      other people.

> *Boku wa Toda san ni mite*   I got Mr. Toda to look.
> *moratta*

A use so similar to this that it is doubtful whether it ought to be differentiated occurs in "potential" sentences. E.g.:

> *Anata ni wa kore ga*   Can you do this? (Is it possible
> *dekimasu ka*   to you?)

For further examples see under -ERU and -RERU.

4. Use after Words Indicating Places

As *ni* has no meaning in itself its exact effect cannot be determined until the two concepts it connects are both known. It may be stated, however, that when *ni* is used after words describing places the following concept is not one of specific action at that· place. If the second concept is one of specific action the place-name is marked by *de*. (See DE.)

"Living" (said of a person), "blowing" (said of the wind), etc., are of course not specific actions.

Kyōto ni sumu	Live in Kyoto.
Tōkyō ni tsuku	Arrive at Tokyo.
Suichū ni kuguru	Dive into the water.
Miyako ni chikai tokoro ni sumitai	I would like to live at a place near the capital.
Miyako ni natte Edo wa Tōkyō to kawatta	Becoming the Imperial capital, Edo changed (its name) to Tokyo.
Tōkyō ni taishite . . .	In regard to Tokyo . . . (As compared to Tokyo . . ., etc.)
Sanjō ni tō wo tateru	Build a tower on a mountain top (the reference is to the finished result).
Shina ni iku	Go to China (when thinking of being there).

Ni is sometimes confused with *de* and *e* by careless speakers, but even they would probably say *sanjō de to wo tateru* if they were thinking of the actual building operations, or *Shina e yuku* if they were thinking of the actual journey.   Compare with the examples above.

5. Use Connecting Line 2 Verb Forms and
Verbs of Going and Coming

When the first concept is the Line 2 form (*renyōkei*) of a verb, and the second concept is a verb of self-movement such as "go," "come," and the like, *ni* will mark the first concept as the purpose or object of the action.

Mi ni iku to dare mo inakatta   When (I) went to look, nobody was there.

6. Use Connecting Forms of the Same Verb

There is one use of *ni* that seems confined to the colloquial. This is its use between two forms of the same verb.

This doubles the force of the verb.   The first concept may be either:

(a)   In the Line 2 form (*renyōkei*).

Sakebi ni sakenda	He shouted and shouted.
Hitohashiri ni hashiru	He runs without stopping.

(b)   In the Line 3 form (*shūshikei*).

Iu ni iwarenu	He couldn't speak (a word).
Naku ni nakarenu	She couldn't cry (a tear).

7. Use in Connecting Nouns

When used between nouns the effect of *ni* is simply to connect them together additively.

Fude ni empitsu ni kami . . .   Brush and pencil and
paper . . .

Tsuki ni murakumo *hana ni kaze* (an epigram)	The moon—and clustered clouds; Blossoms—and the wind! (I.e., nothing remains per- fect.)

8. Other Uses

Various examples illustrating uses common to both bungo and colloquial follow:

Fune ni notte kokyō ni kaeru	I will get on board a boat and go back to my birthplace.
Senaka no itami ni kurushimu	She suffers from a pain in the back.
Kare no bengo ni tōdan shita	I took the platform in his defense.
Ryūgaku ni shuppatsu suru	He leaves for study abroad.
Kono tebukuro wo oji ni itadaita	I received these gloves from my uncle.
Obi ni mijikaku tasuki ni nagai	It is too short for an *obi* and too long for a *tasuki*.
Shizuka ni	Be quiet!
Go en ni mittsu	Three for five yen.
Hi ni sando tabemasu	We eat three times a day.
Mizu ga kōri ni kawaru	Water changes into ice.
Hachiji ni Tōkyō wo shuppatsu suru	I leave Tokyo at eight o'clock.
Dōjōshin ni toboshii	He is deficient in sympathy.
"A" wa "B" ni hitoshii	A is equal to B.
Maneita ni konai	Though I invited him he did not come.

In the above sentence *ni* replaces the more common *noni*. Compare with the bungo uses of *ni*, and see also under NONI.

BUNGO

In bungo *ni* has all the uses found in the colloquial (with the possible exception mentioned in part 6) and others besides.

Bungo does not use the substantival *no*, so *ni* may come directly after attributive forms (*rentaikei*, that is, the -*ki* form of adjectives and the Line 3A form of verbs). These forms may then be considered substantives.

Bungo does not use the particle *de*. Instead, *ni* is used with *ari*, in the form *ni ari* (*nari*), and performs the same functions as the sentence-ending *de aru*. The *ari* may of course be conjugated; *ni aru* (*naru*), etc. Note that the *ni* may be separated from the *aru* by particles, as in:

> *Imashimubeki wa sake ni*   What is to be guarded against
>   *koso are*   is, in particular, sake.

The special uses of *ni* in bungo are:

1. Its use after clauses to give an effect similar to that of *no ni* in the colloquial, i.e., "in connection with the fact that," and hence sometimes the adversative effect "in spite of the fact that."

> *Aki to iu ni atatakashi*   They call it autumn and yet
>   it's warm.

But note that even in the colloquial the substantival *no* may be omitted, as in: *Aki to iu ni atatakai* 'They call it autumn and yet it's warm!'

The "adversative" effect, however, like that of *no ni,* seems to be derived primarily from the context. It is, for instance, very light indeed in such a sentence as:

> *Hi kurekakaru ni yadorubeki*   The sun is setting and the
>   *tokoro tōshi*   place where we are to lodge
>   is distant.

2. Its use with a conjunctive adverb, such as *moshi* 'if' to express a condition.

Moshi tsune ni haibutsu no	If people would always pay
riyō wo kokorogakemu ni	attention to the disposal of
wa kanarazu sono yōto wo	waste products they could
hakkensuru wo ubeshi	certainly discover a use for
	them.

Sir G. B. Sansom ("Grammar," p. 278) points out that in such cases the *-mu* form ("future") of the verb is generally required.

-NI. A bungo suffix, added to the Line 2 form (*renyōkei*) of verbs. It is itself the *renyōkei* of the bungo "perfect" suffix *-nu*. (See -NU.)

Other "past" tense particles, such as *-keri, -ki, -shi,* or *-shika* may be further suffixed to *-ni*. When two such "past" particles are used together the combination indicates a past more definite and more distant than is indicated by either form taken alone.

NI MO, NI WA. There is a special honorific use of these compounds.

When the designation of some very honored personage is followed by *ni wa,* or *ni mo,* the *ni* may have no meaning other than that of a polite circumlocution. (It has been described as a device used to avoid treating the Emperor as a subject.)

Heika ni wa honjitsu go-kankō	His Majesty returns today.
araserareru	
Sensei ni mo goshusseki	Also you, professor, please
kudasai	attend the meeting.

NI NARU. A combination of the postposition *ni* and the verb *naru* 'become', 'get to be', 'develop (into)', etc.

Once the meaning of *naru* is understood, it presents no difficulties in its ordinary uses, such as *kanemochi ni naru* 'become a rich man', *byōki ni naru* 'fall ill', etc.

It does, however, present difficulties to foreign students in its honorific use. In this it is preceded by some noun indicating an action, to which is usually prefixed an honorific particle like *o* or *go*. This noun is usually either the Line 2 form (*renyōkei*) of a verb, or else a Chinese expression.

When so used *ni naru* is probably best considered as having no meaning in itself, but as simply making a phrase longer and more respectful.

   O-tabe ni natta   He ate.
   Goran ni naru toki . . .   When you see . . .

The *o-tabe ni natta* means simply *tabeta;* the *goran ni naru* means simply *miru;* but the longer phrases do indicate respect to the person performing the action.

NI OITE, NI OKASERARETE, NI OKERU, etc. A combination of the postposition *ni* with certain verb forms apparently originally derived from the verb *oku* 'set'.

It may be considered as having no meaning beyond that of the simple postposition *ni.* It does, however, give an effect of formality, politeness, and a certain slight emphasis.

The *oite* and *okeru* forms are quite common. Longer forms (*okaserareru,* etc.) are reserved for sentences having to do with very highly placed personages such as the Emperor.

Students should note that the *oite, okeru,* etc. is usually written with a special Chinese character 於 not normally employed for the verb *oku.*

   zenkyoku ni oite   in its general aspect
   konnichi ni okeru   today
   doko ni okeru   where?
   tōjisha-kan ni oite   among the persons concerned
   ōzora no shita ni oite   underneath the broad skies
   kanraku zengo ni oite   about the time of the fall (of the city)

A distinction should of course be made between the *oite,* which is a *-te* form and hence may be used adverbially, and the *okeru,* which is a Line 3, 3A form and hence may be used as a sentence-ending, attributive or adjectival form, etc.

NI SHITE. A combination of the postposition *ni* with the *-te* form of the verb *suru* (bungo *su*). Its use will vary according to the context. (Cf. with TO SHITE.)

It presents difficulties to foreign students chiefly because of its great number of possible uses. The function of *ni* of course depends on the nature of the concepts that it connects, and the verb *suru* may have the meaning of "make," "do," "act," "be," etc.

The presence or absence of a word marked by *wo* is usually sufficient to show whether the *shite* is used transitively or intransitively, and there is usually no great difficulty in understanding the use of *ni shite* when the *shite* is used in an active sense (make, do, act).

Examples with *wo* are:

Kodomo ga kame wo omocha ni shite imasu	The children are making the turtle a plaything.
Shunuri no shaden ga yama no midori wo ato ni shite taisō kirei ni miemasu	The red-painted shrine has (puts) the green of the mountains behind it, and shows very beautifully.

Examples without *wo* are:

Ossharu tōri ni shite . . .	Doing as (one) is told . . .
Roma wa ichinichi ni shite narazu	Rome was not built in a day.

There is, however, one special use of *ni shite* which often puzzles beginners. This is a bungo use which has survived in the colloquial.

In bungo *ni suru* is often used as *de aru* is used in the colloquial, that is, as a copula with the meaning of "is." In the colloquial this use survives in the form *ni shite*, which, especially at the end of clauses, may be practically equivalent to *de*.

Typical bungo examples of this use of *ni shite* are:

Kin wa kiiro ni shite gin wa shiroshi	Gold is yellow and silver is white.
Kan ni shite tsukuseri	It is brief and (but) sufficient.

Hence, even in the colloquial, *ni shite* may be used where the English form would simply be an apposition. E.g.:

Washinton wa Beikoku no miyako ni shite daitokai de aru	Washington, the capital of the United States, is a large town.

NI SHITE MO. In general this may be regarded as simply a combination of *ni, shite,* and *mo.* However, in most uses of this combination the *shite* has the sense of "being," and the phrase has much the force of *de atte mo* 'even though it be'. There is, however, likely to be the suggestion of "even though we consider that it be." (Cf. also -TEMO.)

Go en ni shite mo takaku wa nai	Even though (we consider that) it be five yen, it is not expensive.
Yotte ita ni shite mo sore wa ii wake ni wa naranu	Granting that you were drunk, that is no excuse.
Kau ni shite mo minakereba naranu	Even though (we consider that) it is bought, we must see it.

There is also a special use which should be mentioned. In this usage *ni shite mo* has the meaning "even such as a" or "and the like," a usage corresponding to that of the colloquial *demo,* which derives from *ni shite mo* through the contracted form *nite mo.*

This usage is found in the colloquial as well as in bungo. E.g.:

Higashiyama ni shite mo sō desu	It is true of even such as Higashiyama.

NI SHITE WA. In the colloquial this phrase may be used to convey the idea that something is to be considered in the aspect indicated. (Cf. TO SHITE WA.) It is often contracted to *ni shicha*

Yasui ni shite wa sono kutsu wa ii	Considering that they are cheap, those shoes are good.
Kodomo ni shicha kanshin da	Considering that he's a child, we admire (his accomplishments).

Note that the above meaning of *ni shite wa* is possible only if *suru* is not used "transitively," with the sense of "make" or "do." E.g.:

Sonna hito wo sensei ni shite wa ikenai	It won't do to make a person like that a teacher.

Here the *ni shite wa* is practically equivalent to *ni suru no wa.*

NITE.   A bungo particle.

The history of its origin is not clearly known. Apparently it is a contraction from various verb-forms, including *ni arite* 'being', *ni shite* 'acting in-connection-with', *ni oite* 'put in connection with', and possibly others.

As a contraction of *ni arite*, it corresponds to the colloquial *de* in its use as a verb (*de atte*).

As a contraction of *ni shite*, it corresponds to the colloquial *de* in its use as a postposition.

As a contraction of *ni oite*, it corresponds to the colloquial *ni* in its meaning of "at."

It should be noticed that the form *nite ari* is usually contracted, through *ni ari*, to *nari*.

Kare wa kenkō nite katsu kimbenka nari	He is healthy, and furthermore is a hard worker.
Ato nite hanasamu	I will tell you later.
Byōki nite shiseri	He did on account of an illness.
Shiken nite isogashi	He is busy with examinations.
Fude nite ji wo kaku	(I) write characters, using a brush.
Ani mo Kyō nite hōshi nite ari	His brother too is a priest, at Kyoto.
Kare wa gakusha nite ari	He is a scholar.

NI TOTTE.   This is a combination of the postposition *ni* and the *-te* form of the verb *toru* 'take'.

It has a special use which is usually best translated into English as "for (somebody)." In this use the *ni totte* is usually, but not always, followed by *wa*.

Kore wa watakushi ni totte muzukashii n'desu	This is hard for me.
Ren-ai wa fujin ni totte wa seimei de aru	Love is life, for women.

NI WA.   In this combination both particles keep their normal uses.

It therefore has a feeling somewhat like "as for in connection

with," but of course is not to be translated by any such monstrous
phrase.

For what may be called a special case, when used in reference to
exalted personages, see under NI MO.

Tsukue no ue ni wa pen to	On the desk there are pens
empitsu ga aru	and pencils.

Note that whatever comes before the *ni wa is* treated as a substantive, even if it is a verb in form. Thus we may have:

(Q) *Ame ga futte imasu ka*	Is it raining?
(A) *Furu ni wa futte imasu*	To be literal, it is raining, but
ga kosame desu	it's only a drizzle. (As-for
	in-connection-with "rain," it
	is raining, but . . .)

Mazu A san ga iimasu ni	First Mr. A said: ". . ."
wa . . .	

This locution with *ni wa* is often used to introduce long speeches,
which then do not have to be closed with *to itta* or its equivalent.

There is even a substantival feeling given to phrases such as
Tō ga aru kara in the following example.

Tō ga aru kara ni wa tera mo	Because there is a pagoda, I
aru ni sōi nai	am sure that there is also a
	temple.

NI YORU. The difficulties with the phrases *ni yoreba, ni yori,*
and *ni yotte,* apparently all derive from the meaning of the verb
yoru.

This verb is now written with various Chinese characters.
These characters have different meanings in Chinese, and each
corresponds to a particular use of *yoru.* In exact writing (e.g.,
legal language) the distinctions between them must be observed.
In ordinary writing, however, the distinctions tend to disappear,
and the word is often written in *kana.* Apparently all the various
uses of *yoru* have grown out of a single root.

The verb *yoru* seems to have a root meaning of "making or
having a connection with something else." That "something

else" may be thought of as a base on which something stands, or from which or out of which it grows. Hence the meaning of "to lean on," "to base on," or "to be a consequence of." E.g.:

Kabe ni yoru	(He) rests against the wall.
Fuchūi ni yoru	It is due to (has its basis in) carelessness.
Kangun wa shirizoite Yoshinoyama ni yotta	The imperial army fell back and took its stand at Yoshinoyama (made Y- its base).
Yorubeki kisoku ga nai	There is no rule to go by (to base on).
Kare wa senkō ni yori kinshikunshō wo sazukareta	He was given the Order of the Golden Kite on account of his services in war.
Gakusha ni yotte setsu ga chigau	Opinions differ, depending on the scholar. (I.e., according to, or conditioned by, which authority they come from.)

Note that our phrase "depending on" is often used to give a connective idea like that of *ni yotte,* but that it means "hanging from" instead of "based on."

The postpostion *yori,* which marks what it follows as a "base," is undoubtedly derived from *yoru.* And the *yoru* which means "to draw near," "to come together," although it is written with a special Chinese character, 寄, seems also to have derived from the idea of "make a connection with."

COMPARISON OF "NI YOTTE" AND "NI YOREBA"

A general rule for distinguishing these is to remember that the *-te* form is usually used adverbially, and that the subject of *-ni yotte* is normally the subject of the following sentence.

On the other hand . . . *ni yoreba* . . . is usually used elliptically, to mean, "if one takes . . . as a basis, one finds that . . ."

A san wa shimbun ni yotte hon wo tsukutta	Mr. A has written a book, taking the newspapers as a basis for it.

A san wa shimbun ni yoreba hon wo tsukutta	If one takes the newspapers as a basis (i.e., according to the newspapers) Mr. A has written a book.
A san wa shimbun ni yoreba hon wo tsukutta to kaite aru	If one takes the newspapers as a basis, one finds that it is there written that Mr. A has written a book.

Note that if one wishes to translate the last two sentences, it is quite possible to say for both "according to the newspapers, Mr. A has written a book." In other words, the *to kaite aru* of the last sentence may be omitted, in English as well as in Japanese.

For other examples of ellipsis, see under -BA.

COMPARISON OF "NI YOTTE" AND "NI YORI"

The difference between *ni yotte* and *ni yori* is basically that between any *-te* form of a verb and its Line 2 form (*renyōkei*). See under -TE, particularly the Special Note on p. 284.

As a connective, the Line 2 form suggests a larger gap than a *-te* form does, and makes a somewhat different kind of connection. Thus *ni yori* suggests an action preceding the action or state of the following sentence, rather than a state co-existing with it.

A san wa tegami ni yotte hon wo tsukutta	Mr. A has written a book, taking the letters as a basis for it.
A san wa tegami ni yori hon wo tsukutta	Mr. A has written a book, following (the suggestion or instructions in) the letter.

Of course the examples given above have been specially manufactured for the purposes of comparison. They are grammatically correct, but not to be taken as examples of good colloquial Japanese. Such examples may be found in any dictionary.

As an example of the bungo use of *ni yori*, the following may be useful. It is taken from Article 70 of the Japanese Constitution.

Kōkyō no anzen wo hōjisuru   In case of urgent need for the
tame kinkyū no juyō aru   maintenance of public safe-
baai ni oite naigai no jōkei   ty, at times when, owing to
ni yori seifū wa teikoku-   the internal or external
gikai wo shoshū-suru koto   condition of affairs, the
atawazaru toki wa chokurei   Government is unable to
ni yori zaiseijō hitsuyō no   convoke the Imperial Diet,
shobun wo nasu koto wo u   it may, by means of an Im-
                                 perial Ordinance, take all
                                 necessary financial measures.

Here the first *ni yori* is translated as "owing to," and the second
ni yori by "by means of."

The first *yori* is written with the Sino-Japanese character *yu*
(由) meaning 'reason' or 'cause'. The second is written with the
character 依 'to depend on'.

In both uses, however, *ni yori* shows what is "taken as a basis"
for subsequent action.

-NJIRU. A phonetic change from *-nzuru,* quite widely used
in colloquial speech.   (See -NZU, -NZURU.)

-NN-. In Japanese the consonant "n" is often lengthened or
doubled, usually for emphasis, but often apparently just because
the speaker feels that he wants to.

When this is done, a long vowel preceding the "n" sound may
become short.

The student is warned to be on the lookout for such words.
E.g.:

> *minna,* for *mina* 'all'
> *nanni,* for *nani* 'what?'
> *sonnara,* for *sō-nara* 'if it be so'

NO. There are two words *no,* the postpositional *no* and the
substantival *no.* They are quite different, and are therefore
treated separately.

They are fortunately not easily confused. In bungo one finds
only the postpositional *no.* In the colloquial the general rule is
that a *no* used after a substantive is the postpositional *no;* the
substantival *no* is used after adjectives or verbs.

For special cases see also NO . . . NO, NO DE, NODE, NO DE WA, NO DESU, NO NI, NONI, NO NI WA, NA NO, NA-NO-DE, NA NO DESU, NA NO NI, MONO NO.

THE POSTPOSITIONAL *NO*

This *no* is a particle (postposition) used to join two substantives.

Its function is to indicate that the first substantive in some way characterizes the second. This characterization may be of almost any description.

A substantive followed by *no* may be regarded as adjectival in function, and in fact is quite often equivalent to an adjective. See introductory Note on Adjectives. See also -TARU.

As explained in the introductory Note on Nomenclature, in Japanese a substantive idea is not necessarily expressed in the form of a noun.

In early Japanese *no* could be used to mark the subject of a final verb. In the modern colloquial this is no longer possible, and there is an increasing tendency to have the two ideas connected by *no* not only "psychological substantives," but substantives in form as well.

For this reason it has seemed best to consider first the uses of *no* in the modern colloquial, and then to give examples of its use in bungo.

THE COLLOQUIAL

1. It is simplest to start with examples of the uses of *no* when both substantives are substantives in form.

Natsu no kimono	Summer clothes
Beikoku no jidōsha	American automobiles
Migi no hō e	Toward the right (direction)
Isu no shita ni	Under the chair (at the underneath of the chair)
Kin no yubiwa	A gold ring
Kin no omomi	The heaviness of gold
Anata no hon	Your book
Go on no tame ni	On account of the Imperial favors

Fujiwara no Mitsunobu	Mitsunobu of the Fujiwara (family)
Bosuton no machi	The city of Boston
Gakusha no Yamada hakushi	Dr. Yamada, the scholar
Hitsuyō no mono	A necessary thing
B san no migi no te no koyubi no tsume no katachi no fushigina koto	The queerness of the shape of the nail on the little finger of Mr. B's right hand.

This is a manufactured phrase, given here to illustrate the Japanese order of expression which is regularly from large to small, from general to particular.

These examples illustrate some of the ways in which the first substantive may characterize the second. It would be impossible to give examples of all conceivable ways.

It should be noticed, however, that whenever the first substantive is particularized or otherwise dominant it tends to characterize the second as in some way belonging to the first.

Ume no hana	Plum-tree flowers (i.e., plumblossoms in general)
Ano takai ume no hana	That tall plum-tree's blossoms
Beikoku no jidōsha	An American automobile
Beikoku no ōkisa	America's size or "the size of America."

There will usually be very little difficulty in determining from the context what kind of characterization is implied, though unfortunately *no* is such a convenient word that there is a natural tendency to overwork it, rather than to go to the trouble of accurate definition.

But it must be remembered that what puzzles foreigners is often quite simple to natives. We in America have no trouble with such phrases as "the Washington Monument" or "puppy love," while foreigners may need to have it explained whether the monument is at, by, in, or, from, or to Washington and whether the love is by puppies, for puppies, or like that of puppies.

If there is any doubt as to what kind of characterization is intended, a more exact method of characterization should be used. For example, *Kōrin no byōbu* may mean a screen owned

by Kōrin, one painted by him, or even one so called because it is
painted in the Kōrin style. The simple phrase may be replaced
by:

Kōrin no motteru byōbu	Screen owned by Kōrin
Kōrin no kaita byōbu	Screen painted by Kōrin
Kōrin ni nite iru byōbu	Screen like Kōrin's, etc.

It is important to note that the "second substantive" does not
necessarily follow the *no* immediately. Adjectives, verbs, or whole
clauses may be inserted. Such insertions then also characterize
the second substantive. (The only exception to this rule would
come if the insertions were obviously interjections.)

If the insertions are adjectives no difficulties are presented.
E.g.:

Watakushi no okii tokei	My large watch

However, if the insertions are verbs or complete clauses it is
often more in accordance with English idiom to use relative
clauses in the translation.

Kōrin no kaita byōbu	A screen which Kōrin painted.
Watakushi no, kinō ojisan ga kudasaimashita tokei	My watch, which my uncle gave me yesterday.

A literal translation of this last sentence would be "My yesterday-
uncle-gave watch." Such placing of the *kinō* is more common in
speech than in writing. The use of the comma is referred to below.

Notice that the subject of the inserted verb may or may not be
the word marked by *no*. However, the subject will normally be
taken as being the word marked by *no* unless some other subject
is expressly indicated.

In loosely constructed sentences it may be necessary to guess
what substantive the word marked by *no* actually does characterize. E.g.:

Watakushi no ojisan ga kudasaimashita tokei	(a) My watch which (my) uncle gave me. (b) The watch, which my uncle gave (possibly to someone else).

Here one has to judge from the context whether the *watakushi no* characterizes the *tokei* to give meaning (a), or the *ojisan* to give meaning (b). In speech, if meaning (a) is intended, there would usually be a short pause after *watakushi no;* in writing, such pauses may be indicated by a punctuation mark corresponding to a comma.

The whole subject of the use of *no* in subordinate clauses is really quite simple. The student can usually avoid trouble by not trying to apply preconceived notions derived from European grammars. Consider, for example:

Kono ue no nai rippana mono   A thing than which there is
                                    nothing more splendid.

Such phrases as these are hard to parse, and the ordinary Japanese does not attempt to do so. He simply understands that the first substantive is used in characterizing the second, and that it acts as the subject of the verb.

It is true that if we substitute *ga* for *no* in such subordinate clauses, we get phrases that are easy to parse.

Kōrin ga kaita	Kōrin drew.
Kono ue ga nai	There is no superior to this.

It is, however, an error to consider such clauses as derived from the *ga* form. People do not think that way.

Either *no* or *ga* may be used to mark the subject of a verb in attributive clauses. Which is used depends on context and the exact meaning intended. At times the two would be practically interchangeable. But consider the following sentences:

1. *Kōrin no kaita byōbu*   Is it a screen painted by Kōrin?
   desu ka
2. *Kōrin ga kaita byōbu*   Is it the screen painted by
   desu ka   Kōrin?

The English translations are, of course, only approximate. In (1) the *Kōrin no* connects with and characterizes the substantive *byōbu*. In (2) the *ga* lays stress on *Kōrin* and links it closely with *kaita,* so that *byōbu* is characterized by *Kōrin-ga-kaita* as a whole.

Possible answers might be:

1. *Ha, Kōrin no kaita byōbu desu.*
2. *Ha, Kōrin ga kaita byōbu desu.*
3. *Ha, Kōrin no kaita no desu.*
4. *Ha, Kōrin ga kaita no desu.*

The first would be a quite common form of assent. The second would be very seldom heard and, if used at all, only to convey an idea like "Yes, it is the screen we were talking about as being 'painted by Kōrin'." The meaning of (3) is approximately "Yes, it is (one) painted by Kōrin," and that of (4) "Yes, it is Kōrin who painted it."

2. In the examples given above the substantives connected by *no* have both been substantives in form as well as in meaning. However, it is not necessary that this rule should be followed on all occasions. As pointed out in the introductory Note on Nomenclature, in Japanese there is no absolute correspondence between grammatical categories and logical categories. Furthermore, in Japanese, as indeed in most languages, obviously unnecessary words may be omitted.

Phrases in which the two substantives connected by *no* are not both in noun form are of the following types:

(a) Phrases in which the first substantive is expressed in words or phrases which may also be used as adverbs.

(b) Phrases in which the second substantive is omitted.

(c) Phrases in which the second substantive is a verb-form.

(d) Phrases in which neither substantive is expressed in noun form.

(a) The first substantive may be a word which has its most common use as an adverb. It may also be a descriptive phrase ending with *kara, e, made, yori,* or *to.*

Adverbial phrases ending with *ni* cannot be used as substantives. It is of interest that in the very earliest days *ni* seems to have been a verb. *Kara, e, yori,* and probably *made* seem to have been nouns. *To* had uses as a pronoun.

tokidoki no okonai	occasional happenings
massugu no michi	the road straight ahead
hitsuyō no mono	a necessary thing
kono chikaku no yama	mountains near here
anata kara no tegami	the letter from you
Tōkyō made no kishachin	the trainfare up to Tokyo
Tachi san to no sōron	the dispute with Mr. Tachi
itsumo no tōri ni	in the usual way (as always)

Note, however, that if the word or phrase is also one that may be used as an adjective, a following *no* may be, not the postposition, but the substantival *no*. E.g.: the phrase *hitsuyō no de . . .* This may be considered as equivalent to either:

hitsuyō no mono de . . .	being a necessary thing . . .

or to:

hitsuyō de aru no de . . .	since it is necessary . . .

The point here is that *hitsuyō* may be treated as an adjective which takes the suffix *-na, hitsuyōna.*

(b) The second substantive is omitted only if its inclusion is obviously unnecessary. The English idiom is practically the same. E.g.:

Ue no ga kimi no de shita	The upper is yours and the
no ga boku no da	lower is mine.

If one happens to be talking about lockers, for instance, it would be as unnecessary in Japanese as in English to say "The upper locker is your locker, and the lower locker is my locker."

As another example:

Kimi no no ue ni oite	Please put it on top of yours.
kudasai	

Here some word like "hat," "overcoat," "book," etc., has obviously been omitted. For further discussion of two *no* coming together see under part (a) in the treatment of the substantival **no.**

The general rule is that the omission of the second substantive is indicated whenever a postpositional *no* is immediately followed by another postposition.

(c) The second substantive may be a verb form, either the Line 2 form (*renyōkei*) or the Line 3 form (*shūshikei*). If it is the Line 2 form it is always regarded as a noun, and functions exactly like any other noun. If it is the Line 3 form, it may or may not be followed by a substantivizing *no*. When it is so followed we have, of course, a definitely substantival form. See the discussion of the substantival *no*.

Tegami no kuru wo matsu	Await the arrival of a letter.
Tegami no kuru no wo matsu	

Note that in this sentence the *no* after *tegami* is a postposition. The *no* after *kuru* is the substantival *no*.

(d) The first substantive may be of the adverbial type described above in part (a), joined by *no* to a substantival idea which is not expressed, having been omitted for the reasons described in part (b). This omitted second substantive is of course usually a simple noun. Even if it were expressed it would in practice always be substantival in form.

Kono ringo wa Beikoku kara no ni taishite . . .	These apples, compared with the ones from America . . .
Shintō no go sono mono wa yahari kono igi de no de aru koto wo kangaeru to . . .	The word "Shintō" itself, when we consider the fact that it is one used with this meaning also . . .

BUNGO

The bungo uses of *no* are much the same as those of the colloquial, that is, it joins two substantive ideas. The few differences are connected with the second substantive. Strictly speaking, this can never be omitted, but practically any verb-form may be regarded as a substantive. E.g.:

Yukiki no shaba no taezareba mukō no kawa e yukikanetsu	Since the coming and going vehicles and horses had no cessation, (she) was unable to cross to the other side.

For discussion of the use of verb-forms as substantives see the

NO

introductory Note on Nomenclature. It should be noted that the substantivizing *no* is not used in bungo.

In bungo both *no* and *ga* are used to connect nouns. The Japanese say that when *no* is used the connection is less strong and less possessive than when *ga* is used. Sansom illustrates this point with the phrase:

Shizunoo ga ono no oto   The sound of the peasant's axe.

Both *no* and *ga* may be used in attributive clauses as if they were marking the subject of an attributive verb. When they do so, however, the distinction between them is not quite the same as in the colloquial. About all one can say is that such a phrase as *Kōrin no egakishi byōbu* sounds somehow softer than *Kōrin ga egakishi byōbu*. They both refer to "Kōrin-painted" screens.

In phrases of this sort it seems more accurate to consider that both *no* and *ga* mark words as performing an attributive function rather than as being subjects of a verb. This, however, is primarily a matter for nomenclaturists. The important thing for the student is to be sure that the meaning is clear.

THE SUBSTANTIVAL *NO*

This *no* is a colloquial word, which may be regarded either as a substantive (meaning approximately "thing"), or as a substantivizer of what precedes it. (See the introductory Note on Nomenclature.)

Whether or not this *no* was originally derived from *mono* seems to be an open question. There is no harm in so regarding it if the student finds it helpful to do so. It does not occur in bungo, and is used in the colloquial:

(a) After adjectives or adjectival phrases
(b) After complete clauses or verbs in sentence-ending form
(c) At the end of a sentence

In all uses the effect is to substantivize the whole *no* phrase.

(a) After an adjective or adjective phrase, *no* is like the English "a one," "the one," "ones," or "the ones."

Nagai no wo kashite kure	Please lend me the long one.
Kireina no ga hoshii	He wants a beautiful one.
Akai no ga kimi no de, shiroi no ga boku no da	The red one is yours and the white one is mine.

In the last example the *no* after *akai* and *shiroi* is obviously the substantival *no*; the *no* after *kimi* and *boku* is the postposition. There may, however, be some confusion when two *no* come together. E.g.:

Nagai no no hō ga ii	The long one is better.

Here the first *no* is substantival, the second is the postposition. We also have examples where both *no* are postpositions, as in:

Kimi no no ue ni oite kudasai	Please put it on top of yours.

In general there is an avoidance of a double *no* where the first *no* is the postposition, but very occasionally one meets forms like:

Dai ni no no wo kudasai	Please give me the second one.

Triple *no,* with the center one the substantival *no* are theoretically possible but are apparently never used.

(b) After a complete clause or a verb in sentence-ending form (i.e., the simple Line 3 or "dictionary" form or with the *-ta, -da,* or *-u, -yō* endings), the whole phrase, including the *no,* may be regarded as a substantive. It is a question for specialists to decide whether this *no* is in itself a substantive, or whether it simply substantivizes what precedes it.

Sakura no saku no wa haru no sue de aru	The blooming of the cherries is the end of spring.
Ikitai no wo gamanshite iru	They are patient about their desire to go.
Hito ga kuru no wo matte imasu	(We) are waiting for somebody to come.
Hito no kuru no wo matte imasu	(We) are awaiting somebody's arrival.
Doko ni iru no ka	Where are you?

(c) After complete sentences, *no* gives an effect of gentle emphasis. This *no* is used mostly by women and children.

Grammatically, a *no* so used may be considered as an abbreviation of *no desu.*   (See NO DESU and cf. NA NO.)   It seems, however, to be rather more comparable to NA and NE in their use as exclamations,

Kirei da no	It is pretty!
Doko ni iru no	Where is it you are?

NŌ   (Kyushu dialect). An interjection equivalent in meaning to NEE.

NO DE.   This combination may consist of either the postposition *no* or the substantival *no,* followed by *de.*   It is used in the colloquial only.   (See NO, DE, and NODE, and compare with NO NI and NONI.)

The distinction is usually easily made.

1. If *no de* directly follows a substantive, normally the *no* is a postposition, and an obviously implied "second substantive" has been omitted. See under NO, p. 218.

Kore wa anata no de are wa *watakushi no de gozaimasu*	This is yours, and that is mine.
Boku no de koshiraete kure	Please make it of mine (i.e., using my bricks or stones, or whatever it may be).

Note that there are some phrases, not uncommon in loose speech, where it is not clear whether a substantive has been omitted, or a verb-phrase such as *to iu* or *de aru.* It usually doesn't matter. E.g.:

Kotae wa hai no de . . .	The answer being "hai" . . .

This is probably thought of as equivalent to *hai de aru no de, hai na no de,* or *hai to iu no de,* but it would be equally possible to think of it as *hai no kotae de.*

2. If *no de* directly follows an attributive verb or adjective, or an attributive phrase, the *no* substantivizes the attributive.   (See pp. 220, 221.)

Akai no de koshiraeyō	I will make it of the red ones.
Akai no de yoku miemasu	Being a red one it is easily seen.

3. If *no de* directly follows a statement, it may often be regarded as a single word, *node*. (See NODE.)

As all adjectives (in the *-i* form) and adjectival verb-forms (Line 3A, *rentaikei*) are in the colloquial the same as the sentence-ending forms (*shūshikei*), it is sometimes difficult to distinguish between them. Fortunately the context usually makes this point clear.

When *no de* occurs after a statement or after any expression that can stand by itself as a complete sentence, technically that expression may be regarded as modifying the *no,* and hence as being an attributive phrase. However, when *no de* stands between two such expressions, and is not immediately followed by *wa,* it is often regarded as if it were one word, *node,* used as a conjunction, and indicating that the first state of affairs is the cause of the second.

For example, in the Japanese sentences given in paragraph 2 of this section, if *akai* is taken as a statement "it is red," the phrase *akai no de* would mean "because it is red." This assumption would make the first sentence practically meaningless, but would hardly at all affect the meaning of the second.

NOTE. If the second phrase is some form of *aru* or an equivalent, the *de* becomes part of the copula, and the *no de* is not to be regarded as one word. For examples see DE ARU and NO DESU (NO DE ARU).

NODE. A colloquial combination, formed from the substantival *no* plus *de.*

When it occurs between statements in sentence-form, it is usually regarded as a conjunction, and pronounced as a single word.

When so used it indicates that the first state of affairs is the cause of the second. It may be translated by such conjunctions as "and so" or "consequently," or by an initial "because."

When treating *node* as a conjunction, remember that it is, of course, attached to the first clause. In English the "and so" or "consequently" is thought of as attached to the second.

Note that *no* followed by *de* does not necessarily form the conjunction *node.* Compare with examples under NO DE, NO DE WA, and NO DE ARU. See also NA NO DE.

Amari samui node sampo ni   As it was too cold, (I) did not
   dekakemasen deshita   go out for a walk.
Ame ga futta node   It rained, and so I was (made)
   ikaremasen-deshita   unable to come.

NOTE ON

COMPARISON OF "NODE" AND "KARA"

When *kara* and *node* are used as conjunctions their effect is so
similar that in most sentences they may be considered as practically interchangeable in meaning. There is, however, a distinct
difference in usage. This difference is partly grammatical, partly
due to emphasis, and partly to formality.

When *kara* is used after a statement it marks that statement as
a starting-point or cause of action, and tends to focus attention
on the following result. On the other hand, when *node* is used
after a statement it tends to focus attention on the condition
described, which is then taken as an accepted fact.

Consider the following phrases:

Tenki ga ii kara . . .   As it is (or was) fine
                                 weather . . .
Tenki ga ii node . . .   The weather is (or was) fine,
                                 and so . . .

The English translations naturally are not to be taken as
absolute equivalents suitable in all circumstances, but they do
illustrate the difference in emphasis.

There is also a difference in formality. *Kara* is rather light and
informal, and tends to be used in statements concerning the
actions or decisions of the speaker. *Node* is rather ponderous and
formal, and tends to be used more in general statements, or those
in which the speaker is not the person primarily concerned.
Thus, usually,

Tenki ga yokatta kara   As the weather was fine (I)
   sampo shita   went for a walk.
Tenki ga yokatta node   The weather was fine, and so
   sampo shita   (they) went for a walk.

The one real grammatical difference between them seems to be that *kara* may be used after a "future" (*-u, yō*) form. *Node* is not so used. This is apparently because *kara* simply points out a reason for action, while *node* emphasizes an accepted fact.

Kore wa muzukashii darō	As this is likely to be difficult,
kara jisho wo kasō	I will lend you a dictionary.

In such a sentence as the above, *node* would not be used.

NO DESU (NO DE ARU).

NO DESU (**NO DE ARU**). A phrase often found at the end of a sentence complete without it. Grammatically the *no* substantivizes the sentence and the *de aru* form predicates its existence. The effect is to make the preceding sentence more clear and definite.

In English we sometimes begin a sentence with "It is a fact that . . . " or tack on a "That is the case" at the end. The effect of *no desu* is somewhat similar, though it must be remembered that its use is so common in Japanese that it does not attract so much attention as the English phrases. It is usually better not to try to translate it by any special English phrase.

Shōgun ga seiji wo suru	A situation in which a *shōgun*
tokoro wo bakufu to iu no	administers the government,
de aru	we call a *bakufu*.

This use of *no desu* or its equivalents, such as *no de aru* or *no de gozaimasu,* etc., is rather more common in speech than in writing. Thus in sentences like

Uso ni mo hodo ga aru	There are limits, even in lying.
(*no desu*)	

the form without the *no desu* is a general statement. In speech it is felt as more clearly and definitely applicable to the person addressed if a *no desu* is added.

The exact effect of *no desu* in making a statement somewhat more definite naturally depends on the context.

In public speaking, sentences are quite often ended, for the sake of emphasis, with *de aru no de aru.*

The compiler has even heard an after-dinner speaker end with
. . . *de aru n'de aru n'de aru.*

There is also a special use which implies an idea of frequent or
habitual action.   The context is usually sufficient to show the
meaning.

Taka wa tonde kite Jingisu	The falcon used to fly to
Kan ni shiraseru no deshita	Genghis Khan and show him.

For further examples and discussion see under NO and NA NO
DESU.

NOTE.   Note that when *no desu* occurs after an adjective form in
-i, we cannot tell from the form whether we are dealing with an
adjective or a verb.   For example, *Kore wa akai* means "This is
red," and by adding *no desu* to the sentence we get

Kore wa akai no desu	(The case is that) this is red.

But the same form with *akai no,* thought of as "red one," will
mean "This is a red one."   It will be noticed that for practical
purposes there is very little difference in the meanings.

It should also be noted that a sentence which ends in an
adjective *-i* form (e.g., *kore wa akai*) is felt as somewhat harsh and
unsatisfactory in speech.   It is therefore usually rounded out by the
addition of *no desu, n'desu,* or *desu.*   This last is in quite common
use, but is still regarded by many as incorrect Japanese.

NO DE WA.   When *no de* is followed by *wa,* so that we get the
combination *no de wa,* it shows that *no de* is not to be considered
as a conjunction and that the relationship with the second statement is not a causal one.

Tenka wo tairageyō to	Have the intention to conquer
kokorozashitemo yatto	the whole country, and still
chūgoku gurai shika	in the end one will not be
torenai	ᵎable to seize more than the Central Provinces.

Chūgoku wo tairageyō to shita   Have an intention to conquer
no de wa dōshite chūgoku   the Central Provinces and
wo toru koto ga dekiru ka   (with that as a basis) how
    will the taking of the Central Provinces be possible?

NOMI. Bungo word meaning "only." In the colloquial it is replaced by *dake* or *bakari*.

It may be used after nouns, verbs, adjectives, or adverbs. After nouns which are governed by postpositions it may come after the postposition or between the postposition and the noun.

Nichiya shushoku ni nomi   Day and night he spends his
fukeru   time only in eating and drinking.

Gō-kaku seshi mono wazukani   Those who passed in the ex-
sūmei nomi   amination were only a few.

NO NI. A combination of *ni* with either the postposition *no* or with the substantival *no*. (See NO and NI, NONI, NO NI WA and compare with NO DE and NODE.)

In the colloquial the distinction is easily made.

1. If *no ni* directly follows a substantive, the *no* is always a postposition.

2. If *no ni* directly follows an adjective or an adjectival phrase, the *no* is substantival.

3. If *no ni* directly follows a statement, it may be often regarded as one word. (See NONI.)

In bungo no distinction is necessary, as the substantival *no* is not used. (Cf. under NI.)

1. After substantives (nouns or pronouns), when *no ni* follows a substantive the phrase is always a contraction formed by omitting a substantive. (For such omissions see under NO, p. 218.) The *ni* is then a postposition modifying this omitted substantive. What substantive has been omitted should be obvious from a previous context. E.g.:

Kono hon wa kimi no ni katte kita no da yo	This book I bought to be yours!
Boku no ni taishite . . .	Compared with mine . . .
Kono jidōsha wa Beikoku no ni makenai	This automobile is not inferior to the American ones.

2. After an attributive verb or adjective, or after an attributive phrase, the *no* substantivizes the attributive. (See NO.) The *ni* of course performs its usual function of establishing connection with a second concept.

As all adjectives in the *-i* form and adjectival verb forms (Line 3A, *rentaikei*) are, in the colloquial, the same as the sentence-ending forms (Line 3, *shūshikei*), it is sometimes difficult to distinguish between them. Fortunately the context usually makes this point clear. For further discussion see NONI.

Akai no ni shiroi no ni kuroi na ga aru	There are red ones, white ones, black ones.
Ano byōbu wa Kōrin no kaita no ni yoku nite imasu	That screen is very much like the ones that Kōrin painted.
Jibiki wa kotoba no imi wo shiru no ni tsukau	One uses a dictionary for learning the meanings of words.
Genki no sakanna no ni makasete . . .	Carried away by his own exuberance . . .
Sore wo kiru no ni naifu ga irimasu	To cut that (I) need a knife. (Literally "a knife is needed.")
Hanasu no ni tsugō ga yokatta	It was (more) convenient to have a talk.
Kome wo tsuku no ni ue nimo usu wo okeba . . .	When one hulls rice, if one puts a mortar on top as well (as below) . . .
Totsugeki suru no ni yamiyo wo riyōshita	In making the sudden attack (they) took advantage of a dark night.

Otona ni sae wakaranai no ni   When it is not clear even to
  kodomo ni wakaru hazu   adults it is not to be ex-
  ga nai   pected that it will be clear
                            to a child.

3. After a statement: When *no ni* occurs after any expression which can stand by itself as a complete sentence, technically that expression may be regarded as modifying the *no*.

However, when *no ni* stands between two such expressions and is not iself followed by *wa,* it may often be regarded as if it were one word used as a conjunction. There seems to be a quite general and growing tendency to use it as such. When it is so used, it is often written and pronounced emphatically as one word, *nonni,* especially in the Tokyo district.

There is a similar tendency to regard *no ni* as one word when it is used at the end of sentences.

Compare the following sentences with the somewhat similar ones in section 2 above.

Akai no ni umaku nai kono   They are red but yet have a
  ichigo wa   poor taste, these strawber-
                           ries.

Ano byōbu wa Kōrin ga   As for that screen, Kōrin
  kaita no ni Kanoha   painted it, and yet it resem-
  (no saku) ni nite iru   bles (the work of) the
                         Kano school.

For further examples see NONI, NA NO NI, and NO NI WA.

NONI (NONNI).   A combination formed from the substantival *no* plus *ni*. It is confined to the colloquial.

1. When it occurs between statements in sentence form it may be and often is regarded as a conjunction. It may then be pronounced as one word, *noni* or *nonni*.

When so used it indicates that after the first state of affairs described, the second is in some way unexpected. When regarded as a conjunction (and only then), it may be translated into English by such conjunctions as "and yet" or "but," or sometimes by an initial "although" or "in spite of the fact that."

Note that the combination of *no* and *ni* is not necessarily a conjunction. Compare examples under NO NI, paragraphs 2 and 3.

When treating *noni* as a conjunction remember that it is, of course, attached to the first clause. In English the "and yet" or "but" is thought of as attached to the second. When it occurs between statements *noni* may be regarded as giving an idea equivalent to " (that) matter in-connection-with." This will help to make it clear why *no ni* is sometimes equivalent to a conjunction and sometimes is not. Technically a verb before *no ni* ought always to be regarded as in the Line 3A form *(rentaikei)*. Practically, however, when people use *noni* as if it were a conjunction rather like *keredomo* or *ga,* the verb is used as if it were in the sentence-ending Line 3 form *(shūshikei)*.

Shiken ga chikai noni asonde bakari iru	The examinations are near, and yet he goes on just playing.
Anna kanemochi da noni mada manzoku shite inai	He is such a rich man as all that, and yet he still is not satisfied.
Hitotsu hitotsu tameshite mita no ni machigatte wa inai	(I) tried testing them one by one, but there are no mistakes.
Aki da to iu no ni mada nakanaka atsui	One calls it autumn, but it's still terribly hot.

Any "adversative" or "although" feel of *noni* seems to derive from the context, rather than from anything inherent in *no ni* itself. Thus:

Yonde iru no ni henji mo shinai	I keep calling and (yet) there isn't any answer at all.

This might be rendered, perhaps less colloquially, but at least with equal literalness, "To my continued calling there is not even an answer."

And there is certainly no "adversative" suggestion of "although" in the following:

Shōgatsu made mō go-roku nichi shika nai no ni konna taikin wo otoshite wa sazo komaru darō	There are now only five or six days (left) till New Year, so (all the more) the loss of such a large sum of money will surely trouble him greatly.

Here the literal rendering of *no ni* is still approximately "in connection with the fact that." The sense is that the loser would be troubled anyway, but more troubled at the near approach of New Year's Day, when all bills are expected to be paid.

In such a sentence as this, however, *no ni* is not used as a conjunction. The *no* and *ni* are separate. See other examples under NO NI, part 2.

Note that in bungo the substantivizing *no* is not used, the phrase being recognized and treated as a substantive without being so marked.ʹ Hence this *no* is often omitted in speech. The Tokyo standard colloquial requires its use, but it nevertheless often is dropped even in Tokyo.

Hence, in place of the *to iu no ni* of such a sentence as *aki to iu no ni mada atsui,* one might have *aki to iu ni* or *aki to iu nonni.* The former is more common in Western Japan, the latter more common in the Tokyo district.

> The way in which *no ni* is getting to be a conjunction is a good example of how the modern Japanese language is changing. It is interesting to compare this development of *no ni* with that of *no de,* which has progressed further along the road to becoming a true conjunction.

2. When *noni* occurs at the end of a sentence, it acts as an expression of emotion. The adversative force is retained.

Oyafukōna yatsu da to bakari omotte ita noni	I was thinking only that he was an unfilial wretch! (. . . and yet he wasn't!)
Hayaku ike to iu noni	(I) say to go quickly! (and you aren't doing it!)

Kono heya wa mō sukoshi	It would be nice if this room
hirokereba ii noni	were a little larger! (It
	isn't—I wish it were!)

NO NI WA. When this combination occurs the *no ni* cannot be used as the adversative conjunction *noni* 'in spite of the fact that'.

The three particles each keep their normal uses.

NO . . . NO. There is a special use of *no* in parallel sequence. This use is always followed by some verb indicating "saying."

When so used, the *no* separates and "piles up" the words or clauses which it follows and which are to be taken as being said separately.

Note that in accordance with the regular rules of Japanese idiom the verb of "saying" may be omitted if it is sufficiently implied by the context.

Imasara ii no warui no nan no	As it is, the saying "It's good,"
ka no iu koto wa shōchi	"It's bad," and this and that
ga naranu	and the other thing, isn't
	getting to an agreement.
Shinu no ikiru no to (iu)	He made an uproar (shouting)
sawagi wo shita	about dying or staying alive.
Yuku no kaeru no to bakari iu	(He) says only "I will go" and
	"I will come back."

-NTA, -NTE. Local contractions of the *-ta* and *-te* forms of (B) (N) (M) verbs of the first conjugation, for which the standard contractions are *-nda* and *-nde*. E.g., *tonte* instead of *tonde* 'flying'. (See introductory Note on Verbs.)

-NU. A suffix. It has two uses, depending on what verb-form it follows. It may be added to:

1. The Line 1 form *(mizenkei)*, e.g., *sakanu*.
2. The Line 2 form *(renyōkei)*, e.g., *sakinu*.

Both these uses are found in bungo. Only use (1) is found in the colloquial.

In use (1) *-nu* is a negative suffix. In use (2) it is used as the sign of a perfect tense.

Some grammarians claim that there are in Japanese vestiges of a now wholly obsolete verb, *nu*, meaning "to be." They presume this verb to have belonged to the first *(yodan)* conjugation, and to have had the four forms *na, ni, nu,* and *ne.* The vestiges found indicate that this verb, if it did exist, was used in combination with other verbs, following their Line 2 form *(renyōkei).* The subject is interesting, but outside the scope of the present discussion. The hypothesis of the existence of such a verb does, however, seem to make it easier to grasp certain uses of, for example, the postposition *ni.*

1. When added to the Line 1 form *(mizenkei)* of verbs, *-nu* always indicates negation.

In the colloquial it is often contracted to *-n.* Like *-nai,* it is used both as a sentence-ending form and attributively, as a true adjective. It may be regarded as the Line 3, 3A form *(shūshikei* and *rentaikei)* of an incomplete conjugation.

> Line 3, 3A   *Shūshikei, Rentaikei*   *-nu*
> Line 4   *Izenkei*   *-ne*

For other forms, sometimes considered as part of the conjugation, see *-zu.*

Ikkō shiranu hito ga	A man whom I did not know
watakushi wo yobimashita	at all hailed me.
Ikkō wakaranu	I don't understand at all.
Benkyō seneba naran	You must study.
Hana mo sakazu tori mo	Neither do the flowers bloom
nakanu	nor do the birds sing.

In bungo the negative *-nu* is always used as an attributive form. It can never end sentences. It may be regarded as the Line 3A form *(rentaikei)* of a partial conjugation:

> Line 3A *Rentaikei*   *-nu*
> Line 4 *Izenkei*   *-ne*

The place of the other forms, except that of the imperative (which does not exist) is taken by the suffix *-zu.* (See *-zu,* and also the negative imperative NA.)

Benkyō senu hito . . .	A person who does not study . . .
Hana mo niowanu yamazato . . .	A mountain village where even the blossoms have no scent . . .
Yukue shiraneba . . .	Since (I) do not know where (you) have gone . . .

2. When *-nu* is added to the Line 2 form (*renyōkei*) of verbs, it forms, in bungo, what is practically equivalent to the English perfect tense. In the colloquial it is replaced by *-ta*.

Some grammarians say it indicates a comparatively recent past. Others say that it describes action completed "from inside" and therefore that it is generally suffixed to intransitive verbs. Some derive it from *inu* 'to go away', others from an obsolete verb *nu* 'to be'. The problems are interesting but rather academic.

It may be regarded as the Line 3 or sentence-ending form of a full conjugation. But it should be noted that in present-day bungo, all but the Line 3 form (*shūshikei*) *-nu* are obsolescent. (Cf. -NA.)

Line 1	*Mizenkei*	*-na*
Line 2	*Renyōkei*	*-ni*
Line 3	*Shūshikei*	*-nu*
Line 3A	*Rentaikei*	*-nuru*
Line 4	*Izenkei*	*-nure*
Line 5	*Meireikei*	*-ne*

Hana sakinu	The flowers have bloomed and are blooming.
Tsuki mo kakurenu	The moon, too, has hidden itself.
Aki wa kinikeri	Autumn has come.

Special Note

Students should note that the two bungo *-nu* suffixes cannot be confused with each other. Even when the Line 1 and Line 2

forms (*mizenkei* and *renyōkei*) are the same, the uses make confusion impossible.

The rule is that the negative -*nu* is always an attributive form
(*rentaikei*), while the perfect-tense -*nu* is always a sentence-ending
form (*shūshikei*). E.g.:

kakurenu tsuki	a moon not hidden
Tsuki kakurenu	The moon has hidden itself.
kakurenuru tsuki	a moon that has hidden itself
Tsuki kakurezu	The moon is not hidden.

-NUDE. A colloquial suffix. It is equivalent to -*naide* or
-*nakute* (not . . . ing).

It is always contracted to -*n'de* in speech and sometimes written
-*nde,* but as it is added to the Line 1 form (*mizenkei*) of verbs,
it cannot be confused with the contraction -*nde,* which is equivalent to -*nite,* -*bite,* or -*mite.* E.g.:

tobande	not flying
tonde	flying

-NURU. See under -NU.

NYA, NYĀ. Informal pronunciations, or mispronunciations, of
ni wa. See -YA, -YĀ.

-NZU, NZURU. A phonetic change from -*ku suru,* especially
where the -*ku* is a suffix added to an adjective root.

This phonetic change took place, apparently, first through the
dropping of the harsh "k" sound, and then by a change of the
-*u su* sound to -*nzu.*

For example, from the adjective *omoki* (colloquial *omoi*), used
in its sense of "important," we first get the verb-form *omoku suru*
'to treat as important', etc. Then *omou-suru, omou-zuru,* and
finally *omonzuru* 'attach importance to (something)'.

In the present colloquial we may have a further phonetic
change to *omonjiru.*

O. Normally the Romaji transliteration of the fifth character of
the *kana* syllabary, the *Go-jū-on* or "Table of Fifty Sounds," お.

Sometimes used as the Romaji transliteration of the 47th character of the *Go-jū-on,* を, which is in this book transliterated as *wo.*

For its use as a postposition, see wo.

-Ō. A transliteration of the *kana* of *-a* plus *u, -o* plus *u, -e* plus *u, -a* plus *fu (hu), -o* plus *fu (hu),* or *-o* plus *ho.*

(See -U, -YŌ, and the introductory Notes on Adjectives and Verbs.)

-PPOI. A suffix with two uses, in both of which it forms a regular adjective.

1. Suffixed to nouns, including the Line 2 form *(renyōkei)* of verbs, it has the meaning of "being inclined to," in the sense of showing a trait of character.

hara-tachi -ppoi	inclined to get angry
namida -ppoi	inclined to tears (i.e., to weep easily)
aki -ppoi	easily bored (fickle)

2. Suffixed to adjective roots it indicates a sort of "-ishness."

kuro -ppoi	blackish
yasuppoku mieru	appear cheapish (undignified)

WARNING. This is a very informal form, almost vulgar. A certain number of compounds with *-ppoi,* such as *akippoi* and *yasuppoi,* have reached the dignity of being included in dictionaries as separate words, but students are advised not to use other *-ppoi* compounds until they are very familiar with the language.

-RA. Suffix added to nouns and pronouns. It is for the most part, but not always, added to words denoting people.

This suffix simply denotes plurality. It is, however, used primarily where the chief one of several persons or things is singled out to represent the rest. For example, *daijintachi* means simply "ministers," while *daijin-ra* might include others, not ministers. It is used in familiar speech, and does not in itself indicate politeness, impoliteness, humility, or the like. For comparison with other "plural" suffixes see -DOMO, -GATA, -NADO, -TACHI, and TŌ.

kimi-ra	you and the others
kore-ra	these people and others
kodomo-ra	children, and such
Suzuki, Kimura,	Suzuki, Kimura, Takahashi,
Takahashi-ra	and others.

When added to pronouns indicating place it serves to give a certain vagueness, i.e., "that place and others connected with it." Apparently this indication of vagueness was the original function of *-ra*.

| *sokora* | thereabouts |
| *kokora* | around here |

This *-ra* may be written with the same character 等 as the suffixes *-nado* and *-tō*.

-RA, -RABA. Verb-endings, not true suffixes. For these forms occurring after the *-ta* or *-da* forms of verbs, see -TARA.

WARNING. In very colloquial speech *-ra* is quite often used as a contraction of *-ru wa*. This *-ru wa* itself is usually a contraction of *iru wa*. E.g.:

Sensō na no ni	In spite of its being wartime
bura-bura shitera	he hangs about doing noth-
	ing! (Just think of it!)

Here the *shitera* is a contraction of *shiteru wa* which is itself a contraction of *shite iru wa*.

-RAME, -RAMU, -RAN. Bungo suffix, added to the Line 3 form (*shūshikei*) of most verbs, but to the Line 3A form (*rentaikei*) of the verbs *aru, oru,* and *haberu*. It indicates supposition on the part of the author or speaker, and corresponds approximately to the colloquial *darō*.

It has a partial conjugation only, the following forms being known:

Line 3	*Shūshikei*	*-ramu*
Line 3A	*Rentaikei*	*-ramu*
Line 4	*Izenkei*	*-rame*

Note that the *-ramu* form is often written *-ran*.

Neko ni kuwareshi wo	For those eaten by the cat
Korogi no tsuma wa	The crickets' widows wail
Sudakuran	together—
	I suppose it's that!
Kumo no izuko ni tsuki	Where in the clouds may the
yadoruramu (ka)	moon dwell?
Hito wo korosuramu	He has killed someone, I
	suppose.
Mizukara wa imiji to	They themselves think their
omouramedo ito kuchioshi	status very fine, I suppose,
	but (to me) it is utterly
	distasteful.

The original forms were *arame* and *aramu* meaning "probably be," but in the course of time the initial "a" has been lost. These forms seem to lend themselves to contraction. E.g.:

> *Miru ran* 'may see, I suppose', elides to *miran*
> *Ōkaranmere* 'suppose are many', elides to *ōkanmere*
> *Aru ramu* 'may be', elides to *arurō* (*arō*)

-RARERU. A colloquial suffix added only to the Line 1 forms (*mizenkei*) of *kuru, suru* and verbs of the second (*ichidan*) conjugation. (Note that it is never added to verbs of the first (*yodan*) conjugation which take *-reru* instead.) It forms a new verb of the second (*-eru*) conjugation.

This form is apparently made up of *ari* plus *eru*, i.e., *areru* with the initial *r* inserted for ease of speech.

For meaning see discussion under -RERU.

Kuru	forms *ko-rareru.*
Suru	forms *se-rareru, shirareru,* and *sareru.*
Miru	forms *mi-rareru.*
Taberu	forms *tabe-rareru.*

Note that one may have *-rareru* added to causatives, so that from *tabesaseru* 'cause to eat' is formed *tabesase-rareru,* etc.

-RARU, -RARURU. Bungo suffix, corresponding to the colloquial *-rareru.* The Line 3 form (*shūshikei*) is *-raru,* the Line 3A form (*rentaikei*) is *-raruru.* It is added to the Line 1 form (*mizenkei*) of *kuru, suru* and verbs of the second conjugation, forming a regular verb of the *Shimo-ni-dan* or lower-two-vowel part of the second conjugation.

As examples of formation from *miru* 'see' and *tabu, taburu* 'eat':

Line 1	form	*Mizenkei*	*mirare*	*taberare*
Line 2	form	*Renyōkei*	*mirare*	*taberare*
Line 3	form	*Shūshikei*	*miraru*	*taberaru*
Line 3A	form	*Rentaikei*	*miraruru*	*taberaruru*
Line 4	form	*Izenkei*	*mirarure*	*taberarure*

Note that the forms derived from *suru* 'do', are *seraru* and *seraruru*. These, however, are usually contracted to *saru* and *saruru*.

For uses see the colloquial examples under -RERU.

-RASHI (-i, -ki, -ku). A suffix, meaning "seeming" or "apparent," with the implication of seeming that way to "me," whatever the seeming or appearance may be to other people.

THE COLLOQUIAL

In the colloquial it is added to nouns, adverbs, clauses, or sentences. It forms a regular adjective.

kodomorashii	childlike, childish
otokorashii	manly, courageous, chivalrous
gakuseirashii	looking like a student
kotosararashii	seemingly on purpose
Mado kara haitta rashii	He came in through the window, it seems.
Shiro no hō ga katsu rashii yō da	It seems as if the white were going to win.
iku no rashii	seem to be going (*iku no de aru rashii*)

Note that -*rashii* is a regular adjective. Hence the -*i* form may be either adjectival or sentence-ending. Of the "conjugated" forms -*rashikatta* and -*rashiku-nai* are the most common.

Shitte iru rashiku omowareru   One may take it that he seems
                                                    to know.
Mō sugu kaerurashikatta   It seemed that he would soon
                                                    be back.

The *-kere* forms, such *-rashikereba, -rashikeredo,* etc., are grammatically possible, but in practice very seldom used.

Japanese grammarians make a careful distinction between the
-rashii that is added to sentence-ending forms and that added to
nouns or adverbs.   E.g.:

1. *Ano hito wa gunjin de*   He seems to be a soldier.
   aru rashii
2. *Ano hito wa gunjinrashii*   He seems a soldier.

They point out that (1) may mean "I understand that he is a
soldier," while (2) means rather "He has the air, or appearance,
of a soldier."   However, as the English word "seems" also conveys
both ideas, it seems unnecessary to elaborate the point here.

It may be well, nevertheless, to point out that in such sentences
as:

Sore wa omoshiroi-rashii   That seems to be interesting.

the *omoshiroi* is a sentence-ending form, i.e., a verb, not an
adjective.

NOTE.   It should be noted that there are a few adjectives, such
as *kawairashii* 'lovely' and *kitanarashii* 'unsightly', which have
been formed by adding *-rashii* to adjective roots.

These, however, are special words which can be found in the
dictionaries.   As a general rule *-rashii* cannot be added to
adjective roots.   The few words formed by doing so usually have
special uses.

For example, *kitanarashii* indicates a direct disgust experienced
by the user, while *kitanai rashii* indicates that he considers something to be dirty, not necessarily on account of direct observation,
but perhaps judging from indirect evidence.

In bungo, the suffix *-rashi* has the same meaning and use as in the colloquial. It may be added to nouns but not to adverbs. It may also be added to clauses or sentences, which normally end with verbs in the Line 3 form (*shūshikei*). The exception is that if the final verb belongs to the *ari, ori, haberi* conjugation the Line 3A form (*rentaikei*) is used (e.g., *aru, -zaru,* etc.).

In the older bungo the one form *-rashi* was used for the *shūshikei, rentaikei,* and *izenkei* (Line 3, 3A, and 4 forms). In modern bungo, however, due to the influence of the colloquial one may find both the *rentaikei, -rashiki,* and the *izenkei, -rashikere,* though they are not common.

It is even possible, though I have not yet found examples of this, that very modern bungo may use *-rashi* attached to adverbs.

WARNING. Note that, especially in the older bungo, a *-ru* sound used to be quite frequently dropped before the *-rashi,* so that one not infrequently finds forms like *narashi* for *narurashi* 'seems to be'; *samukarashi* for *samukarurashi* 'seems to be cold', etc.

-RAU. See -RŌ and -U.

-RE. A suffix, very seldom used. It may occasionally be found:

1. Added to the Line 1 form (*mizenkei*) of second conjugation verbs. It then is used as an imperative. E.g., *mire* 'look!', *tabere* 'eat!'

It is, however, doubtful whether in this use the *-re* can be considered a true suffix. See the introductory Note on Verbs and the section on Imperatives.

2. Added to the Line 4 form (*izenkei*) of first (*yodan*) conjugation verbs, or to the *se* form of *suru* 'do', 'act'. It is then the now obsolescent Line 4 form of the bungo "perfect tense" suffix *-ri.* (See under -RI.)

-RERU. A colloquial suffix. It is added to the Line 1 form (*mizenkei*) of verbs of the first (*yodan*) conjugation. It combines to make a new verb of the second (*-eru, shimo ichidan*) conjugation.

It has the same uses as the suffix *-rareru,* which is added to all verbs not of the first conjugation. (See -RARERU.) The two suffixes are therefore treated together.

> The *mizenkei* of all *yodan* verbs ends in the sound "a." This -*a* plus -*reru* gives -*areru,* which is presumably a contraction of -*ari* -*eru.* The meaning of -*areru* is roughly "to get" or "to get a being." This statement, while not absolutely accurate, may help in understanding the uses of the form. It may also help to consider this -*areru* as equivalent to a semi-independent auxiliary verb.

The suffixes -*reru* and -*rareru* may be used for the purpose of indicating:

1. A passive use
2. Potentiality
3. Politeness

The context will usually make it quite clear which use is intended.

I. The Passive

The Japanese "passive" is not quite the same as the English passive. Basically both are used to indicate that the subject of a verb undergoes an action performed by some other person or thing. In Japanese, however, we may have "passives" for any verb; in English there are passive forms for transitive verbs only. It therefore sometimes is necessary to translate Japanese "passives" by non-passive English expressions.

> The student might find it of interest to try using some form of the word "got" in the following English translations.

Examples in which the English and Japanese passives correspond exactly are of the following type:

Genbun ga hito-bito ni yomareta	The original text was read by various people.
Daitoryō ni erabaremashita	He was chosen President.
Būsu ni pistoru de utaremashita	He was shot with a pistol by Booth.
Meiji no hajime ni kakareta hon . . .	A book which was written at the beginning of the Meiji era . . .

Subete no mado wa hirakareru	All the windows are opened.
Kodomo ga haha ni kusuri wo nomaserareru	The child is caused by the mother to drink the medicine.
Kodomo ga densha ni hikareru	The child is run over by the street-car.

Examples in which the force of a Japanese "passive" cannot be rendered by literal translation into an English passive are of the following type:

B wa A ni tokei wo nusumaremashita	B had his watch stolen by A (i.e., underwent the stealing).
Kyaku ni korareta	(I) had guests come (i.e., underwent the arriving—presumably unexpected).
Haha ga ko ni shinareta	The mother had her child die. (Cf. the Irishism "was died on.")
Hito ni tansho wo mirareru	One's shortcomings are seen by others (i.e., one undergoes the seeing).
Sando made umaku kangaerareta	He was outwitted as many as three times (i.e., He had done to him clever thinking as many as three times).
Ame ni furareru	(I) get rained on (i.e., undergo a falling by rain).
Tarō kun wa shiken ga warukatta to sensei ni iwareta	Taro was told by his teacher that he had done badly in his examination.

Here the *iwareta* gives much the same suggestion of admonishment or reproof as would the English "he underwent a talking to." This is its normal force in conversation. In newspapers *iwareta* usually means "we are told," and has the same effect that an introductory "It is said" would have in English.

It will be noticed that in the above examples the subject undergoes an action performed by persons or definite things. Japanese grammarians draw a distinction between such "passive" sentences and those in which an emotion is caused by some state of affairs.

There is a real distinction, and it is suggested that in translating sentences of this second type the *-reru, -rareru* form be rendered by recasting the sentence and using an English active form like "(one) can but" or "cannot help but."

Literal translation is impossible, but in the following examples an attempt at literalness is given in the parentheses.

Yukusue ga anjirareru	One cannot help but worry about the future. (The future gets a being worried about, or undergoes a worrying-about.)
Natsu-kyūka no kuru no ga matareru	One cannot help but (impatiently) await the coming of the summer vacation. (The coming gets a being awaited, or, undergoes an awaiting.)
Take no nai tokoro e iku to imasara no yō ni take no kōyō no hiroi no ni odorokareru	When one goes to places where there is no bamboo, more than ever one cannot help but be amazed at the wide extent of the uses of bamboo. (One gets a being startled.)
Nan to naku fushigi ni omowareru	One cannot help but feel the exceeding strangeness. (It gets a being felt as inexpressibly strange.)

2. Potentiality

The use of the *-reru, -rareru* form to express potentiality does not differ greatly from its use as a passive, although, strictly speaking, there can be no imperative use. (Cf. -ERU.)

Consider the following sentence:

> *Kono katana de wa tetsu demo*   With this sword even iron can
> *kirareru*   be cut.

A more literal translation would be "even iron gets a being cut." If read as a passive it is "even iron is cut." The relation to the potential "can be" form is obvious.

The context will usually make it clear whether a "passive" or "potential" form is the best English translation. When the context does not make it clear, it usually doesn't matter.

In bungo the verb *u, uru* may be used by itself to indicate potentiality. I.e., . . . *koto wo u* means ". . . (thing) can be done," or "one can do the . . . (thing)." Therefore the colloquial *eru* may be used in the same way. The colloquial idiom corresponding to the bungo . . . *koto wo u* is . . . *koto ga dekiru*.

> *Getsumei ni mo suitei no suna*   Even in moonlight the sand-
> *ga funmei ni kazoerareru*   grains at the bottom of the
>   water can be clearly
>   counted.
> *Sekai-seikatsu ni tsuite mo*   And this can be said also about
> *mata kono koto ga iwareru*   life throughout the world.

These examples show "passive" potentiality, but occasionally one meets with sentences in which "active" ability is concerned, such as:

> *Kore wo taberarenai*   (One) cannot eat this.

There is, of course, only a difference in the angle of approach between this and such a sentence as:

> *Kore ga taberarenai*   This cannot be eaten (or, is
>   uneatable).

It is a question for nomenclaturists to decide whether it is "passive potentiality" or "active ability" that is shown in such a sentence as the following. It is quite possibly chiefly politeness. Whatever the decision the meaning is clear:

> *O-taku no jochū ni chotto*   Could I get your maid to just
> *tsukai wo shite*   deliver a message for me?
> *morawaremashō ka*

For further examples and discussion see under -ERU. The so-
called "potential" -*eru* verbs may be regarded as, and quite
possibly actually are, contractions of the -*reru* form.

3. Politeness

A -*reru* or -*rareru* form may be used to express politeness or
respect. (Perhaps simply because it is a longer form than the
original verb.)

It is used in the same sense as the simple verb, hence usually
with an active meaning. It shows respect to the person who is
the subject of the verb.

Go shujin wa oraremasu ka	Is your master at home?
Kyōto e dete, ni san nichi kembutsu shite, kaerareru sō desu	It is said that he is coming back after two or three days sightseeing in Kyoto.
Anata wa honya de donna hon wo kawaremashita ka	What books did you buy at the bookshop?

There is an idea similar to the English "get" inherent in these sentences also. They seem to be formed on the same principle as "What
books did you get to buy?" A sentence like "It is said that he will get
a returning" is of course not idiomatic English, but it is understand-
able.

An even longer and more respectful form may be obtained by
adding -*rareru* to the Line 2 forms of -*seru* or -*saseru*. E.g.:

On tomo no shi wo itamaserareta	He grieved over the death of his friend.

In such sentences as this one the -*se*- or -*sase*- convey no suggestion of
causality. In this particular sentence the *itamaserareta* is exactly
equivalent in meaning to *itanda*. The long form was used because
the writer, a Japanese Christian, wished to show the high position of
the person who grieved, in this case King David. It might be mentioned, however, that present-day chauvinists object violently to
showing such respect to people not of Japanese birth.

WARNING. There are a few non-standard forms like *koreru* 'be
able to come', which are sometimes used to indicate "potentiality."

-RI. A suffix with various uses. It may be added to:

1. Japanese numbers (cf. -TARI).
2. The colloquial *-ta* *(-da)* form of verbs.
3. The Line 4 form *(izenkei)* of verbs of the first *(yodan)* conjugation, or the *se* form of *suru,* and occasionally other verbs.

For *ari, ori, haberi,* see introductory Note on Verbs (Bungo). For *nari* see NARI.

1. As a suffix to Japanese numbers, *-ri* stands for "persons." Formerly *-ri* could be suffixed to any Japanese numeral, but at present the only forms in common use are:

hitori	one person, single, alone
futari	two persons, both
yottari	four persons

For other numbers of people the Chinese number is used together with the classifier *nin.* E.g., *sannin* 'three people'; *hyakunin* 'a hundred people'; etc. *Ichinin* 'one person', and *ninin* 'two people' may be used if desired, but *shinin* 'four people' is usually avoided because a homonym has the meaning "dead people."

2. In the colloquial only, *-ri* may be added to the *-ta* or *-da* forms of verbs.

The forms *-tari* and *-dari* seem to have been actually derived from *-te ari* and *-de ari,* but the question of historical development need not be taken up here. In the modern colloquial *-ri* behaves as if it were a real suffix, and it seems simplest to treat it as such. (Cf. -TARI.)

The form *-tari* *(-dari)* indicates repetition of the action or state shown by the verb to which it is attached. This form is usually used in sequence, followed by some form of verb meaning "to do" *(suru, nasaru, itasu)*, but this rule is not absolute.

Hito ga ittari kitari shite nakanaka nigiyaka da	What with people going and coming, it is very bustling.
Dore wo mite mo noshi wo tsuketari mizuhiki wo kaketari shite aru	No matter which you look at (they all) have *noshi* on and are tied up with *mizuhiki.*
Nondari kuttari jūbun hara wo koshiraeta	(What with) eating and drinking, he has filled his belly properly.

> *Kui mo kuttari, jippai mo*   Eating and eating, he ate all
> *kutta*   of ten helpings.

3. In bungo only, *-ri* may be added to the Line 4 form (*izenkei*) of verbs of the first (*yodan*) conjugation, also to the *se* form of *suru*, making *seri*. It may occasionally be found added to the Line 2 form (*renyōkei*) of verbs of the *shimo nidan* conjugation to give forms like *ukeri* or *hajimeri*, but this is not standard practice.

Apparently this *-ri* is derived from a contraction of *ari* added to the Line 2 form. For example, *kaki-ari* 'have written' became *kakeri*, etc.

It usually indicates a recent past, but sometimes also indicates a present continuance. It forms, therefore, what is practically equivalent to an English perfect tense. In the colloquial it is replaced by *-ta*.

It may be considered as the Line 3 or sentence-ending form of a partial conjugation:

Line 1	*Mizenkei*	*-ra*
Line 2	*Renyōkei*	*-ri*
Line 3	*Shūshikei*	*-ri*
Line 3A	*Rentaikei*	*-ru*
Line 4	*Izenkei*	*-re*

Note that forms other than the Line 3 and 3A forms *-ri* and *-ru* are obsolescent. The present compiler has been unable to find an example of the *-ra* form even in old bungo, though this form theoretically should exist.

Ame fureri — It rained. / It has been raining. / It is raining.

Tori nakeri — Birds sang (and are singing)
Fumi wo tsukureri — He has composed a letter.
Moteru kuni to motazaru kuni . . . — The "have" and "have-not" countries . . .

-RO. A particle with the effect of a verbal exclamation mark. It is often used with the imperative form of verbs. E.g.:

Miro	Look!
Shiro	Do!
Taberoi	Eat!

It has a somewhat sharp and peremptory effect.

It is one of the particles permissible with imperatives of first conjugation verbs also. For further discussion see the introductory Note on Verbs.

-RŌ. A verb ending, used in the colloquial only. It is usually written with the *kana* for *ra* and *u*.

1. When it comes after the words *da* and *ja* it forms *darō* and *jarō*. These, however, are best thought of as simply contractions of *de arō*, with which they are equivalent in meaning. E.g.:

Mō sugu kuru darō	He ought to (will probably) be here soon.

2. The uses of the suffixes *-tarō* and *darō*, in which *-rō* might be thought of as added to the *-ta* and *-da* forms of verbs are treated under -TARŌ.

3. In certain dialects (e.g., that of *Shikoku*) *-rō* is still used as an equivalent of the bungo *-ramu*. See -RAME, -RAMU. Thus we have:

arurō	may be (equivalent to the bungo *aruramu*)
omoshirokattsurō	may be amusing (bungo *omoshirokaritsuramu*)

-RU. A suffix attached to verb forms. It has several different uses.

1. When it is attached to the Line 1 form (*mizenkei*) of verbs of the first (*yodan*) conjugation, or of *shinu, inu, ari (nari), ori,* or *haberi* it is the *shūshikei* of the bungo *-ru, -ruru* suffix. See -RU, -RURU.

2. When it is attached to the Line 4 form (*izenkei*) of verbs of the first (*yodan*) conjugation it has two sharply distinct uses.

   (a) In the colloquial, to indicate potentiality. E.g.:

Hon ga kakeru	Books can be written.
Kakeru onna	Women who can write.

This function is fully treated under -ERU.

(b) In bungo, to indicate a "perfect" tense. E.g.:

Kakeru onna   Women who have written.

This *-ru* is the *rentaikei* of *-ri*. See -RI.

3. When attached to the *-ta* form of verbs it is part of the suffix *-taru*. See -TARU.

-RU, -RURU. Bungo suffix, corresponding to the colloquial suffix *-reru*. It is added to the Line 1 form (*mizenkei*) of verbs of the first (*yodan*) conjugation and of the irregular verbs *shinu, inu, ari* (*nari*), *ori, haberi,* and *imazukari*.

It forms a new regular verb of the *shimo ni dan* or lower two-vowel division of the second conjugation. See Table II in the introductory Note on Verbs.

For example, from *utsu* 'strike', we get:

Line 1	*Mizenkei*	*utare*
Line 2	*Renyōkei*	*utare*
Line 3	*Shūshikei*	*utaru*
Line 3A	*Rentaikei*	*utaruru*
Line 4	*Izenkei*	*utarure*
Line 5	*Meireikei*	*utare* (*yo*)

The uses correspond exactly to those of the colloquial suffix *-reru*, i.e., passive, potentiality, or politeness.

As with *-reru*, there is, strictly speaking, no imperative (*meireikei*) for the potential use.

For discussion of the uses, see -RERU.

SA. A colloquial word of emphasis used to end a sentence. Grammatically it is practically equivalent to *da* or *no de aru*.

It differs from these, however, not only in being more emphatic, but also in being essentially a word suggesting intimacy.

In general it expresses emphatic affirmation. When it follows a reference to the speaker it has a certain boastful feel. When it follows a reference to the person spoken to it has an effect of rather strong urging.

Okii sa	Certainly it's big!
Muron sa	No question about it!
Watashi mo ikitai no sa	Sure, I want to go too!
Sareba sa . . .	Well, I'll tell you . . . (more
(said in reply to a question)	or less: If you ask, it's this.)
Mada hayai kara asonde yuku sa	It's still early, so *do* come!
Hōtte oku sa	Do leave it alone!
Sugu ni tonde iku no desu to sa	I tell you it's said that it goes flying off at once.
(a) *Kimi wa doko e*	Where are you going?
(b) *Hanami ni sa*	To the cherry-viewing!
(a) *Kyō wa nigiyaka da*	It's very bustling today.
(b) *O matsuri da kara sa*	That's because it's a fête-day.

NOTE. *Sa* is also used as a particle, within sentences, in quite a number of dialects. Perhaps the most important of such dialect uses is as a substitute for postpositions, particularly *ni* or *e,* in such expressions as *gakkō sa itta* 'he went to school'. It may also be found substituting for *wo,* as in *hana sa kaimasen ka* 'won't you buy some flowers?'.

-SA. Suffix added to
  1. The roots of Japanese adjectives
  2. The root *-ta* of the "desiderative" *-tai* or *-tashi*
  3. Words of foreign origin and certain Japanese nouns and adverbs.

It forms a substantive indicating not only the possession of a quality but also showing that the degree is measurable, hence one can compare two *akasa* 'rednesses', or *takasa* 'heights'.

When used with adjectives it may have a certain emotional feel. For example, *Hana no utsukushisa!* may be used exclamatorily, with much the effect of the English, "What beautiful flowers!" or "Oh, the beauty of the flowers."

Examples of its various uses follow:

1. *tōsa*	farness, distance
yosa	goodness, excellence
kanashisa	a state of being sorrowful, sorrow, sorrowfulness
2. *homeraretasa*	a desire to be praised
iwasetasa	a desire to make someone say something
3. *kireisa*	beauty
sumātosa	smartness
tachimachisa	suddenness
fushigisa	strangeness

NOTE. The suffix *-sa* may also be found added to the Line 3 forms (*shūshikei*) of certain special verbs, particularly those referring to change of place. The resultant word is a noun, indicating a time. E.g.:

kaerusa	time of returning
yukusa	time of going

WARNING. The suffix *-sa* is not added to the root *-na* of the negative suffix *-nai*.

The only apparent exception to this rule occurs with adjectives originally formed by adding the suffix *-nai*, but which have come to be regarded as independent words. E.g.:

nasakenasa	miserableness

The adjective *nasakenai* was originally formed from the noun *nasake* 'sympathy', but has long been accepted as a word in its own right.

SAE. A particle with different uses in bungo and in the colloquial.

It seems to have been derived from *sa* 'that' and the postposition *e*(*he*) meaning "to" or "toward." Therefore originally *sae* had a meaning of "to that" or "that far." It keeps this meaning in bungo, but has certain derived uses in the colloquial.

BUNGO

In bungo it is usually translatable by "even," but it is used in a sense equivalent to that of *made*, by which it is replaced in the

colloquial. It may come before or after "case" postpositions like
wo or *ni.*

Ie wo ushinai ima mata koromo sae ubawaretari	He lost his house, and now has been despoiled again, even to his clothes.
Wasurenu sae wo wasuru to ya semu	Forget (even) what is not forgotten—will I do that? (Would that I could!)
Kagiri aru mitsugimono wo sae yurusareki	(She) was given even the rare things brought as tribute. (They) were excused from even a limited payment of taxes.

The meaning of this last example depends on the context. In early
literature it would probably have the first meaning; in later times the
second meaning would be the more probable.

THE COLLOQUIAL

In the colloquial *sae* may follow both substantives and other
parts of speech.

When used after substantives *sae* may take the place of *ga, mo,*
or *wo,* but follows all other postpositions.

For the meaning of *sae,* the general rule is that in conditional
clauses it has the effect of "just" or "no more than." In all other
uses it has the effect of "even."

1. In conditional clauses *sae* may follow not only substantives,
but also the *-ku* form of adjectives or the Line 2 form (*renyōkei*)
of verbs.

O-cha sae kurereba yoroshii	If you give me just tea it will be quite satisfactory.
Kare wa namake sae shinakereba ii hito da noni	If he just weren't idle, he'd be a fine fellow. (But he is idle.)

Tsuyoku sae areba yoroshii   It is not the case that "if (it)
  to iu wake de wa nai   were just strong (it) would
                            be all right."

Kimi dake sae shōchi sureba If just you and no one else
  sore de yoi no da   knows, in that case it is fine.

2. In clauses which are not conditional *sae* seems to be used only after substantives.

This use corresponds roughly to the bungo use of *sura* or *dani*.

Mizu sae nodo ni tōranu   Even water does not pass
                            through his throat.

Ano hito wa namae sae   That man can't write even his
  kakenai   own name.

Ano hito ni sae wakarimasen It was not clear even to him.
  deshita

Anna gōriki de sae motenu   Even with (his) so great
                            strength he can't hold it.

SARERU. Colloquial contraction of *serareru* or *shirareru,* the *-rareru* forms of the verb *suru* 'do', 'act', etc. (See -RARERU, -RERU.)

-SARERU. Colloquial contraction of the causative passive suffix *-serareru.* E.g.:

    nomu   drink
    nomaseru   cause to drink

    nomaserareru
                          be caused to drink (etc.)
    nomasareru

    saseru   cause to do

    saserareru
                          be caused to do
    sasareru

(See -RARERU, -RERU.)

SARU, SARURU. Bungo contractions of *seraru* and *seraruru,* the *-raru, -raruru* forms of the verb *suru.* (See -RARU, -RARURU.)

-SARU, -SARURU. Bungo contractions of the causative passive suffixes *-seraru* and *-seraruru.* (See -RARU, -RARURU, and cf. -SARERU.)

-SASERU. Colloquial suffix added to Line 1 form (*mizenkei*) of the second conjugation (cf. -SERU). It forms a new verb of the second (*-eru, shimo ichidan*) conjugation.

Note that this suffix is never added to the *-reru, -rareru* suffix. The two are combined by adding the *-rareru* form to the Line 1 forms of *-seru* and *-saseru*. E.g., *matsuraserareta* (from *matsuru*).

Its meaning is causative (to make or to let), the same as -SERU, which see.

Kuru becomes *kosaseru* (*kisaseru* is occasionally heard but is not regarded as correct). *Suru* has the forms *shisaseru* and *sesaseru*, which are sometimes used, but usually contract to simply *saseru*. For example, *benkyō suru* becomes *benkyō saseru*.

Daiku ni ie wo tatesaseru	(We) have a house built by a carpenter. (E. g., cause the building of a house.)
Kodomo ni o-kashi wo tabesaseru	(He) gives the children cakes to eat. (I.e., not as strong as "make them eat cake.")
Kodomo ni o-kashi wo tabesasete wa ikemasen	Don't let the children eat cakes.

-SASŌ. See -sō. A suffix, added only to the root *yo* of *yoi* 'good' and the root *na* of the negative *nai*.

It has the same meaning as the suffix -*sō* 'seeming'.

Kono shinamono wa taihen yosasō da	These goods seem to be excellent.
Kono machi ni wa gakkō wa nasasō da	There doesn't seem to be any school in this town.

-SASU, -SASURU. Bungo suffixes.

They are added to the Line 1 forms (*mizenkei*) of *ku* 'come', *su* 'do', and verbs of the second conjugation, forming regular verbs of the *shimo nidan* part of the second conjugation.

The conjugation is therefore:

Line 1	*Mizenkei*	*-sase*
Line 2	*Renyōkei*	*-sase*
Line 3	*Shūshikei*	*-sasu*

Line 3A *Rentaikei*   *-sasuru*
Line 4 *Izenkei*   *-sasure*
Imperative *Meireikei*   *-sase (yo)*

Note that the verb *suru,* which should normally have the forms
sesase, sesasu, sesasuru, sesasure, in practice actually contracts
these to *sase, sasu, sasuru,* and *sasure.*

This suffix is used to indicate "causation," in exactly the same
way as the colloquial suffix *-saseru.*

For examples of this use see under -SASERU, -SERU, and -SHIMU.

-SEBA. Bungo suffix, added to the Line 2 form *(renyōkei)* of
verbs. It indicates a supposition contrary to fact. (The independent word *seba* is the *mizenkei* of *su* plus *-ba.*)

Teki to shiriseba   If I had known you as an
  yorazaramashi wo   enemy I would not have
                               come. (But I did not know,
                               hence the situation I now
                               face.)

SEN. A form of *su* or *suru,* which may be an abbreviation of:
1. *Semu* 'probably do, act, or make'. This is primarily a bungo
usage, but may occasionally be found in the colloquial. See -MU
and -N.
2. *Senu* 'not do, act, or make'. This is, strictly speaking,
properly a purely colloquial usage. See -NU and -N.

SERI, SERU.   Bungo forms of *suru,* indicating approximately
a present perfect tense. *Seri* is the sentence-ending, *seru* the
attributive form. (See -RI.)

Japanese grammarians have said that it normally indicates a
recent past, but sometimes indicates a present action.

Kurushiki omoi seri   He has (had) painful feelings.

-SERU. Colloquial suffix added to the Line 1 form *(mizenkei)*
of first conjugation *(yodan)* verbs only (cf. -SASERU). It forms a
new verb of the second *(ichidan)* conjugation.

Note that there is a growing tendency to treat these *-seru* words as if
they were *-su* verbs of the first conjugation. In particular the *-te* and

-ta forms are quite frequently sounded and occasionally written as *-shite* and *-shita* instead of *-sete* and *-seta*. E.g., *matashite* instead of *matasete*, etc. This usage, however, is not yet accepted as correct by all grammarians.

A form like *yakuseru* used by a good speaker in formal discourse would be a bungo form equivalent to the ordinary colloquial *yakushita*. (See -RI.) Used by a semi-illiterate speaker it might mean that he was attempting to treat a *-suru* verb as if it were a *-su* verb of the first conjugation, and was forming a potential from it. (See -ERU.) This is of course entirely "incorrect," but is occasionally heard.

It has a causative meaning, that is, "make" or "let" something happen, sometimes weakened to "have" something happen. Its use is the same as that of *-saseru*.

Like *-reru* and certain other suffixes, *-seru* may be considered as performing the functions of a semi-independent auxiliary verb.

Watashi wa isogashii kara jochū wo ikasete kudasai	I'm busy, so please have the maid go!
(Kare wa) kodomo ni muzukashii hon wo yomaseru	(He) makes the children read difficult books.
Furasetaku nai	I don't want to have it rain.

Note that a person caused to perform an action is normally marked by *wo*, as *jochū wo* in the first example, when the stem verb is an "intransitive" one, like *iku*. If, however, the stem verb is "transitive" enough to require that its own direct object be marked by *wo*, as in the second example, where *hon* is the object of *yomu*, then the person caused to act is usually marked by *ni* or *wo shite*. For further discussion of this usage see under NI, WO, and WO SHITE.

NOTE. The compound suffixes *-serareru* and *-saserareru* may be used without involving any suggestion of causality, simply to indicate respect for the person who is the subject of the verb to which they are attached. Cf. -RERU, p. 246.

-SESHIMU. A bungo suffix, added to the Line 1 form (*mizenkei*) of verbs. It makes a new verb of the *shimo nidan* (*-e, -uru*) conjugation. It has exactly the same causative force as *-su*, *-sasu*, or *-shimu*.

It is usually added only to verbs with monosyllabic roots, and seems to be used instead of *-shimu* purely for euphony. (Cf. -SHIMU.) E.g.:

miseshimu	cause to see
miseshimetari	did cause to see

WARNING. Do not confuse this suffix with the *seshimu* found in such combinations as *benkyō seshimu* 'cause to study', where the *se* is the Line 1 form of *su* 'do'.

SEU. The *kana* syllables *se* and *u*, usually pronounced *shō*. In certain dialects the "dubitative" or "future" form of *suru* 'do', is pronounced *shō* and may be written *seu*.

The standard "future" of *suru* is of course *shiyō*.

-SHA. A rather low-class contraction of *-shi* plus the postposition *wa*. E.g.:

Watasha sakanaya	I'm the fish-man.
de gozansu	

SHI. A particle, with different functions in bungo and in the colloquial.

Do not confuse this particle with the Line 2 form (*renyōkei*) of *suru*, which is also *shi*.

1. In the colloquial, *shi* acts as a connective, equivalent to "and" or "so." It is used to connect clauses only, and if it appears at the end of a sentence, it means that there is a clause to be supplied mentally. It is added to the conclusive or *shūshikei* form, the Line 3 form of either verb or adjective.

It usually indicates that the first clause is a reason for the second, but this intimation may sometimes be a very slight one. Two or more adjacent clauses followed by *shi* are often connected closely but without any intimation of causality.

Kimi mo mō kodomo de wa	You too are no longer a child,
arumaishi sukoshi wa	I should think—so pull your-
shikkari shitamae	self together.

Sue no mikomi ga nai wake de wa nai shi amari hikan shitamau na	It is not as if there were no prospects at the end, so don't be too discouraged.
Zaisan wa ushinau shi saikensha kara wa semerareru shi kare wa ōyowari ni yowatte iru	He has lost his fortune and he is being pressed by creditors and so is overwhelmed with troubles.
Sumire tanpopo ga saite iru shi hibari ga saezutte imasu	Violets and dandelions are blooming, and (so) the sky-larks are warbling.
Me mo mienai shi mimi mo kikoenai shi ashi mo kikanai	His eyes are blind, his ears deaf, and his legs crippled.

2. In bungo, *shi* is used within a clause or sentence to impart further emphasis to an already emphatic statement. (See SHIMO, -BASHI.)

Tare shi no hito ka shiramu	(They) probably know to whom this man belongs.

This use of *shi* occurs in the colloquial only in a few stereotyped phrases derived from bungo, usually in the form of *shi mo,* e.g., *kanarazushimo* 'necessarily'.

-SHI. A suffix, primarily bungo, with different uses depending on what it follows. (Cf. -KI.)

1. When it is suffixed to adjective roots it has the force of a verb meaning "be," and is used as a Line 3 or sentence-ending form (*shūshikei*).

Adjective roots which end in *-shi* or its sonant form *-ji* do not have to add this *-shi* in order to act as sentence-ending forms, and in practice it is usually not added. Short roots ending in *-shi* seem to add the suffix *-shi* more often than long ones. For example, *ashishi* 'is bad' does not sound as strange as *utsukushishi* 'is lovely'.

Bungo		Colloquial
Yama takashi	The mountain is high	*Yama ga takai*
Hana utsukushi	The blossoms are charming	*Hana wa utsukushii*

Note that very occasionally it is still heard in speech. With a few words it is still common:

Yoshi	It is good—used for "Stop," i.e., "It's O.K."
Yoroshi	It is satisfactory.
Medetashi	(A polite phrase used at the end of stories.)
Nashi	There is not.
-tashi	(I, you, he, etc.) want (something). (When *-ta* is the root of the desiderative suffix *-tai*.)

At present *yoshi* seems to be dying out, and to be superseded by *oke,* the origin of which should be obvious.

There seems to be a tendency to use *-shi* in colloquial tales. When so used the form often has an adverbial feel, and seems to have some sort of connection with the colloquial connective *shi.* (See SHI.)

Kurasa wa kurashi, michi wa *nashi, heike-gata ga tani e* *ochimashita*	In utter darkness, and with no road, the Taira (army) fell into the valley.

2. It may be added to the Line 2 form *(renyōkei)* of regular verbs; also to the verb suffixes *-tsu, -re, -ri,* and *-tari.* (*Kuru* may become *kishi* or *koshi; suru* becomes *seshi.*)

When so used it is an attributive or adjectival form, equivalent to the colloquial *-ta,* but more definitely indicating an action completed in the past.

mishi hito (mita hito)	a person who saw or was seen

It has also other uses as a regular Line 3A form, as in *agetarishi ga ochitari* 'I lifted it up but it fell'.

Japanese grammarians often put it in a partial conjugation with *-ki* and *-shika.* (See -KI and -SHIKA.)

Line 3	*Shūshikei*	*-ki*
Line 3A	*Rentaikei*	*-shi*
Line 4	*Izenkei*	*-shika*

NOTE. There is also a dialect *-shi* equivalent to *dake.* E.g., *dekishi = dekiru dake* "as (much) as possible."

-SHIDAI. In addition to its other uses as a noun and as an adverb, *-shidai* has two special uses as a suffix. In both these uses it retains its original meaning of "next-in-order," specifically applied to events.

It may be of interest to point out that as an adverb (*shidai-ni*) the meaning is "next-in-order-ly" in the sense of "without omitting any intermediate steps," and hence usually, though not necessarily, equivalent to "gradually." As a noun *shidai* may be considered to have as its basic meaning "the next in order of events." As the word is used at present it has come to mean either "order (of events)" or simply "event (s)" or "circumstance (s)."

1. There is a special use as a suffix to verbs in the Line 2 form (*renyōkei*). This occurs only between clauses.

In this use the *-shidai* has the effect that an initial "as soon as" would have in English. If one translates in the Japanese order of thought the effect is that of "A, and, next in the order of events, B."

This *-shidai* may or may not be followed by *ni*. It seems to be used only in reference to the future.

Kyōto ni tsuki-shidai hoteru ni yuku	As soon as (I) reach Kyoto (I) will go to the hotel.
Kikai no ari-shidai ni yuku	(I) will go at the first opportunity.

2. There is a special use as a suffix to substantives. In this use the substantive is marked as the controller of the events next in order. If the *-shidai* comes at the end of a sentence, the feeling is that some word like *da* or *desu* has been omitted.

Kore wo kettei-suru no wa kimi shidai	In the matter of deciding this, you're the boss.
Ne wa shina-shidai de chigau	The price varies according to the quality.
Jigoku no sata mo kane shidai	Even the sentences given in hell depend on money.

-SHIKA. Bungo suffix, added to the Line 2 form (*renyōkei*) of verbs. (*Kuru* becomes *kishika* or *koshika; suru* becomes *seshika*.)

Japanese grammarians often put *-shika* in a partial conjugation with *-ki* and *-shi,* as:

> Line 3   *Shūshikei*   *-ki*
> Line 3A *Rentaikei*   *-shi*
> Line 4   *Izenkei*   *-shika*

(See also -KI and -SHI.)

It indicates a past tense. When standing alone it is only used with *koso.* It is usually followed by *-ba, -do,* or *-domo.*

Tanen kokorozase-shika-do tsuini suihō ni kishinu	Although I strove for many years, in the end it came to nothing.
Tomo Amerika ni yukishikaba ware wa sabishi	Because my friend went to America I feel lonely.

WARNING. Do not confuse this with the *-shi* past tense suffix followed by a *ka* used to express emotion. E.g.:

Katsute wa tomo ni tsuki wo medeshi koto mo arishi ka	Once there was a time when, with my friend, we admired the moon! (This *ka* is a little like, "Ah, me!")

Also do not confuse it with the *shika* which means "more than" or "other than" and is used in negative sentences, such as:

Ano otoko wa kyōjin to shika omoenakatta	I could not think other than that he was mad.

The combination of an emphatic *shi* and an emotional *ka* may occasionally be found in bungo, but it is so rare that the average student need not bother about it.

-SHIMERU. Colloquial suffix. It may be added to the Line 1 form *(mizenkei)* of any verb, making a new verb of the second *(-eru, shimo ichidan)* conjugation.

It is added to the *se* form of *suru,* making *seshimeru.*

It has practically the same "causative" force as *-seru* or *-saseru.* It has a sort of semi-literary flavor, and is not ordinarily used in conversation. Cf. with -SHIMU, and WO SHITE.

SHIMO. An intensive particle, formed by combining the intensive *shi* with *mo*.

> *Ima shimo*   This very instant

-SHIMU. A bungo suffix, equivalent to the causative *-su,* except that it is longer and therefore more "polite." It is much used in newspapers and normally should concern dignified doings.

It may be suffixed to the Line 1 form (*mizenkei*) of all verbs (but see also -SESHIMU). It forms a new regular verb of the *shimo nidan* (*-e, -uru*) conjugation.

Bungo *-iru* (*kami ichidan*) verbs practically always add *-seshimu* rather than *-shimu*. *Uru* becomes *e-seshimu* rather than *e-shimu*.

Note that the *-shimu* form may follow a previous causative. E.g.:

> *Sute-sase-zara-shime-ki*   Caused (him) not to let throw
>   away.

It is customary, when a *-shimu* form is used, to mark by the compound *wo shite* the person who is caused to perform an action (or, with a negative, who is not allowed to perform it). The person marked by *wo shite* is therefore sometimes called the "indirect subject."

> *Shujin genan wo shite machi*   The master sends the servant
>   *ni shinamono wo kai ni*   to the town to buy goods.
>   *yukashimu*
> *Hito wo shite shiru koto*   (They) make it impossible
>   *atawazarashimu*   for a person to know.

SHITE. Originally the *-te* form of the verb *suru* (bungo form *su*). This verb means not only "to do" or "to make," but is also very widely used in the sense of "to be." Although this sense of "to be" is found more in bungo than in the spoken language, it is by no means uncommon in speech, especially in the form *shite*.

The following examples illustrate certain special uses of *shite*. For other special uses see also NI SHITE, NI SHITE MO, NI SHITE WA, TO SHITE, TO SHITE MO, TO SHITE WA, WO SHITE.

1. After expressions indicating number, *shite* is usually practically interchangeable with *de*:

Hitori shite suru	(He) does it alone.
Sannin bakari shite kuru	They arrive (a party of) only three people.
Kyōdai shite dekakeru	Go out, brothers and sisters together.
Mikka hodo shite yokunatta	In three days' time it got better.

2. With *kō* 'this way', *sō* 'that way', *dō* 'what way?' and *dō ka* or *dō zo* 'some way', *shite* forms expressions which are almost compound words.

Sō-shite	"So-being" or "that-way-doing," etc. (Often used as an introductory word in a sentence, practically equivalent to "thereupon.")
Dō-shite	"How-being?" or "What-way-doing?" (Often used as equivalent to "how?" or "why?". As an introductory or connective, sometimes like the English "why! . . .")
Dō-ka-shite sō shitai	(I) want to do it somehow (in some way or other).
Kanjō no doyō wo jibun de dō-shite ii ka wakaranakatta	He himself did not know what he ought to do about the excitement he was feeling.

3. After most adverbs *shite* retains all, or at least much, of its force as a verb form. It depends on the adverb whether or not the addition of *shite* changes the meaning.

shibaraku . . .	
shibaraku shite . . .	after a while . . .
shibaraku suru to	
shibaraku shite kara . . .	
sude ni . . .	already . . .
sude ni shite . . .	after a while . .

Not infrequently the verb force is shown chiefly in suggesting a
continuance of the state indicated by the adverb.

Towazu (ni) shiru *Towazu shite shiru*	(He) knows without asking.

There is really only a slight difference between these two sentences. The second is perhaps more nearly "He doesn't ask, and
still he knows." It definitely has a bungo flavor.

4. There are certain expressions in which *shite* seems to have
no effect other than that of giving a slight emphasis, and in which
it may be omitted without at all affecting the sense. This use of
shite is most marked when it occurs after *kara* or *ka*.

Wakai toki kara shite *jimbutsu ga chigatte ita*	He was an outstanding person from his youth up.
Habuita kara shite mienai	It is because it was left out that it can't be found.
Kokoro ga kawatta ka shite *dete konai*	He has not come, perhaps be- cause he changed his mind.

5. When *shite* is used to start a sentence it has no clearly
defined meaning. It obviously refers back to something that has
just occurred, and so is much like an English "well . . ." or "well
then, . . ." or "and . . ."

Shite anata wa jissai ni *o-ide-ni-naru no desu ka*	And are you really going?
Shite sore kara . . .	Well then, after that . . . (If not followed by a statement this expression can be used as a question.)

SHITE NO. Especially in the form *to shite no* and *ni shite no*,
this is a neologism derived from the English "as a."

For example, the phrase "Byron as a poet" would be translated
into Japanese as *Shijin to shite no Bairon*. The form was found
useful, and has been adopted by many modern writers.

Technically, the *to shite no* should always follow a substantive.

| Umare nagara ni shite no sabetsu | Discrimination based on birth (and continuing in the present). |

SO. In old bungo and occasionally in later poetry, *so* may be used together with a previous *na* to make a negative imperative. (See NA.)

| Haru na wasure so | Do not forget the spring! |

-Sō. A suffix derived from *sayō, sō* 'that way'. It is usually written with the *kana* for *sa-u*, さ う.

It has two uses, depending on what it follows.

1. It may be added to adverbs, the Line 2 form (*renyōkei*) of verbs, and the roots of adjectives, including the suffix *-ta.*

Note that after the negative *na* and the root *yo* of *yoi* 'good,' *sa* is inserted before *so*, apparently for the sake of euphony. (After the negative *na*, this *sa* is sometimes omitted.)

When so used *-sō* has the connotation of "apparently" or "seeming." Words thus formed by adding *-sō* are substantive in form. They can be used as adjectives by adding *-na,* and as adverbs by adding *ni.*

Takusan-sō	Seemingly many or much.
Taisetsu-sō	Apparently important or valuable.
Iki-sō (or *ikisō desu*)	It looks as if he would go.
Ikita-sō (desu)	It looks as if he wants to go.
Oishi-sō desu	It looks appetizing.
Ureshi-sō ni	With a look of delight.
Yosa-sō desu	It looks good, or seems good.
Nasa-sō (desu)	Apparently there is not any. (It seems not to be here.)
Chigatte i-sōna ki ga suru	I feel that it seems wrong.
Mizudeppō ni nari-sō na fushi	A (bamboo) joint which looked as if it could become (be made into) a water-gun.
Mizu ga tsumetasō da	The water gives the impression of being cold.

2. After statements in sentence form, and followed immediately by *desu* or *da,* the combination *sō desu* or *sō da* has the effect of the English "so they say" or "so I hear."

Some grammarians do not consider this -*sō* as a true suffix, and consider the statement preceding it as being in the attributive form. As there is, in the colloquial, no difference between attributive and sentence-ending forms, the question is academic.

Iku sō desu	They say he will go.
Itta sō desu	He is said to have gone.
Ii sō desu	They say it is good.
Kirei na sō desu *Kirei da sō desu*	They say (she) is beautiful.
Oishii sō desu	It is said to be delicious.

Note that *sō* when used in this way is always followed by some form of *de aru* or *de gozaru,* or its equivalent, *na.* (See NA.)
However, the extremely soft sound of such a sentence as

    Kirei na sō na   They say (she) is beautiful,

would make it unusual in Tokyo, at least in men's speech.

-SU. Suffix added to the Line 1 form (*mizenkei*) of verbs. It always makes a "causative," with uses equivalent to those of -*seru.* (See -SERU.)

It has not, however, the same forms in the colloquial as it has in bungo.

BUNGO

In bungo -*su* is a "causative" suffix, equivalent to the colloquial -*seru* (which see).

It is added to the Line 1 form (*mizenkei*) of verbs of the first (*yodan*) conjugation, also to Line 1 forms of *shinu, inu, ari, nari, ori,* and *haberi.*

It forms a new verb conjugated regularly according to the *shimo nidan* column of the second conjugation.

Line 1	*Mizenkei*	-*se*
Line 2	*Renyōkei*	-*se*

Line 3	*Shūshikei*	*-su*
Line 3A	*Rentaikei*	*-suru*
Line 4	*Izenkei*	*-sure*
Imperative	*Meireikei*	*-se (yo)*

THE COLLOQUIAL

In the colloquial *-su* may be added to the *mizenkei* of first (*yodan*) conjugation verbs only.

It forms a new *yodan* verb which is equivalent in meaning to a *-seru* verb. It may be regarded as a contraction of *-seru,* one which is in the process of displacing *-seru,* but which has not yet wholly done so. Its use in the spoken language seems to be constantly increasing, but for most verbs the *-su* form is not yet regarded as standard. It is certainly not a polite form.

In practice both *-su* and *-seru* forms seem to be used. It depends on circumstances which is preferred.

It is impossible to give rules, but as an example of forms, it may be said that:

> *Kikasu* and *kikaseru* are both used for "make hear."
> *Kikasanai* and *kikasenai* are both used for "not make hear."
> *Kikashita* is replacing *kikaseta.*

The form *o kikase mōshimashita* (used as an apology for having made someone listen) seems to be a permanency. In such phrases *kikashi* is apparently never used for *kikase.* However, the language is changing, and what is true today may not be true tomorrow.

WARNING. There is a very natural confusion of the strictly colloquial forms of *-seru* and *-su* verbs with the strictly bungo forms of *-su, -suru* verbs. The foreigner must learn to make allowance for this.

Thus in speech the idea "if make hear" may be expressed by:

1. *Kikasereba.* (This is the "standard" form, from *kikaseru.*)

2. *Kikaseba.* (This is the "new colloquial" form, from *kikasu.*)

3. *Kikasureba.* (Technically wrong, but occasionally used by the insufficiently educated. This form is derived from the bungo *kikasu* and in bungo would mean "because make hear.")

SURA. An emphatic particle, with somewhat different uses in bungo and in the colloquial.

In bungo, *sura* indicates that what it follows is an example used as an analogy. It has much the force of the English "even" in this use.

> Apparently the bungo *sura* had a conditional sense, somewhat like "if we take (that)." It may possibly derive from *suru nara.* If this conjecture is true, *sura* ought not to be used in conditional clauses. I have not been able to find any example of its being so used. If any reader should happen to come across one, I would be grateful if he would let me know.

Kakaru koto wa shōni sura kanō nari	Such a thing as that even a child can do.
Chōjū sura nao on wo shireri	Even birds and beasts have shown that they know gratitude.

The colloquial counterparts of the above sentences would substitute *sae* or *demo* for *sura.*

In certain colloquial dialects *sura* is widely, and rather loosely, used in the sense of "even." When so used it is practically equivalent to *sae,* and is not subject to the restrictions of the bungo *sura.* (See SAE.)

Yomikaki sura dekinai	He can't even read and write.

-TA. Suffix added to the Line 2 form *(renyōkei)* of verbs.

1. It may be a purely colloquial tense suffix.

> This *-ta* may be regarded as a contraction from both of the bungo forms *-tari* and *-taru.* (See -TARI.)
> For the standard colloquial contractions see the introductory Note on Verbs.

This *-ta* indicates completion of an act and hence forms what in general corresponds to past or perfect tenses in English. It is, however, important to note that the time element does not necessarily enter into the meaning of this form. All past actions are completed and therefore the *-ta* form may be used when in English we would use a past tense. However, not all completed actions are necessarily past; therefore the *-ta* form may be used in some sentences when the English past tense would be inapplicable.

It acts as both a Line 3 form (*shūshikei*) and Line 3A form (*rentaikei*) and so may be used either to end a sentence or to modify a noun.

Kinō kita	He came yesterday.
Tadaima kaerimashita	He has just come home.
Kinō mita hito . . .	The person I saw yesterday . . .
Arimashita	Here it is, or (I've) got it, (I've) found it!
Wakatta n'desu ka	Do you understand completely?
Arigatō gozaimashita	Thank you very much.

These last English sentences are equivalents rather than translations.

2. It may be the "root" of the desiderative suffix *-tai* (colloquial) or *-tashi* (bungo). (See -TAI and -TASHI.)

This *-ta* is always followed by one of the suffixes attached to adjective roots, such as *-i, -ku, -ki, -shi, -sa,* etc.

-TACHI. Sign of plural, added only to substantives denoting persons.

-Tachi, like *-ra*, has no thought of politeness or impoliteness. It differs from *-ra* in that it simply expresses plurality. (See -DOMO.)

For example, *daijin-tachi* means simply "ministers," but *daijin-ra* might include others of whom the ministers were representative.

daijin-tachi	ministers
kimi-tachi	you (intimate)
o-mae-san-tachi	you (to inferiors)

-TAI. Colloquial suffix added to the Line 2 form (*renyōkei*) of verbs. It forms a regular adjective, performing its verb functions in the usual way.

It is used to express desire and therefore is often referred to as a "desiderative."

Myōchō wa hayaku okitai	I want to get up early to-morrow morning.
Mitakereba mite mo yoi	If one wants to look at it, one may.
Zehi aitō (a-hi-ta-u) gozaimasu	I very much want to meet him.
Kimi mo kitakattarō	I suppose you wanted to come too.
Mitaku nakereba minaku-temo yoi	If one does not want to look at it, one needn't.
Dōzo shite kyō wa furasetaku nai n'desu	Whatever happens, I do hope it won't rain today. (Literally: I do not wish to have it rain.) (Rather a woman's expression.)
Ikitai tokoro desu	It is a place I wish to go to.
Sake wa nomitai shi, kane wa nashi	I want to drink sake, and have no money.

The *-tai* form is comparatively easy to understand and to use. The only grammatical difficulty in connection with it arises when it is used with a verb which is normally transitive, and this is concerned with the proper postposition to be used in these circumstances. E.g.:

(Watakushi wa) sake ga nomitai	I want to drink some sake.
(Watakushi wa) sake wo nomitai	

The answer seems to be that both forms are correct.

In bungo (where *ga* is not used to mark the subject), one can find examples corresponding to both *sake wo nomitashi* and *sake nomitashi,* either of which means "I want to drink some sake."

At least as early as Tokugawa and Meiji times the colloquial forms using *ga,* such as *sake ga nomitai,* seem to have been fairly firmly established as "correct." This is a construction parallel to such "desiderative" forms as *sake ga hoshii.*

In the last generation, however, the pendulum seems to have

swung back toward the older bungo use of *wo,* and it is probable
that a large proportion—possibly more than half—of the recent
college graduates actually do use forms such as *sake wo nomitai.*

-TAKERE, -TAKI, -TAKU. Literary (bungo) suffixes. (See
-TASHI.) For *-taku* (colloquial) , see -TAI.

TARA. See -TTARA.

-TARA (-dara). A colloquial suffix added to the Line 2 form
(*renyōkei*) of verbs. It takes the same standard contractions as
-ta (see introductory Note on Verbs) .

> From the point of view of the colloquial, *-tara* and *-dara* may be re-
> garded as made up of the *-ta* and *-da* forms plus the suffix *-ra.* It is,
> however, very unlikely that this *-ra* is a true suffix. The historical
> development is somewhat difficult to follow, but in all probability
> this *-tara* and *-dara* are contractions of the bungo *-taraba.*

It indicates a completed condition, but one which is to be
followed by another statement. It therefore has the meaning
"if (or when) . . . had been (has been, or is) completed." It is
this envisaging of completion that differentiates it from the
simple colloquial *-ba* form (cf. -BA) .

It may be used:

1. For pure supposition
2. For statement of actual condition

In both cases the *-tara* (*-dara*) form is used to indicate a "condition precedent." The general rule is:

1. If this condition precedent is followed by another statement which is non-definite (i.e., indicating doubt or referring
to the future) , the *-tara* (*-dara*) clause shows pure supposition.
This supposition may refer to the past, present, or future. (IF.)

2. If this condition precedent is followed by another statement
which is definite (i.e., referring to a past or present completion) , the *-tara* (*-dara*) clause is a statement of actual fact. This
fact is of course completed or "past" fact. (WHEN.)

I. Indicating Pure Supposition

Note that in the following examples we may throughout substitute
for the *-tara* (*-dara*) form the *-taraba* (*-daraba*) , *-ta* (*-da*) *nara* or *-ta*

(-da) naraba forms. This does not change the basic meaning of the clause, though in general the longer the form, the more formal it sounds. (Cf. -BA.)

Yuki ga futtara chūshishiyō	If it does snow (I) will probably stop (i.e., suspend operations).
Sotsugyō shitara gaikoku e iku tsumori desu	It is my intention to go abroad when (and if) I graduate.
Ima tondara abunai yo	If you jump now it will be dangerous. (It's dangerous to jump now.)
Yonde mitara omoshirokatta deshō	(a) If you had tried reading it, you (probably) would have found it interesting. (b) If you did try reading it, you probably found it interesting. (c) When you tried reading it, you probably found it interesting (didn't you?).

This last example is rather typical of certain aspects of the Japanese language, where the exact meaning of a sentence depends on the context. If in such a sentence one wishes to bring out clearly the idea of "supposition contrary to fact," one would probably add some such expression as *noni* or *ga*.

2. Statement of Actual Fact

When the *-tara* (*-dara*) form is so used, the condition following is never one that necessarily follows. It is one which is to some extent unexpected (or at least not necessary). Note that in the following examples we may substitute the *-taraba* (*-daraba*) form for *-tara* (*-dara*) without change of basic meaning. The *-ta* (*-da*) *nara*, *-ta* (*-da*) *naraba* or other *-ba* forms should not be used in these examples. (See -BA.)

Kare wo sasottara konakatta	When I invited him—he did not come. (Almost equals "although I invited him . . .")

Rondon ni itte mitara angai tsumaranakatta	When I went to London it was more boring than I had expected.
Tondara ōkega wo shita	When he jumped he got seriously injured.
Yonde mitara omoshirokatta	When I tried reading it, it was interesting.

-TARABA. 1. In bungo, a suffix added to the Line 2 form (*renyōkei*) of verbs. It is made up of *-tara* plus *-ba*. It means "if (or when) completed." Cf. -TARI.

| *Kachitaraba dempō nite shirasubeshi* | If (or when) you have won, let me know by telegram. |

2. In the colloquial *-taraba* and its sonant form *-daraba* may be regarded as made up of the suffix *-ba* added to the colloquial *-tara* and *-dara* forms of verbs. They have about the same meaning as the *-tara* and *-dara* forms, but sound a bit more formal and emphatic.

| *Kattaraba dempō de shirasete kudasai* | If (or when) you have won, let me know by telegram. |

TAREBA. A bungo form.
When standing alone it is equivalent in meaning to *to areba* 'since it be that way'. Its main use is after a verb in sentence-ending (*shūshikei*) form, where it is practically equivalent to a colloquial *kara* or *node*.

Bungo:

| *Natsu kitari tareba . . .* | As summer is come . . . |

Colloquial:

| *Natsu ga kita kara . . .* | As summer is come . . . |

-TAREBA. A bungo suffix, made up of the Line 4 form (*izenkei*) of *-tari* plus *-ba*. It is added to the Line 1 form (*mizenkei*) of verbs.

This form -tareba is practically equivalent to the colloquial
-ta kara, with the sense of "when, since, because, completed."

Hito wa mina kaeritareba	Since all the others had gone
ware mo kaerinu	home I have come home
	too.

-TARI. A suffix which has different uses in the colloquial and
in bungo.

THE COLLOQUIAL

In the colloquial the suffix -tari is added only to the Line 2 form
(renyōkei) of verbs. It normally undergoes the same contractions
with the Line 2 forms as does the suffix -ta. For a list of these see
the introductory Note on Verbs. Note that in consequence of
these changes -tari sometimes becomes -dari.

These forms (-tari and -dari) seem to have been actually derived
from contractions of -te ari and -de ari, but the question of historical development need not be taken up here.

The forms -tari and -dari indicate repetition of action or state.
They usually are used in sequence and are followed by some form
of verb meaning "to do" (suru, nasaru, itasu), but this rule is not
absolute, especially when a verb is repeated, as in the last
example.
They are often called "frequentative" forms. Their use should
be obvious from the examples given.

Dore wo mite mo noshi wo	No matter which you look at
tsuketari, mizuhiki wo	(they all) have *noshi* on and
kaketari shite aru	are tied up with *mizuhiki*.
Nondari kuttari jūbun hara	(What with) eating and drink-
wo koshiraeta	ing, he has filled his belly
	properly.
Tattari suwattari	(They are) fidgeting around,
sowasowashite iru	constantly getting up and
	sitting down again.

Utsukushii e wo kaitari	The painting of beautiful
rippana ji wo kaku no mo	pictures and the writing of
te no hataraki desu	splendid characters also are
	work done by the hands.
Kui mo kuttari, jippai mo	Eating and eating, (he) ate
kutta	all of ten helpings.

Note that it depends on the context whether or not an alternation of actions or states is suggested. If the context allows, other similar actions or states may also be suggested.

BUNGO

In bungo -*tari* has three distinct uses, each of which had its own particular derivation. It may be added to:

1. The Line 2 form (*renyōkei*) of verbs. This -*tari* is a contraction of -*te ari*.

2. A substantive form. This -*tari* is a contraction of *to ari*.

3. Any of the Japanese numerals, from three to nine inclusive. The derivation of this -*tari* is not clear.

1. As a suffix added to the Line 2 form (*renyōkei*) of verbs -*tari*, which is derived from -*te ari*, gives the effect of a "completion" tense which is partly a "perfect" and partly a "progressive present." It may be, and often is, used in conjunction with other conjugated tense suffixes.

The above remarks have to do with the original and "correct" use of -*tari*. In modern prose, however, the tendency is to treat it as equivalent to the colloquial -*ta*, that is, to use it for the past tense as well.

For a more detailed discussion of its uses see Sansom's "Historical Grammar of Japanese," pp. 177*ff*, 211*ff*.

It is conjugated as follows:

Line 1	*Mizenkei*	-*tara*
Line 2	*Renyōkei*	-*tari*
Line 3	*Shūshikei*	-*tari*
Line 3A	*Rentaikei*	-*taru*
Line 4	*Izenkei*	-*tare*

The imperative is now obsolete, but is found in early writings. Its form is of course the same as Line 4 (*-tare*).

Kenji no shoku ni aru mata wa aritaru mono . . .	Persons who are or have been in the post of Procurator . . .
Hana wa migoro wa sugitare domo nao shichibun no nioi ari	Though the blossoms are past their glory most of their beauty still remains.
Ame furitari	Rain has fallen. Rain fell

2. As a suffix added to substantive forms *-tari*, which is derived from *to ari*, indicates that what it follows is to be taken as a state or quality. This quality may be apparent, inherent, or both.

It may be considered as part of a conjugation, equivalent to that of *ari* 'be'.

Line 1	*Mizenkei*	*-tara*
Line 2	*Renyōkei*	*-tari*
Line 3	*Shūshikei*	*-tari*
Line 3A	*Rentaikei*	*-taru*
Line 4	*Izenkei*	*-tare*
Imperative	*Meireikei*	*-tare*

I have not, however, come across examples of the last two forms.

There is some doubt among grammarians as to whether or not this *-tari* should be considered a true suffix. In the examples it has therefore been printed in three different ways, namely, as a true suffix, as a separate word, and as forming part of a compound word.

Yōyō-taru Tonegawa . . .	The immensely wide Tonegawa . . .
Yo ga katsute gakusei tarishi toki . . .	Formerly, when I was living the life of a student . . .
Hito ni shō taru mono . . .	One who impressed me as a leader among men . . .
Hito ni shō taru wa moto yori yōi narazu	To be a leader of men is not easy from the start.

Keitari gataku teitari gatashi   It is hard to see any difference. [Literally: "Older-brother-quality-is" is difficult (to say) and "younger-brother-quality-is" is difficult (to say).]

3. Apparently at one time *-tari* was quite widely used as a suffix to Japanese numerals to convey the idea of "persons." At the present time the only standard examples of this use are *yottari* (*yotari*) 'four persons', and *ikutari* 'how many persons?' One may, however, occasionally also come across *mitari* 'three persons', *mutari* 'six persons' and *yatari* or *yattari* 'eight persons'.

-TARŌ (-**darō**). A colloquial suffix, formed from the suffix *-tara* (*-dara*) by the addition of the further suffix *-u*. The *-au* is pronounced *-ō*.

It is added to the Line 2 form (renyōkei) of verbs, and forms a so-called "probable past" tense. It is now becoming obsolescent, being usually replaced by *-ta darō* or *-ta deshō*.

Note that this suffix combines with the *renyōkei* in the same way as *-ta*. For the usual contractions see the introductory Note on Verbs. The *-ō* represents the usual pronunciation of the vowel-sequence *-au*.

It serves to express supposition or expectation. The *-ta* form (see -TA) indicates completion and hence usually refers to the past. Consequently the *-tarō* form can never refer to the future, even when the *-ta* is not past.

Mō ikimashitarō   I suppose he has (had) already gone.

It has also the slightly extended use of asking for confirmation as to the past.

Ano hi Tanaka san ga kite imashitarō   Mr. Tanaka was here that day, wasn't he?

This indicates not only that you wish confirmation, but that you wish to make sure that the other person is aware of the truth of what you are saying.

-TARU. A suffix with various uses.

THE COLLOQUIAL

In the colloquial it may be:

1. A contraction of *-te aru*, usually considered rather provincial. When so used it is suffixed to the Line 2 form (*renyōkei*) of verbs. The verb-form to which it is added undergoes the normal euphonic changes given in the introductory Note on Verbs. See also the introductory Note on *Aru, Iru,* and *Oru*.

> *Koko ni chawan ga oitaru wa*   Teacups have been left here!
>   (Please take them away!)

2. A contraction of *to aru*. When so used it is suffixed to substantive forms. The combination is now used only as an adjective which indicates an observed quality. (Cf. introductory Note on Foreign Words.)

> *Shōjōtaru tokoro da*   It's an empty and lonely place.

Even when used in the colloquial, this form has a distinctly "literary" flavor. When such a flavor is not desired, the tendency seems to be to replace it by *to shite iru* or *to shite oru*.

BUNGO

In bungo *-taru* may be:

1. A contraction of *-te aru*
2. A contraction of *to aru*

Whichever it is, it is the Line 3A form (*rentaikei*) of the conjugated suffix *-tari*.

Its meaning is given under the bungo use of *-tari*, paragraphs 1 and 2.

-TASHI. A bungo suffix. It is added to the Line 2 form (*renyōkei*) of verbs.

It conveys the idea of desire, and is equivalent in meaning to the colloquial *-tai*.

It is an adjective in form, consisting of the root *-ta* plus the suffix *-shi*. To the root *-ta* may be added the other suffixes that regularly are added to adjective roots (*-ki, -ku, -sa,* etc.).

Ware mo yukitashi	I too wish to go.
Tazune-kikitaki koto ari	There are things which I wish to ask.
Yukitakariki	(He) wished to go.
Yukitagaru	He shows his desire to go

TATTE. 1. This may be a colloquial contraction of *de atte* used as an equivalent of *de atte mo* 'although it be'.

Okashii tatte warattewa ikenai	Although it is funny, it won't do to laugh.

2. It may be a contraction of other colloquial verbal forms, such as *to itte* (*mo*), or *to atte* (*mo*).

Na wa ie tatte (*to itte mo*) *sonna hito wa arimasen*	You ask me to tell you his name, but there is no such person.

There is some doubt about the derivation of the *tatte* used after *-ku* forms. It may be, as some say, from *to atte mo*. In any case, the effect is that of a strong *-temo*.

Donna ni yokutatte . . . *shinakutatte*	However good it be . . . even if not do

-TATTE. See -TTE.

-TCHA (-TCHYA). (See -CHA.) A contraction of *-tte wa*, very often heard in speech. Cf. -DJA or -JA, contraction of *-de wa*. In *kana* it is usually written *tsu-chi-ya* つちや.

> *Itte wa* becomes *itcha*.
> *Totte wa* becomes *totcha*.

Sō itcha bachi ga ataru	If you talk that way, punishment will come upon you.

-TCHAU. A contraction of *-te shimau*. It may be conjugated. Cf -CHATTA, -CHAU.

TE. This may be either a very informal equivalent of *to*, or a contraction equivalent to *to itte* or *to iu*.

It does not occur in ordinary writing, except in such recognized compounds as *tote*. Cf. TOTE.

It is, however, fairly common in very familiar and rather vulgar speech. Cf. NANTE.

-TE. Suffix, added to the Line 2 form (*renyōkei*) of verbs. (See -TSU.) If used in any other way, it is to be regarded as a contraction. For examples see NANTE, TATTE, TE FU, etc.

The uses of the -*kute* form of adjectives, including *nai* and the suffixes -*nai* and -*tai*, are much the same as those of the -*te* forms discussed here. The differences are noted under -KUTE.

In the colloquial it combines with the Line 2 verb-form to give the contractions listed in the introductory Note on Verbs. These of course include -*de* forms. In bungo contractions are ordinarily not used.

In early bungo it may also be found suffixed to other forms, such as the negative suffix -*zu*. It may be regarded as part of the conjugation of the suffix -*tsu*, which is now nearly obsolete except for the -*te* form. (See -TSU.)

The -*te* is primarily a verb-form. Its uses differ slightly in bungo and in the colloquial. They are therefore treated separately here.

For special uses of the -*te* form not treated here, see under the headings: -TEMO, -TE WA, -TARI, -TSU, -KUTE, NITE, TOTE, NI SHITE and TO SHITE.

For the combination -*te kara* see under KARA; for -*te yori* see YORI.

THE COLLOQUIAL

When not followed by a postposition, the suffix -*te* serves as a link between two descriptions of action or state; that is, between the word to which it has been suffixed, and a following verb or adjective.

This -*te* suffix has no tense significance in itself but has much the force of an English "and" or "-ing."

Students are warned that while -*te* corresponds very roughly with "-ing," the correspondence is by no means absolute. What is said here about the uses of the -te form of course applies equally to the contracted forms ending in -de, a list of which is given in the introductory Note on Verbs, and also to the negative forms *naide, -naide,* and *-masende.*

It is a pure connective, and cannot be used to close a sentence grammatically. If it is used to end a sentence it definitely calls for something to follow. In Tokyo speech sentences ending in -te are quite often used as questions, or exclamations.

The exact significance of the connective force of -te depends largely upon the context. The chief uses of this form are given below, under the following headings:

1. The use of the -te form in connecting two clauses.
2. Special verb-combinations in which the -te form has special uses.
3. Words in the -te form which have developed an individual adverbial meaning.
4. The use of the -te form to end a sentence.

The preceding paragraph refers only to the uses of the -te form of a verb when it is not followed by a postposition. For use of the -te form in connecting adjectives, see under -KUTE.

1. The Use of -TE in Connecting Clauses

The general rule is that if the first clause describes a definite single act, that act precedes whatever action or state is described by the second clause. If the first clause describes continued action or state, this is to be taken as existing along with the action or state of the second clause.

In all such linkages, the context may suggest that the first statement is the cause or origin of the second, but does not necessarily do so.

Note that there are many verbs in Japanese which use the same forms to describe both state and action. Which is meant will usually be quite obvious from the context. Adjectives and all verbs meaning "be" of course necessarily describe state only.

Examples are given below. These have been analyzed to show the various kinds of linkage possible. The student should remember, however, that for a Japanese it is not necessary to analyze in this way; and that the sooner a foreigner can get the "feel" without analysis, the better it is for him.

(a) Act linked to act

Any number of successive actions may be linked together in temporal sequence by means of the -*te* form but, whether these actions be two or many, any idea of tense has to come from the form of the last verb in the sequence.

Uma ni notte dekaketa	(He) got on his horse and started out.
Shitamachi e itte hon wo katte sugu kaerimashita	(He) went downtown, bought a book, and immediately returned home.
Shitamachi e itte hon wo katte sugu kaerimashō yo	Let's go downtown, buy a book, and return home immediately.
Ōame ga futte ōmizu ga deta	Heavy rains falling, a flood arose.

(b) Act linked to state

In such linkages the emphasis is on the state existing after the act has taken place.

Hi wa kurete michi wa tōi	The sun has set and the road is long.
Hi ga ochite nanimo mienai	The sun has set and nothing can be seen.

(c) Continued action or state linked to act

The -*te* form normally characterizes the act, and so may be regarded as "adverbial." If the subject of the -*te* form is not mentioned, it may be taken as the same as that of the verb.

Uma ni notte nōfu gà chikazuku	Riding on a horse, a farmer draws near.
Tokuhon wo koe wo dashite yomu	(He) reads the book in a loud voice.

(d) State linked to state

The emphasis is usually on the second state. The -*te* form, if

it does not suggest cause or origin, is often translatable by an
English adverbial word or phrase.

Jidōsha wa hayakute benri desu	Motors are fast and (therefore) convenient.
Kawa ga kira-kira hikatte nagarete imasu	The river is sparkling and flowing along (i.e., flowing along sparkling).
Ta ga konjiki ni hikatte mieru	The fields are seen (appear) sparkling goldenly.
Shōnin no shinsha ni Shijō Kingo to itte Ejima Tōtomi no kami no rōshin ga atta	Among the followers of the holy man was an old retainer of the Lord of Tōtomi in Ejima, called Shijō Kingo.

SPECIAL NOTE ON COMPARISON WITH THE LINE 2 FORM (RENYŌKEI) WHEN CONNECTING CLAUSES

It has been mentioned in the introductory Note on Verbs that
a *renyōkei* may be used to connect clauses. This use is similar to,
but not quite the same as, the use of the *-te* form for this purpose.

The main difference seems to be that the *-te* links simply the
two adjoining clauses. The *renyōkei* indicates a larger break in
the thought, and may be used to link together quite long and
complicated parts of a sentence. These parts are often composed
of shorter clauses more intimately linked by *-te* forms. E.g.:

Gozen wa toshokan e itte hon wo yomi gogo wa bijutsukan e itte e wo mita	In the morning I went to the library and read books, and in the afternoon I went to the. art museum and looked at the paintings.
Kaite mise yonde kikase iwasete mita ga ano seito wa chittomo oboenakatta	I wrote it and showed it; I read it and made them listen; I tried making them say it; but those students did not remember it in the least.

2. Special Verb Combinations

It is impossible to give a complete list of these, as their use usually depends on the meaning of the second verb. For example, *shimau* may form a sort of perfect tense, but has other uses besides. Practically all such uses will be illustrated in the dictionaries.

For a far more extensive treatment than is given here, see "A Dictionary of Japanese Compound Verbs," by C. K. Parker, Maruzen, Tokyo, 1939.

(a) With verbs meaning "be."

Iru and its grammatical equivalents *oru, irassharu, ketsukaru,* etc., form true auxiliaries with a *-te* form, and indicate continuation of the action or state described.

Aru and its grammatical equivalents *arimasu, gozaru,* etc., can follow the *-te* form of transitive verbs only. The subject of the *aru* is the direct object of the *-te* verb.

For examples and further discussion see the introductory Note on *Aru, Iru,* and *Oru.*

The *-te iru* and *-te aru* forms may also be considered as examples of "state linked to state."

(b) With verbs meaning to give or to receive, e.g., *ageru, chōdai (suru), itadaku, kudasaru, kureru, morau, yaru.* To these may be added *oide* or *oide nasai* when used as an equivalent of *kudasai.* Here the *-te* is used to mark the action which is given or received.

Tarō wa funsui wo uchi no hitobito ni mite moraimashita	Taro got the people of the house to look at the fountain. (Literally: received the seeing . . .)
Hon wo yonde kudasatta	(He) was good enough to read the book (for us). (Literally: condescended (gave) the reading . . .)

(c) With verbs meaning to see, e.g., *miru, goran ni naru,* etc. These verbs are very often used after a *-te* form in the sense of "to test." The full suggestion seems to be "try (doing something) and see how it turns out." The -*te* suffix marks what action is tried.

Atete goran nasai	Try getting at it! (E.g., the answer to a riddle.)
Tabete miru	To try eating

Sometimes these verbs have an utterly untranslatable softening effect, especially in the polite imperative form.

Ocha wo motte kite goran nasai	Just bring the tea, please.

(d) With verbs meaning to come or go, such as *iku*, *kuru*, or *mairu*. If the reference is to physical coming or going, and if the context permits it, the -*te* verb will be practically adverbial.

O cha wo motte kite kure	Please bring tea. (Literally: come holding . . .)
hashitte iku	to run (literally: go running)

Iku may act as a semi-auxiliary, indicating passage of time and so continuation of action.

Chokin wo shite ikimasu	I will keep on putting money in the bank.

However, when it follows a -*te* verb that itself indicates a passage of time or space, it normally simply reinforces the idea, as in:

Yo ga fukete iku	The night is growing late.

Kuru is also often used as a semi-auxiliary, to convey the idea that a certain state or condition has been reached (has "come to pass").

Ame ga futte kita	It has begun to rain.
Bukkyō wo shinjite kita	They came to believe in Buddhism.

There is also a special use of *kuru* in which the English idiom exacts the use of the word "go."

kiite kuru	(to) go and inquire
sagashite kuru	(to) go and search for

Such a use does not necessarily imply a return to the place from which one starts.

3. Words in the -TE Form Which Are Used Purely as Adverbs

There are quite a number of these, most of which, however, will be found as separate words in the dictionary.

hajimete	for the first time (from *hajimeru* 'start')
tsuzukete	continuously (from *tsuzukeru* 'continued')
kaette	contrariwise (from *kaeru* 'change')

4. The -TE Form May End a Sentence

This is not "standard" Japanese, but is quite often used in Tokyo, especially by women of the upper classes. It usually means that the grammatically unfinished sentence is meant as a question.

Kimi wa hitori de itte	Are you going alone?
Kyō hima atte	Are you free today?

It may also be used as a sort of exclamation at the end of an unfinished sentence, as in:

Onna datera ni taisoreta koto wo shite . . .	That she—a woman—should do (such) an impertinent thing . . . ("is inexcusable" or the like).

BUNGO

In bungo the *-te* form is used in almost exactly the same way as in the colloquial.

There are, however, certain additional uses, deriving from the fact that *-te* is at the same time the Line 1 form (*mizenkei*), the Line 2 form (*renyōkei*), and the imperative form (*meireikei*) of the "perfect tense" suffix *-tsu*. See -TSU.

At present forms of *-tsu* other than the *renyōkei* are obsolete or obsolescent. As a Line 2 form, however, *-te* may take further suffixes, so that, especially in the older bungo, one may come across such forms as:

Ame furiteki   It did rain.

-TE FU, -TE (H) U. This combination of *kana* (てふ.) may indicate a contraction of *to iu* (*to i-* (*h*) *u*), to be pronounced as *chō*.

-TEKI. Suffix, with two uses.

1. Both in the colloquial and in bungo *-teki* 的 is suffixed, particularly in Chinese words, to make a new "Chinese" word, which may be regarded as an adjective.

However, though it usually has the effect of an adjective in Chinese, it is from the Japanese standpoint not an adjective *in form*. Hence it has to be treated like other Chinese words which are unconjugated and so correspond to nouns in form. (Cf. the introductory Note on Foreign Words.)

> In Chinese this suffix originally was a noun meaning "target." It has developed into a sort of adjective suffix, meaning approximately "having to do with."

kakkan-teki no midokoro	an objective viewpoint
shukan-teki ni	subjectively
keizai-teki ni suru	to economize (time, etc.)
biteki-seikatsu	an aesthetic life
biteki no seikatsu	

Note that *bitekiseikatsu* without the *no* may be regarded as one word.

2. In old bungo, *-teki*, suffixed to the Line 2 form (*renyōkei*) of verbs, is a combination of the Line 2 form of the "perfect" suffix *-tsu*, plus the further "past" suffix *-ki*. E.g.:

Ame furiteki   It did rain, or "had rained." (Cf. under -TE, -TSU, and -KI.)

-TEMO (-demo). Colloquial suffixes. They may be regarded as made up of the particle *mo* added to the *-te* or *-de* end-forms of verbs or conjugated adjectives. (See -TE, -DE; -KUTE; -UTE.)

For adjectives, one may consider *-temo* as added to the *-ku* (or *-u*) suffix to the adjective root, e.g., *shiro-ku-temo*. For verbs, one may consider *-temo* as added to the Line 2 form (*renyōkei*) and then contracted in accordance with the contractions of the *-te* form given in the introductory Note on Verbs. For example, from *kaku* 'write', *kakitemo*, contracted to *kaitemo*; from *yomu* 'read', *yomitemo*, contracted to *yondemo*. For the negatives *nai*, *-nai* and *-masen*, one may consider *naidemo*, *-naidemo*, and *-masendemo* as special forms.

The *-mo* retains its usual additive effect (see MO). The *-te* or *-de* is of course an "unfinished" form (see -TE and cf. with -TE WA). Consequently the *-temo* (or *-demo*) is always used in an introductory clause. Cf. also with DEMO.

1. The primary use of the *-temo, -demo* form is as a concessive, which may often be translated by an introductory "although," "even," or "even if." In this use *mo* has the sense of "even."

Senmannin itemo ikō	Though there be a million men, I'll go!
Kanashūtemo kokoro wo yaburu na	Though you are sorrowful, do not break your heart! (*Kansai* speech.)
Osokutemo shuppatsu-shiyō	Even if it is late, let us start out!
Ikudo kokoromitemo sono kai ga nakatta	Although I tried several times, it was without success.
Ano ko wa karada-bakari ōkiku-temo kara akambō desu	Even if that child is big in body, he is an utter baby.
Chūi-gurai shite kuretemo yokari-sōna mono da	You might at least pay attention! (I don't think it would do any harm even if you did do something of the sort!)
Tatoe mangan no sho wo yondemo seijin to naru koto wa muzukashikarō	Even if one were to read ten thousand books, it would be hard to become a sage.

This form may be used, particularly with *ii* 'good', in asking and giving permission.

(Q) *Ikanakutemo ii ka*   Is it all right even if I don't go?

(A) *Ikanakutemo ii*   Quite all right.

(Q) *Ittemo ii n'desu ka*   May I go?

(A) *Ittemo ii*   You may.

2. When the *-temo* (*-demo*) comes at the end of a clause containing an interrogative word the *mo* has its usual effect of turning the interrogative into an indefinite. (See under MO and DEMO.) In translation it is usually more idiomatic to avoid the "even if" or "although" construction.

Ano onna wa doko ni itemo   That woman is not satisfied,
  manzoku shinai   wherever she lives. (Even
                                   if she lives anywhere she is
                                   not satisfied.)

3. In certain contexts the *mo* has the sense of "also." When it has this sense the *-temo, -demo* form is usually repeated. (Cf. MO . . . MO and DEMO, section 5.)

In these contexts the *mo* indicates that the situation described in the words preceding it is to be added to situations previously referred to. (Cf. discussion under MO.)

For example, in a context where a young man's good behavior has been referred to, the text goes on:

Aisatsu wo shite mo teinei de Also in his greeting he was
  chittomo namaikina fū ga   polite and without any trace
  naku nani wo kiitemo ichi-   of affectation, and whatever
  ichi hakkiri to kotaeta   (questions) were asked he
                                   answered clearly, one by
                                   one.

-TERU (-TETA, etc.). Contraction of *-te iru,* common in colloquial speech. E.g.:

Mainichi kō suru koto ni   I make it a rule to do so every
  kimeterunda (kimete iru   day.
  no da)

Note that similar contractions, made by dropping the *i* of other forms of *iru,* are not uncommon, especially in rather low-class speech. E.g.:

matteta hito *matte ita hito*	The people who were waiting
Mattero *Matte iro*	Wait!

-TE WA (-de wa). When *wa* follows the *-te* *(-de)* form of a verb it performs its usual function of marking what it follows as a psychological subject, which may or may not be also the grammatical subject of a sentence. (See under wa.)

The *-te* *(-de)* form may indicate an action or a state, or may be used adverbially. [See under -TE (-DE).]

In treating of the uses of the *-te wa, -de wa* form, it is convenient to group the examples together under the following headings:

1. When it is found between what are obviously two separate descriptions of act or state.

2. When it is followed by certain special verbs, which obviously do not describe a second separate act or state.

3. When the *-te, -de* word is used abverbially, as in the phrases *ni oite, ni kanshite,* etc.

1. When two separate statements are connected by a *-te wa, -de wa* form, the connection is much like that made by the *-te, -de* form.

The difference is that the first statement does not refer to only a single instance of the act or state described, but to any instance of it. It marks the first statement as a condition precedent, and so indicates that when the first act or state occurs, the second naturally follows.

Normally, if the first statement is positive, the equivalent English idiom will use "when"; if it is negative, the English idiom uses "if." Occasionally other idioms are preferable.

Kō nobite wa totemo *taberaremasen*	When they (bamboo-shoots) grow this way, they are wholly uneatable.

Kō natte wa susumu yori hoka ni michi wa nai	When things get like this, there is no other road (of action) than to advance.
Gakumon wa dekitemo karada ga yowakute wa shikata ga nai	Even though he is a good student, when the body is weak there is nothing to be done.
Kochira wo mite wa waratte imasu	When he looks this way, he laughs (and keeps on doing it).
Totte wa kurai totte wa kurai hara ippai kuratta	When he took (one) he ate, when he took he ate, and he ate till his belly was full.
Tonde wa ochi ochite wa tobi shimasu	When jump, fall; and when fall, jump—(that is what) he does.
Nani wo suru nimo kane ga nakute wa komarimasu	In doing anything at all, it is hard when one hasn't money.
Sonna koto wo sarete wa tamaranai	When one has such things done to one, it is not to be borne!
Tokuhon wo yoku benkyō shinaide wa Nihon no omoshiroi hon ga yomeru yō ni naranai	If one doesn't study one's reader well, one won't get to be able to read interesting Japanese books.
Jissen ni yaku ni tatanakute wa nanimo naranu	If (it) is not useful in actual warfare, (it) does not amount to anything.

2. When the second clause is obviously not the description of a separate action or state, the force of the *-te wa, -de wa* is much like that of an English "as for . . . -ing."

It is not possible to give examples of all such "second clauses," but the following types are among the most important:

(a) When the "second clause" is some form of a verb meaning "to be."

Tsukue no mae ni suwatte wa iru ga hon wo yonde wa inai	As for sitting in front of the desk, (he) is, but as for reading the book, (he) isn't.
Q. *Ano kami ni wa nanika kaite aru no ka*	Is there anything written on that paper?
A. *Kaite wa aru ga usui kara totemo yomarenai*	There's something written, all right, but it's so light that it can't possibly be read.

It will be noticed that this use of the *-te wa, -de wa* form is exactly equivalent to that of *de wa* in the common negatives such as *so de wa nai* 'as for being that way, it isn't', etc.

(b) When the "second clause" repeats the verb of the first clause, the effect is practically the same as in (a).

| *(Ame ga) futte wa furimasu ga kosame dake desu* | As for "raining," it is "raining" but it's only a drizzle. |

The more common form for expressing this idea is *furu ni wa furimasu ga* . . .

(c) When the "second clause" is a verb like *naranai* or *ikemasen,* the first clause shows what it is that "will not do," and becomes a grammatical as well as a psychological subject.

| *Kaze ga fuitara uchi wo dete wa naranai* | You must not go out of the house when it is windy. (Literally: . . . as for going out, it won't do.) |
| *Waratte wa ikenai kara dō shimashō?* | As it won't do to laugh, what shall I do? |

(d) When the "second clause" is a verb like *oku,* the first clause becomes practically a direct object.   (Cf. under WA.)

| *Kotowatte wa okimashita* | As for the (act of) refusing, I made it firm (with the implication that my final decision is not yet made). |

3. When the *-te, -de* form is obviously adverbial, the *wa* simply shows what we are talking about.

Under this heading come phrases like *ni tsuite wa*, etc. For other examples see under TO SHITE WA.

Kono koto ni kanshite wa	Concerning this affair I have
nanimo kiita koto ga nai	heard nothing at all.

TO. A connective particle, with an additional reflexive force, somewhat like "that" or "that way."

In all its uses *to* indicates a union. Furthermore it makes what it follows very clear and distinct. For special uses see TOMO, TO SURU, TO SU, TO KA, TO IU, TO WA, TO ZO, NARI TO.

Historically, *to* seems to have been originally a demonstrative pronoun. In early texts, as Sansom points out, there are such locutions as *Chichi to masu hito* 'the person that is my father', where *to* corresponds almost exactly with the demonstrative "that" in English, in its use as a relative. This meaning survives in certain phrases (e.g., *tokaku*, which is basically "that (!) —this"), and accounts for its strong reflexive force, which still corresponds somewhat to the force of "that" as used in "that (thing)," "that (way)," "that (happening)," etc.

To has developed such a wide variety of uses that it has seemed best to treat it under the following heads, namely, when it is used:

1. After quotations
2. After clauses in sentence form which are not quotations
3. After the Line 2 form (*renyōkei*) of verbs
4. After adverbs or adverbial phrases
5. After substantives

This is, of course, not a scientific division. It has, however, seemed the most practical one. The student should have no great difficulty in deciding, for example, whether a word or sentence marked by *to* is or is not used as a quotation in a particular text.

AFTER QUOTATIONS

1. *To* is used after quotations to mark them as such.

In Japanese all quotations of what is said or heard are direct quotations. Thoughts are also given in the form in which they were conceived.

When *to* marks a quotation it joins it to an idea of saying, hearing, or thinking. This idea may be expressed in definite words but does not have to be so expressed if the context makes the meaning obvious.

The demonstrative force of *to* after quotations is fairly clear. E.g.:

    Ha to iu   *He says Ha!*

might be literally rendered: "Ha! that he says."

Colloquial examples:

Ikitai to omoimashita	I wanted to go. (I had the thought, "I want to go.")
Mō kesshinshita to kikimasu	I hear that he has already made up his mind.
Kuji ni koi to no koto deshita	It was a matter of "come at nine!" (I was told to come at nine.)
Damare to donatta	He yelled "Silence!"
Nai to wa iemasu ga . . .	It is possible to say that there aren't any, but . . . (there are a few).

The English idiom would probably be phrased: "One can hardly say that there aren't any, but . . . (there are only a few)."

There are many common colloquial expressions in which some form of *iu* 'say' has obviously been omitted. E.g.:

nan to naku	indefinably, inexpressibly, etc. (*nan to ienaku* 'unable to tell what').
ikutabi to naku	a countless number of times (*iwanaku* or *ienaku* 'do not say or cannot say how many').
Takai yama ga kanarazu nadakai yama da to wa kagiranai	To say that high mountains are necessarily famous ones does not fit the facts. (*To wa* equals *to iu koto wa, to iu no wa, to no koto wa,* etc.

Bungo examples:

Kare wa mokka Ōshu ryugakuchū nari to kiku	I hear that he is at present studying abroad in Europe.
Zeni nashi to iu	He says he has no money.
Sono dempō iwaku Kansai chihō ni kōzui ariki to	The telegram says that there has been a flood in the Kansai district.
Omoeraku teki kōgeki shi kitaru beshi to	He thought that the enemy would come to the attack.
Yukamu to omou	I am thinking of going.
Kore wa kore wa	"This is . . .! This is . . .!"
To bakari hana no Yoshinoyama	That was the measure— Blossom-covered Yoshino mountain.

This last example was the answer given by the poet Teishitsu when he was asked what poem he had composed when he saw the cherry-blossoms at Yoshino-yama. It might be rendered:

> "Oh!" and "Oh!" and "Oh!"
> That's all—upon the blossom-covered
> Hills of Yoshino.

Note that, strictly speaking, the adjective or verb before *to* should be in the sentence-ending form (*shūshikei*), but custom allows the use of the Line 3A form (*rentaikei*) also. Occasionally the verb which introduces a quotation is placed at its head, but *to* always marks the end of the narration.

AFTER CLAUSES NOT QUOTATIONS

2. *To* may be used after clauses in sentence form which are not quotations.

The bungo and colloquial usages are not all the same when *to* is used in this particular way. They are therefore treated separately.

The demonstrative as well as the connective force of *to* is strong when it connects clauses.

Bungo

(a) When the *to* is immediately followed by a word or phrase meaning "seem," "be," "act," or the like, the *to* has a force like "that way," or "thus."

This usage is so similar to that after quotations that it is hard to draw the line between them. For instance, if "I think" something, that is the way the thing "seems" to me. Take also, for example, the two sentences:

Ikan to ieri	He said he would (probably) go.
Ikan to seri	He started to go (made to go).

From a Japanese point of view the first is, "Will-probably-go thus he said"; and the second is, "Will-probably-go thus he acted." There is obviously no fundamental difference in the action of the *to*. The student will note also the close relationship that this use of *to* has to its use after adverbs, and in such phrases as *ano hito wo teki to miru* 'look upon that person as an enemy', etc.

Tekizei kudaru to miete imada ugokazu	It appears that the enemy will surrender, but they have not yet moved (to do so).
Ya wo nukan to su	He tries to draw out the arrows.
Kimi yukan to areba . . .	Since you mean to go . . . (since it is that you are going . . .)
Kakuru to suredo arawarenikeri	Though he tried to hide he was detected.

The *su* in *to su*, it will be noted, may often be rendered as "try to do" rather than simply "do." In other words, the "act-that-way" effect of *to su* avoids a definite statement that the action of the verb before the *to* is effectuated.

At the end of explanatory sentences *to su* is often best left untranslated. It has a tying-up effect, approximately equal to "that is what it comes to." It is a bit like the colloquial *no desu*. After an explanatory summing up it has a slightly softening effect:

Sore wa kandō wo arawashitsutsu shushi suru mono nari to su	These (particles) are things that put an end (to a sentence) at the same time they show emotion.

However, after the statement of laws, in proclamations, etc.,
to su rather adds to the force and clarity.

(b) When the *to* is not followed by a suggestion of saying,
thinking, hearing, seeming, acting, etc., it is used as an equivalent
of *to mo* 'even though', 'although'. (See TOMO.)

This usage is not very common, and may be regarded as a contraction of *to mo*. (See also NARI TO.)

E ni kaku to fude oyobaji	Even though you paint it your brush will not succeed.

The Colloquial

(a) There is a use of *to* corresponding to the bungo use discussed in paragraph (a) above. This is, however, in practice
almost wholly confined to instances in which the *to* is followed
by some form of *suru* or its equivalent. (See TO SURU.)

Ikō to shimashita	He started to go. He made as if to go.

(b) When *to* follows a "dubitative" suffix (*-u, -yō,* or *-mai*),
and is not followed by some form of *suru* or its equivalent it usually has the effect of *to mo*. Cf. paragraph (b) above.

Shinō to kamawan	Even if I die, I don't care.

When the *to* is repeated, the English idiom "whether . . . or"
may be used in translation.

Ame ga furō to kaze ga fukō to shuppatsu suru	Whether the rain fall or the wind blow, I shall leave. (Even though the rain fall, etc.)
Ikō to ikumai to kimi no katte da	Whether you go or don't go is entirely up to you.

Note the effect after interrogatives.

Dare ga sō iwō to uso sa	Whoever may say so, it's a lie!

(c) When *to* follows a verb in the simple conclusive Line 3 form (not *-ta* or *-u*, *-yō*), its most common use is to join two sentences, giving the effect that when or if the first happens, then the second happening follows more or less immediately.

Here the demonstrative force is like that of "that (happen) and (then) . . . " Note that in this use *to* never follows a *-ta* form. (When it does follow a *-ta* form it indicates a quotation.) Note also that an imperative cannot follow this use of *to*.

This use of *to* may occur after either suppositional statements, or accounts of some particular happening.

When it occurs after suppositional statements, the effect is that "when" or "if" this happens, then a second happening follows necessarily.

When it occurs after the description of a particular happening the effect is that "when" this did happen, the second happening did follow more or less immediately.

The context will usually make it quite clear whether the first statement is suppositional or a statement of fact.

Ochiru to kowareyō	Drop it and you'll break it.
Ame ga furu to suzushiku naru	When it rains it will get cooler.
Guzu guzu suru to chikoku suru	Idle along and (so) be late.
Amari nagai to oreru	Break it off when it is too long.
Ie e kaeru to hi ga kureta	When he got home the sun had set.
Mon ni hairu to hito ga oru zo	She entered the gate and — somebody was there!
Ano hito wa itta ka to omou to kaette kimashita	He had hardly gone before he returned.
Kaite okanu to wasureru	If (you) don't write it down (you) will forget.
Hayaku ikan' to ma ni awan	If we don't hurry, we won't be in time.

It has been suggested that this use of *to*, which occurs only in the colloquial, derives from a contraction of *toki* 'time.' This suggestion is interesting, and whether it is true or not may assist the student in getting the "feel" of sentences in which *to* is used in this way.

AFTER LINE 2 FORMS

3. *To* may join the Line 2 form (*renyōkei*) of a verb with another form of the same verb. This gives an effect of emphasis.

Ari to aru mono . . .	All there are . . .
Naki to naku tori . . .	Birds that sing and sing . . .
Kaze fuki to fukinu	The wind blew and blew (blew with all its might).

Such forms as the above are primarily literary, and have a bungo flavor even when used in speech. There are, however, a few similar expressions which are primarily colloquial, such as:

Ari to arayuru hon . . .   All the books there are . . .

Arayuru is a special form, apparently derived from *ari-uru* or *ari-eru*.

AFTER ADVERBS

4. *To* is used after adverbs or adverbial phrases. When so used it joins them to a verb.

It is used only with adverbs or adverbial phrases which are vivid to start with. These are often duplicated or onomatopoetic words. It is also affixed to compounds formed with the Chinese adverbial suffixes, *-zen, -jo, -ko,* etc.

The demonstrative force of *to* after adverbs (i.e., "that way") is akin to that after quotations. Thus:

                kara-kara to warau   to laugh harshly

is literally "*kara-kara* that-way laugh," and could well be translated "to laugh, making the sound *kara-kara.*"

chiri-jiri to naru	to be scattered (become "scatter-scatter")
hira-hira to tobu	to flutter (fly flutteringly)
ran-man to	luxuriantly
kakko to	solidly
funjo to	confusedly
totsuzen to	with a rush

For comparison with *ni* see note at end of the article.

AFTER SUBSTANTIVES

5. *To* is used after substantives. When so used it joins them to other substantives.

It may be put as a grammatical rule that these "other substantives" are joined on in such a way as to put them on a plane of parity with the substantives marked by *to*.

These "other substantives" may or may not be actual words in the sentence. For example, they may be personal pronouns which are omitted because they are the obvious grammatical subjects, etc.

Bungo and colloquial usages do not differ in this use of *to*. However, as the subject is rather complicated, it seems simpler to confine the examples to the colloquial.

> The demonstrative force of *to* after substantives is not always clear, as it may be overshadowed by its connective force. It nevertheless exists, and the student should get the "feel" of it from the following examples. It will be noted that in the discussion below, the examples with the greatest amount of connective force have been given first. In these, as the full force of *to* cannot easily be given in English, it is usually best translated by "and" or "with."

(a) When the other substantive is also followed by *to*, the union between the two is necessarily grammatical as well as psychological, and the reflexive force of *to* gives the effect of an enumeration.

> By a grammatical union it is meant that the joined substantives act as a compound noun, which may be the grammatical subject of a verb, or its object, etc.

Tōkyō to Ōsaka to Kōbe to ni yōji ga aru no desu	I have business in Tokyo, in Osaka, and in Kobe.
Chichi to oji to no tateta ie desu	It is a house built by my father and my uncle.

Note that in such sentences Japanese custom allows the dropping of a *to* if it is not needed to make the sense clear. The omitted *to* is usually the final one.

Take to suzume to tora wa tsukimono da	Bamboos, tigers, and sparrows are things that belong together. (The reference is to an artistic tradition.)
Yama to kawa wo miru	(I) see mountains and rivers.

Note also that the final *to* cannot be dropped if there is any danger of misunderstanding. E.g.:

Doyō to suiyō no gogo to wa yasumi ni natta	Saturdays, and Wednesday afternoons became times for rest.
Doyō to suiyō to no gogo wa yasuma ni natta	The afternoons of (both) Saturdays and Wednesdays became the times for rest.

But if the final *to* were omitted, we would have a sentence whose meaning might be either of the above.

Doyō to suiyō no gogo wa yasumi ni natta	. . . . . . ??

(b)   When the other substantive is not also followed by *to* the union may or may not be a grammatical one. The exact nature of the union will depend on the context. So also will the exact nature of the reflexive effect.

It may be said that in all cases *to* makes a substantive clear and vivid. It is somewhat as if it drew a frame around it.

Kare wa sensei to isshōni sampo shita	He took a walk with the teacher.
Kare wa sensei to hanashite iru	He is talking with the teacher.
Kare wa sensei to naru	He becomes a teacher (i.e., begins teaching).
Kare wa sensei to Maeda san wo mita	He saw the teacher and Mr. Maeda.
Kare wa Maeda san wo sensei to omotta	He looked upon Mr. Maeda as a (his) teacher.

Kare wa Maeda san wo   He made Mr. Maeda his
   sensei to shita   teacher.
Kare wa sensei to shite erai   He, as a teacher, is very fine.
    (Cf. under TO SHITE.)

The above examples have been manufactured to assist the
student. The following examples are taken directly from
Japanese books.

Haha to futari de sabishiku   She dwells sadly alone with
   kurasu   her mother.
Anata to isshōni mairimasu   I will go (together) with you.
Ato de yukkuri kimi to   Later on I would like to have
   sōdan shitai   a talk with you at leisure.
Sore wa kore to onaji (da)   That is the same as this.
Ko wa otsu to hitoshii   A is equal to B.
Shiro wa kuro to naru   White becomes (as) black.
Kodomo no na wo Tarō   He recorded the child's name
   to tsuketa   as Tarō. (Here *to* might
    be considered as marking a
    quotation.)

Kare wa watakushi no te-ashi   He is a man whom I depend
   to tanonde iru hito da   on on a par with my own
    hands and feet.

(Yūshi ga) tatakatte hana to   (The heroes) fought and, like
   chitta   the cherry-blossoms, fell.
    (Here the force of *to* is
    stronger than that of "like."
    It is almost "being as blos-
    soms.")

NOTE. In all the uses of *to,* whether used after substantives,
adverbs, or verbs, there is a similar reflexive force inherent in its
original meaning "that." It may be "that" thing, "that" way,
"that" happen, etc.

In the above discussion it has been necessary to discuss the uses
of *to* under the headings of what it follows. The student, however, should synthesize these uses and get the "feel" of *to.* It will
then not be necessary for him, any more than it is for a Japanese,

to feel conscious that he is putting "what *to* follows" into any
particular grammatical category. It would be not only un-
Japanese to do so, but also hardly possible.

Once the "feel" of *to* is obtained, it becomes easy to understand
many elliptical expressions which cannot be gone into here.

For illustration there are subjoined a few special phrases,
together with their English equivalents.

Sore wa sō de arō to . . .	Be that as it may . . .
. . . *to no kiita koto desu*	I understand that . . . I hear that . . .
. . . *nan to itte mo* . . .	Whatever we may say . . . . . . after all . . .
. . . *nan to (mo) ienai*	unspeakable (Literally: can- not say even "What?")
Anata ni sōdan, shiyō to *omotte kimashita* *Anata ni sōdan to kimashita*	I came to consult with you.

NOTE ON "TO" COMPARED WITH "NI"

To, originally a demonstrative pronoun much like "that" or
"that way" expresses correlation, similarity, parity.

Ni, originally probably a form of the hypothetical verb *nu* 'to
be', can express the idea of actual being.

Kin wo gin to kaeru	Change gold for silver.
Kin wo gin ni kaeru	Change gold into silver.
Kare wo sensei to suru	Make him a teacher (in the sense of "appoint," etc.) .
Kare wo sensei ni suru	Make him a teacher (ie., make him a real teacher) .
totsuzen to	with a rush
totsuzen ni	rapidly

It is obvious that when the distinction is a very slight one, even
good speakers or writers will not be particularly careful about
which form they use.

-Tō. A suffix, usually indicating plurality.   It derives from a Chinese noun meaning "class," "grade," "degree."

As a suffix it is practically equivalent to the purely Japanese suffix *-nado,* and hence is not a simple plural, but rather suggests the idea of "such as" the things or persons mentioned. Cf. -NADO. E.g.:

> *yakyū teikū tō*   baseball, tennis, and the like

This suffix is seldom used in conversation, as it sounds rather bookish and affected.   In the common combinations such as *ittō* 'first class,' *nitō* 'second class', etc., the *tō* functions as a regular noun.

NOTE.   The character 等 may be read as *-nado, -tō, -ra,* or *-tachi.* It depends on the context what reading is to be used.

As a general rule it will be read as either *-nado* or *-tō.* The pronunciation *tō* is preferred when the style is Chinese or based on Chinese.

It is to be read *-ra* if one person is obviously singled out as a representative of others.   See -RA.   Also, in poetry or metrical prose the pronunciation *ra* will be used if a single (short) syllable is needed for proper scansion.

It is very seldom read *-tachi,* and the student should normally not read it so unless this particular pronunciation is indicated by *kana.*

TO IU.   A combination of the particle *to* plus the verb *iu,* meaning to "say," "tell" or "speak."

Note that *iu* is actually a first (*yodan*) conjugation, (H) column verb. (See introductory Note on Verbs.)   Nevertheless it is some-times Romanized as *yū,* and even in Japan it is sometimes written with the *kana* for *yuu.* The dialect forms *yutte* and *yutta* are not in-frequently used in place of the standard colloquial *itte* and *itta.*

The phrase *to iu* is very common in Japanese.   It sometimes bothers foreign students, but only when they forget that in Japanese the use of a verb which is active in form does not necessarily involve mention or even implication of any specific subject.

Kono mura wa Kose to iu   This village (they) call Kose.

A sentence such as this might, of course, occur in a context which does imply that some specific person does the calling. It might also, however, appear in contexts in which no specific speaker is implied, and so correspond to the English locution "This village is called Kose," where the English idiom uses the passive as a device to describe an act without reference to the agent. See the introductory Note on Syntax.

In the same way, when *to iu* is used attributively:

Kore wa Kose to iu mura desu	This is a village which we call Kose.
	This is a village called Kose.

Either of the above translations may be equally correct. Which is the better depends entirely on context.

In addition to its regular meaning of "thus say" or "so called," *to iu* is quite often used as a convenient connective, much like *no,* and therefore is sometimes best left untranslated. Even the example immediately above might be rendered in English by such sentences as "This is the village of Kose" or "This is the village 'Kose'."

Nan to iu imi desu ka	What is the meaning?
Seitentaisei fu to iu e okaremashita ga betsu ni kore to iu shokumu mo nai	(He) was put in the district (*fu*) called Seitentaisei, but had no particularly specified duties.

It is not possible to give examples of all possible uses of *to iu,* but a few of the special uses are given below.

A Few Special Expressions

1. *Dochira ka to iu to . . .* "If (someone) say 'which?' " . . .

Byōnin wa dochira ka to iu to kyō wa ii hō desu	Today the patient is a bit better (if I am to answer to "better or worse.")

Boku no tokei wa dochira ka My watch is a bit slow, if
to iu to sukoshi okureru   anything.

2. *Nan to iu . . . deshō*, used as an exclamatory "What . . .
it is!"

Nan to iu ii keshiki deshō   What a beautiful view it is!
Nan to iu ii tenki nan deshō What a fine day it is! (Here
                               the second *nan* is an abbrevi-
                               ation of *na no*.)
Nan to iu baka deshō   What a fool he is!

3. *Nan . . .* (number) *. . . to iu hodo*, "What-(number)-
thus-say-extent-up-to." A periphrastic expression, giving the effect of the English "a number of . . ."

Nanbyakunin to iu hodo   A number of hundreds of
noremasu   people can ride.
Nanzenbiki to iu hodo no I saw several thousand sheep
hitsuji wo mimashita   (. . . thousands of sheep).

4. (Noun) *to iu* (same noun), "(Noun)-thus-called-(noun)."
An expression used for emphasis, to give the effect of *"all* such
things." It may or may not be followed by a reinforcing *mina*
'all'.

shima to iu shima   All (the) islands
hito to iu hito   all (the) people

TO KA. There is a special use of this combination, found
especially in the epistolary style.

In this use the *to ka* is found at the end of sentences, where it
has the effect of "so I hear," "so I think," and the like. E.g.:

Shikashi konogoro wa yohodo I hear, however, that you have
gokaihō ni mukaware soro   been getting much better
to ka   recently.

TOKORO. This word is basically a noun, meaning "place" or
"situation," the latter in both its spatial and other connotations.
It has, however, also certain uses as a conjunction.

When sentences begin with *tokoro* the reference is always to a previously defined "situation." Thus *tokoro de* . . . has the implication "That is the situation, and (consequently) . . . *Tokoro ga* . . . implies "That is the situation, but . . ."

As the uses of *tokoro* within sentences, even where it is a definite noun, is occasionally troublesome to students, a few examples are given:

Ima dekakeru tokoro desu	(I) am on the point of going out.
Tarō wa ima okāsan ga okusuri wo nomu tokoro e kite . . . to itta	Tarō, coming to his mother, who was about to take her medicine, said: . . . (. . . to the now-mother-will-drink-medicine situation . . .)
Ano hito no iu tokoro ni yoreba . . .	According to what he says . . . (if you base on the that-person-say situation) .
Kao wo araō tokoro e tazunete kita	He came to visit me just as I was about to wash my face.
Kao wo aratte iru tokoro e tazunete kita	He came to visit me just while I was washing my face.

Note that in such sentences as the above, English idiom usually avoids translating *tokoro* as a noun. If it is desired to translate it as a noun, "state" or "point" may be better words than "situation."

It might be added that in the epistolary style *tokoro* often seems to suggest the idea of "although," or "but," as in:

Aitazune sōrō tokoro sono gi kore naku sōrō	We inquired about it but there was no such thing.

NOTE. If the student really wants something to work on, he might try the following sentence:

Kore ga jitsu ni waga kokutai no bankoku ni sugure sekai ni tagui no nai tokoro de aru.

A word-for-word attempt at translation would be: "This truly our national-structure's exceed-all-countries-and-have-no-equal-in-the-world point is."

Translated into respectable English it might read: "This in truth is where our national structure is better than that of all other countries and without an equal in the whole world."

However, depending on the context, "how" or "why" might be better than "where." And perhaps the flavor would be best retained by something like: "Truly, it is this about our national constitution that makes it better . . ."

-TOKU. Contraction of *-te oku.*

TOMO. A combination of the particles *to* and *mo,* used in both bungo and the colloquial.

In general, when these particles appear together, each retains its own force, *to* the reflexive "that," and *mo* an additive "also" or "even," and the meanings do not require any special explanation. In such cases they should be written and thought of separately. E.g.:

Zehi to mo . . .	Indeed and indeed . . .; At all costs . . .
"X" to itte "Y" to mo iu	They say "X" and they also say "Y."
Inochi wo suteru koto wo nan to mo omowanu	He sets his life at nothing. (He doesn't think anything at all of throwing his life away.)
Hayai to mo hayai *Hayashi to mo hayashi*	It is very fast indeed.
(Dare ka wo) kami to mo aogu, oya to mo shitau	Revere (someone) as a god, and love (him) as a parent.

There are, however, certain special uses, in which *tomo* acts like a single particle, has a very definite effect, and does require some explanation.

BUNGO

After the Line 3 form (*shūshikei*) of verbs, *-zu,* or the *-ku* form of adjectives, *tomo* has the effect of a concessive conjunction, which joins a supposition to some conclusion about it.

Some grammarians, however, consider it a suffix. It is sometimes shortened to *to*.

This *tomo* marks what precedes it as a hypothesis, a "condition not already determined," and so is usually best translated by a preliminary "even if" or "although." (Cf. -BA.)

Tomo indicates that the clause it follows describes a supposition regarding the present or future. This clause is often introduced by *tatoe*, which serves to strengthen the supposition, but not to change it. The second clause therefore normally refers to the future, and so either ends in *-mu, -ji, -beshi* and like forms, or is an imperative. (Compare with -DO, -DOMO.)

Sen-man-nin ari tomo ware yukan	Even if they be a million men, I will go.
Kanashiku tomo kokoro yaburu na	Even if it be sad, do not break your heart.
Naku tomo kai nakaramu	Even if one weep, it won't do any good.
Hito ni soshiraru tomo kokoro ni kaisuru ni taraji	Even if one were reviled by others, it would not be worth taking it to heart.
Tatoe kono kisoku aratameraru tomo eikyō nakarubeshi	Even if these regulations were changed it would not have any effect.

Apparently when the verb before *tomo* is a *-ru, -ruru* verb, the *-ruru* form (*rentaikei*) is permissible. For example, in the last two sentences the verbs might have been *soshiraruru* and *aratameraruru*. Grammarians do not seem to agree on this point.

THE COLLOQUIAL

In the colloquial there are two special uses of *tomo*:

1. After clauses ending with verbs in the Line 3 (*shūshikei*) or "dubitative" (*-u, -yō*) forms, or with adjectives in the *-ku* form. In this use *tomo* has practically the same concessive effect as in the bungo special use but is used rather more loosely. It is often translatable by a preliminary "even if" or "although," but sometimes requires other English locutions.

Note that after interrogative pronouns the *mo* still has its usual effect.

Shimō tomo kamawan	Even if I die I don't care.
Ashikarō tomo yaru	Even if it is bad I'll do it.
Nani ga koyō tomo osorenai	I'm not afraid, whatever may happen.
Nani ni tsukawareru tomo omae no katte da	Whatever you spend (the money) on, it's your own affair.
Dō suru tomo katte ni shi-nasai	Please do as you please (whatever it be).
Matareru tomo matsu mi ni naru na	Even if you are waited for never get to be the one who waits.

This last sentence is an almost proverbial saying, which might be called "advice to a lover."

2. After the final verb of a sentence. When *tomo* is used in this way it increases the certainty of an already definite statement, and has the effect of "certainly," "of course," and similar expressions.

It is possible, though perhaps not wholly probable, that this *tomo* may be, as Aston suggests, a contraction of *to itte mo yoroshii*. It seems more likely that this use derived from forms like *hayashi tomo hayashi* through omission of the repeated word.

Sō desu tomo	Of course it's so!
Arimasu tomo	To be sure there are!
Hayai tomo	You bet it's fast!

-TORU. A contraction of *-te oru*. (Kyushu dialect.)

TO SHITE. A combination of the postposition *to* with the *-te* form of the verb *suru* (bungo *su*). Its use will vary according to the context. (Cf. with NI SHITE.)

It presents difficulties to foreign students chiefly because of its great number of possible uses. The exact function of *to* depends to a great extent on the nature of the concept it follows, and the verb *suru* (*su*) may have the meaning of "make," "do," "act," "be," etc.

There is usually no great difficulty in understanding the use of *to shite* when the *shite* is used in an active sense (make, do, act, perform, etc.). E.g.:

Kare wa Maeda san wo sensei to shite isshōkenmei ni benkyō shimashita	He made Mr. Maeda his teacher and studied with all his might.
Ikō to shite . . .	Starting to go . . . (acting in the manner of "will go")
Ano onna wa utsu-utsu to shite iru . . .	That woman is sobbing (going "sob-sob").
Moku-moku to shite iru hito . . .	A person who remains perfectly silent . . .

There is, however, a special use of *to shite* which often puzzles foreigners. This is a bungo use which has survived in the colloquial.

In bungo *to suru* (*to su*) is often used much as *de aru* is used in the colloquial, that is, as a copula with the meaning of "is." (See TO SU.) In the colloquial this use survives in the form *to shite*.

As an example of the close relationship of *ari* and *su* note that the bungo equivalent of the phrase given just above is *moku-moku taru hito*, where *-taru* of course is derived from *to aru*.

However, inasmuch as *to* has some of the effect of a reflexive "that" or "that way," *to shite* is not simply a copula equivalent to "being" or "is . . . and . . .," but is more nearly "being that way," or, by a slight extension of meaning, "being considered that way."

Typical bungo examples of this use of *to shite* are:

Shōko hanzen to shite inamu-bekarazu	The proof being clear, it is not to be denied.
Ware ten no shu to shite buō no uchi no buō nari	I, being the Lord of Heaven, am the Warrior King of Warrior Kings.
Oya to shite mata ko to shite mamoru-beki michi ari	Being (considered) as a parent, and again as a child, there are paths (of conduct) which must be maintained.

Hitori to shite somuku mono nashi	Be it (even) a single one, there is no person who disobeys.
Heike no inori no hitotsu to shite shirushi wa nakari keri	For even a single one of all the prayers of the Heike there was no sign of answer.

In the colloquial survival of this use of *to shite* the extended meaning of "considered that way" is the dominant one. It is apparently found after substantives only. E.g.:

Kare wa sensei to shite erai hito da	He, considered as a teacher, is an eminent man.
Ano onna wa onna to shite sei ga takai	She is tall for a woman (considered as a woman).

This is the commonest type of this use of *to shite*. For other examples see under TO SHITE MO and TO SHITE WA.

It is not at all sure, however, that modern Japanese feel this *shite* as an inactive "being considered" and not as an active " (we) considering" or "consider . . . and . . . ."

It is instructive to compare the use of *to shite* when it comes after clauses that are in complete sentence-ending form. Here the feeling of the *shite* is indubitably active, and yet is very nearly the same as in the examples quoted above.

Banji tsugō yoku itta to shite itsu henji ga kuru deshō	Supposing that all goes well, when shall I receive the answer?
Sore wa yoi to shite hoka no mono wo shire	Consider that that is O.K. (i.e., satisfactorily done) and learn something else!

TO SHITE MO. A combination of *to*, the *-te* form of *suru*, and *mo*. It should present no difficulties to students who know the uses of its component parts.

It is referred to here to serve as a sort of appendix to the discussion of the "special use" of *to shite* discussed under TO SHITE.

1. Note that *to shite mo* and *ni shite mo* sometimes have practically the same effect. E.g.:

Katta to shite mo minakereba naranai	Even though we consider it as bought we must look at it.
Katta ni shite mo minakereba naranai	Even though we consider it bought we must look at it.

2. Note that when *to shite mo* is used in sequence, the additive force of the *mo . . . mo* becomes dominant:

Sensō no toki ni wa jōyō to shite mo yusōyō to shite mo taisetsuna mono de aru	In time of war it (the horse) is very important, both from the point of view of its use in riding, and from the point of view of its use in the transportation of materials.

TO SHITE WA. When this compound comes after a substantive, it may convey the idea that something is to be considered in the aspect indicated. Good English translation will of course vary with the context. (See also under -TE WA and NI.)

It may be used in either bungo or the colloquial. When used in the colloquial it usually gives a rather formal effect.

Kodomo to shite wa kanshin da	Considering him (in his aspect) as a child we admire (what he does).
Kanri to shite wa futsugō da	(When we consider him in his aspect) as an official, it is unbecoming conduct.
(Uma) Hashiru koto ga hayakute jōyō to shite wa kore ni masaru dōbutsu ga nai	(The horse) Its running is very fast, and as for its use in riding there is no (other) animal which excels it in this respect.

Note that the above meaning of *to shite wa* is possible only if *suru* is not used "transitively," with an *wo*, in the sense of "make" or "do."

> *Sonna hito wo sensei to shite*   It won't do to appoint a per-
> *wa ikemasen*   son like that a teacher.

Compare with NI SHITE WA. Strictly, *hito wo sensei to shite wa*
should mean "to put a person in the position of a teacher"; *hito
wo sensei ni shite wa* should mean "to turn a person into a
teacher. However, the distinction between *to suru* and *ni suru*
is often rather a fine one, and does not seem to be universally
observed.

TO SU. In addition to its regular uses as a combination of *to*
and the verb *su, suru,* there is a special use in bungo in which *to
su* acts as a copula, practically the equivalent of the colloquial
de aru, or the bungo *nari.* (Cf. TO SHITE.)

It has, however, a further sense of making an explanation and
hence may be added to *nari.*

This use of *to su* is often found in laws, rescripts, textbooks and
writings of that sort.

When *to su* comes after a verb in the Line 3 form *(shūshikei)*, it bears
a fairly close relationship to the colloquial *no desu.* The insertion of
mono before the *to su* does not change the meaning, but makes the
effect somewhat more concrete.

Note that the *to su* has a sort of "is to be considered" effect, like the
colloquial *to sarete iru.* Curiously enough this makes explanations
sound rather softer and less abrupt, but when used in laws definitely
strengthens the imperative force.

> *Sono genshō no shōzuru wa*   The development of that phe-
> *kono genin ni motozuku*   nomenon is due to this
> *mono to su*   cause.
>
> *Kore mo mata meishi no isshu*   This also is (to be considered)
> *nari to su*   a sort of noun.
>
> *Gojin wa ima kono ayamari*   We may now correct this
> *wo tadasamu to su*   error.
>
> *Kono kotoba wa mare ni*   This word is seldom used.
> *mochiyu to su*
>
> *Kaikei-kensainshoku wa*   Subordinate officials of the
> *ni-hyaku-jū-hachi wo motte*   committee for auditing the
> *tei-in to su*   finances are limited in num-
>   ber to 218. (Taken from an
>   *Imperial Rescript.*)

TO SURU. There is a special use of *to suru* which occasionally bothers students.

In this use the *to* is immediately preceded by a verb in the "dubitative" *-u, -yō* form in the colloquial, or the *-mu (-n)* form in bungo.

There is no one English form that will fit all cases. The best rendering depends on the context.

Take for example the phrase *ikō to shita*. Translated as literally as possible, this would be something like: "May-go, that-way he acted." That is. he acted in the "may-go" manner.

It depends on the context whether this means "He started to go," or "He made preparations to go," or "He made to go," or "He acted as if he were going," or "He decided to go," or "He was about to go," or in what particular way he acted in the "may-go" manner. Quite definitely, however, this sentence does not say that he did go.

For further discussion see under TO, part 2, both the bungo and the colloquial sections.

TOTE. A combination of *to* and *-te,* with two uses.

1. It may be a contraction of *to itte* 'thus saying', *to omotte* 'thus thinking', *to shite* 'thus doing', or similar *to . . . -te* forms.

It can probably be best understood as equivalent to "thus-ing."

Hototogisu hototogisu tote	Saying "Nightingale, nightingale!"
Karasu da tote minamina kuroi to wa kagiranu	To say that they are crows is not the same as saying that they are all black.
Sanpo sen tote uchi wo deta	(He) left the house with the intention of taking a walk. (Here *sen* is the bungo form *semu* equal to the colloquial *shiyo*.)
Sukina koto tote yoku yarimasu	It is what he likes and (so) he does it well.

Kono hito wa nani wo shita tote sō utsu no ka	What has this man done that you should beat him so? (More literally: You are beating him so, as having done what?)

There is sometimes difficulty in translating *tote* when it comes after clauses which express an idea of causality. Here *tote* retains its usual functions, but the idea conveyed can often be best rendered in English by some phrase like "take (something) as a reason."

As a bungo example:

Kono koto wo naseba tote aeta hokorubeki ni arazu	He must not dare to be proud, taking the doing of this act as a reason (. . . feeling "because I have done this thing").

As a colloquial example:

Karasu da kara tote kanarazushimo kuroi to wa kagiranai	It is not necessarily correct to say it is black when you take as a reason that it is a crow. (. . . saying "because it's a crow.")

The difficulty probably comes from the fact that in Japanese conjunctive forms like *-ba* or *-kara* are necessarily attached to the end of the first clause, while in English we put their equivalents at the beginning of the second clause.

2. It may be equivalent to *to mo*, or the *tote* of (I) plus *mo*, and so have a sense of "even if" or "supposing that."

(Kare wa) kane ga atta tote tsukaenai	Even if he had money he could not spend it.
(Kare wa) ikani kanemochi da kara tote sore wo kau koto ga dekinai	However much money he had, he could not buy that. (However much it be, "because I have money. . .")

Mō itta tote ma ni awanai	Even if I were to go now I'd be late. (Literally: Even if I had gone by now . . .)
Nani wo sureba tote kane ga nakute wa dekinu	Whatever one does, one can't do it without money. ("Even if it be anything one does . . .")

Naturally, the best English idiom to use in translation depends on the context, and can be determined only after the full force of *tote* is thoroughly understood. E.g.:

Ikani henka shita kara tote watakushi no me wo kuramasu koto wa dekimasen	However much he may count on having changed his appearance, it is impossible to pull the wool over my eyes.

Here the *tote* has much the force of *to iedomo, to itte mo, to omotte mo,* and the expressed order of thought is approximately: "How much 'I have transformed myself, and hence . . .' thus-thinking-even . . ."

TOTE WA. There is a very common use of this combination in which the *tote wa* acts like a sort of compound postposition meaning approximately "one that can be called a . . ." It seems to occur almost entirely in negative sentences.

Shitte iru mono tote wa hitori mo arimasen	There wasn't even a single person he could call an acquaintance.
Onna tote wa inai	There was no one here worth the name of woman.
Jishin no ato de tomaru yado tote wa naku taihen ni komaru	After the earthquake there was no house that could properly be called a place to stay in, and it was very troublesome.

TO WA. This combination may normally be taken as equivalent to *to iu no wa*. Occasionally the context calls for *omou* or some similar verb in place of *iu*.

Suteru kami mo areba tasukeru kami mo aru to wa yoku shita mono da	It is a fine arrangement that if there are deities who abandon you, there are also deities who help.

If it begins a sentence, the *to* of course refers to what has been said before.

To wa iwarenai	*That* can't be said.

If it ends a sentence, the *wa* acts like an exclamation; and the whole phrase has the feel of *to omou no wa*.

Kimi ga sonna koto wo iu to wa	To think that *you* say such things!

TO ZO. At the end of sentences *to zo* has a certain emphatic force. This is primarily a bungo use, and corresponds roughly with a colloquial *to sa*, " . . . so it is said!"

It seems to be most often used after descriptions of something rather unusual, and may then be translated by some phrase like "To think that . . . (this happens)." E.g.:

Ki ni noboru gyorui mo ari to zo	To think that there is a kind of fish that climbs trees!

In the epistolary style *to zo* is often used in the middle of sentences, but using *zo* with a force much like that of *zo* in the colloquial. (See zo.) E.g.:

Nani to zo go kimben kudasaretaku on negai moshi-age-sōrō	I humbly present my hope that you will somehow desire to give me your forgiveness. (I hope that you will please excuse me.)

Here *nani to zo* has almost exactly the force of the colloquial *dōzo*.

TSU. The eighteenth *kana* syllable in the "Table of 50 Sounds" (gojūon). In addition to its ordinary use as a syllable:

1. It may be used in Japanese words to indicate that the consonant sound in the next following *kana* symbol is to be duplicated. Consonants which may be duplicated in this way are k, s, t, and p. For example, the *kana* used in writing:

> *massugu,* are *ma, tsu, su, gu.*
> *katta,* are *ka, tsu, ta.*

2. It may be used in writing foreign words to represent the sound of "tsu," "tu," "ts," or "t." E.g.:

> "truth" would be written: *tsu, ru, -, su.*

Such foreign words are usually written with *katakana*.

3. In archaic times *tsu* was used as a postposition practically equivalent to *no*. Nowadays this *tsu* is found only in place-names and quotations from archaic writings.

-TSU. Bungo suffix added to the Line 2 form (*renyōkei*) of verbs.

It formed, in old bungo, what is practically equivalent to the English "perfect" tense. It is now obsolescent, except for the *-te* form, which is widely used in both bungo and colloquial. (See -TE.)

Some Japanese grammarians speak of it as indicating a quite recent past.

It may be considered as the Line 3 form (*shūshikei*) of the conjugation:

Line 1	*Mizenkei*	*-te*
Line 2	*Renyōkei*	*-te*
Line 3	*Shūshikei*	*-tsu*
Line 3A	*Rentaikei*	*-tsuru*
Line 4	*Izenkei*	*-tsure*
Line 5	*Meireikei*	*-te (yo)*

Kimi wo miteshi ga	Would I had seen you.
Hana sakitsu	The flowers have bloomed.
Hana wo mitsu	I have (just) seen the blossoms.

When *-tsu* is used in parallel sequence it has much the same force as the colloquial *-tari*.

tori no mietsu	the (alternate) appearing and
kakuretsu suru	disappearing of the birds

-TSURE, -TSURU. Bungo verb-endings. See under -TSU.

-TSUTA, -TSUTE. See under -TTA and -TTE.

-TSUTSU. A suffix indicating the continuation of an action. It is added only to the Line 2 form (*renyōkei*) of verbs.

Its use is very similar to that of *-nagara* when that is added to verbs of action except on one point. This point is that *-nagara* is used to indicate that two or more actions take place simultaneously while *-tsutsu* does not necessarily imply the existence of a second action. Thus:

Sake wo nomi-tsutsu danzuru	(They) converse while drink-
Sake wo nomi nagara danzuru	ing sake.

have almost exactly the same meaning; but *-nagara* could not be substituted for *-tsutsu* in sentences like:

Boku wa ima Doitsugo wo	I am now engaged in the study
kenkyū shi-tsutsu aru	of German.
Beikoku kaigun wa kono	The U.S. Navy is frantically
jumbi ni kyōhon shi-tsutsu	engaged in these prepara-
aru	tions.

-TT- A long or doubled "t" sound is not infrequently used in speech in place of a single "t."
Sometimes this "-tt-" sound is put down in writing.

-TTA. Standard abbreviation for the verb-endings *-rita*, *-chita*, and *-(h)ita* of first (*yodan*) conjugation verbs.

Also non-standard (*Kansai* dialect) abbreviation of the verb-ending *-rita* of *-riru* verbs of the second (*kami ichidan*) conjugation.

In *kana* it is written with the two syllables *tsu* and *ta*. (See introductory Note on Verbs.)

-TTARA. A contraction, not a true suffix. It is used only in informal speech, and may be:

1. A contraction of *to ittara*.
2. An indication of emphasis, something like an English "Gosh!", used after nouns or statements to indicate that there is something surprising or unusual about them. The derivation of this *-ttara* is not clear. It is sometimes written and pronounced *tara*.

Ano ko-ttara gambari no tsuyoi yatsu da naa	That kid—gosh!—he's got a lot of stick-to-it-iveness, hasn't he?

The expression *-ttara nai* indicates that something is almost unbelievable.

Hito wo baka ni suru-ttara nai	And the way he treats one like a fool—it's incredible!

-TTATTE. A forceful alternative for *-tte mo*, quite often heard in speech. It has much the force of "even if," "although," etc.

Ittatte dame da	Even if you do go, it won't be any use.
Ikura ibattatte kimi ni wa kore ga dekimai	However much you may swagger, I don't think you can do this.

-TTE. This is a contraction. It is written in *kana* with the two syllables *tsu* and *te*. (つて). (See also -KUTTE.)

It may be:

1. The standard abbreviation for the verb-endings *-rite, -chite,* and *-(h)ite* of verbs of the first (*yodan*) conjugation, or the non-standard (Western Japan) abbreviation for the verb-ending *-rite* of *-riru* verbs of the second (*-iru, kami ichidan*) conjugation. (See introductory Note on Verbs.)

2. An abbreviation of *to iu* or *de atte*. It is found after nouns or at the end of a complete sentence.

Onna-tte sō shita mono sa	That is the way with women.

3. A suffix or pseudo-suffix attached to the colloquial *-ta* or *-da* forms of verbs. This has the force of a strong *-temo* and is usually followed by some expression like *shikata-ga-nai,* meaning "It's no use."

It gives to the verb to which it is attached a subjunctive force, like that of the suffix *-temo.* However, as this verb is already in the *-ta* form, which indicates completion, the final force is more emphatic than that of *-temo.* It is much like that of an English "Even if one did . . ." or "Even if one does . . . ."

The exact derivation is not clear. Its use seems to be commonest after the contracted *-tta* forms.

Asettatte shikata-ga-nai	There's no use hurrying. (Even if one did hurry, no use in it.)
Kangaetatte shiyō-ga-nai	Even if you did think about it, it would not do any good.
Kuyandatte shiyō-ga-nai	Even if you do regret it, there's nothing one can do about it.
Ittatte shiyō-ga-nai	Even if I did (do) go it would be no use.
Nani wo iutatte shinjinai	Whatever (he) may say, (I) won't believe it.

In this last example note that the interrogative is affected exactly as if a *mo* had been expressed. *Iutatte* is a Kyoto form of *ittatte.*

4. An equivalent of *te,* used as a substitute for *to* or *to itte,* or, sometimes, *to iu no wa.* This use occurs only in very informal speech. Cf. TE.

-TTE BA. After an order which has not been obeyed, the order may be repeated with a *-tte ba* added. E.g.:

Hayaku tabero-tte ba	I told you to eat quickly!

The *-tte* is apparently a contraction of *to itte,* and the *ba* an emphatic particle, but the derivation is not wholly clear. The phrase may come from *to ieba.*

-U.   A suffix, with three distinct uses. It may be added to:
1. The Line 1 form (*mizenkei*) of verbs.
2. Adjective "roots."
3. Imperative forms ending in *-e.*

See also -UDA, -UDE and -UTA, -UTE.

1. It may be added to the Line 1 form (*mizenkei*) of verbs. In the standard Tokyo colloquial *-u* is added to the *mizenkei* of verbs of the first (*yodan*) conjugation, and to that of *-masu.* (Cf. under -YŌ.)

The vowel sound at the end of the *mizenkei* is in speech usually combined with the *-u* so as to be pronounced like a long *o* (*-ō*). The usual Romanization is to the *-ō* form.

From *aru* 'be' we get *arau,* usually pronounced *arō.*
From *iu* 'say' we get *iwau,* usually pronounced *iwō.*
From *matsu* 'wait' we get *matau,* usually pronounced *matō.*
From *imasu* 'be' we get *imaseu,* usually pronounced *imashō.*

Note that *deshō* (*desu*) may be considered a contraction of *de arimashō.*

This *-u* was derived from the bungo *-mu,* and apparently at one time was added to all verbs. It is still so added in certain non-Tokyo (and therefore non-standard) dialects. *Kuru, suru,* and verbs of the *ichidan* (*-iru* and *-eru*) conjugations in the standard colloquial add *-yō* in place of *-u.* Examples of the non-standard use of *-u* are:

From	Standard	Dialect	Pronunciation
kuru 'come'	*koyō*	*kou*	*kō*
suru 'do'	*shiyō*	*seu*	*shō*
miru 'see'	*miyō*	*miu*	*miyu, myū*
taberu 'eat'	*tabeyō*	*tabeu*	*tabyu, tabyō*

These forms are used to indicate an "absence of positivity," a suggestion that the speaker or writer for some reason does not wish to make a positive statement.

They are sometimes classed as "dubitative" forms.

Reasons for not being positive may be that the reference is to the future, about which no one can be positive; or that though the reference is to the past or present, the speaker is not sure of his

facts; or that he wishes confirmation from the person spoken to;
or that he simply wishes to be polite; etc.

The -*u* and -*yō* forms thus have a wide usage.   Examples are:

References to the future:

Asu wa ame ga furō	Tomorrow it will probably rain.
Soko de shinō to omotte itta no da	(He) went thinking that (he) would die there.

Doubt about past or present facts:

Tōkyō ni itta n'deshō	It is probable that he has gone to Tokyo.
Sore wa omoshirokarō	I should think it would be interesting.

Wishing confirmation:

Saa, ikō	Well then, let's go. (Shall we?)
Ikō ja nai ka	Let's go—how about it?

Politeness when explaining to others:

Kore goran—Omote dake de ura no hō wa somete nai deshō	Look at this! It is printed only on the front, and not on the back, you see (it seems) .

Supposition:

Hito mo arō ni kimi ga sonna koto wo iu to wa	Of all possible people, that *you* should say such a thing! [With (the fact that) other people too may exist . . .]

Natural expectation:

Akambō ja arumaishi sonna koto wa shitteru darō	You aren't, I think, a babe in arms and so you are expected to know that sort of thing.

It is not possible (nor desirable) to classify all the uses of the
-*u* and -*yō* forms, or to put them into neat little cubby-holes. But
from the examples given the student should be able to get the
necessary "feel."

See, however, also under TO and TO SURU.

2. It may be added to adjective roots. When so used it is
equivalent to -*ku*, from which it is derived. In the standard
Tokyo dialect it is always used before *gozaru*, but may be used
also before *suru, irassharu,* and *zonjiru.* Except before *gozaru,*
its use is rare in the standard Tokyo dialect. (See -KU.)

In the standard speech:

>
> -*au* is pronounced *ō* (long)
> -*iu* is pronounced *ū* (long)
> -*uu* is pronounced *ū* (long)
> -*ou* is pronounced *ō* (long)

In the *Kansai* -*u* is often used for -*ku,* in any position, thus the
Tokyo standard *akakute* will often be pronounced *akaute-akōte.*

In bungo, especially in the Kyoto Court language, this euphonic
softening is practically standard. For example, *mattaku su* 'fulfill'
becomes *mattau su* (pronounced *mattōsu*).

3. It may be used as a colloquial suffix to imperatives, but only
to imperatives ending with an "e" sound.

It combines with the previous "e" to produce a "yo" sound and
is definitely rude and abrupt in feeling. For example, *kureu* is
pronounced *kuryo,* and may be considered a rude form of the
imperative *kure yo.*

The pronunciation of the *yo* sound is usually about half-way
between a long *yō* and a short *yo.*

-UDA, -UDE. Local (Kyoto) contractions of the -*ta* and -*te*
forms of -*mu* (M) verbs of the first conjugation.

For example, standard Tokyo contractions for *nomu* 'drink' are
nonda and *nonde.* The Kyoto forms are *nouda* and *noude.* See
introductory Note on Verbs.

-UTA, -UTE. Contractions, more common in the Kyoto dialect
than in standard Tokyo speech.

1. As verb endings, -*uta* and -*ute* are contractions of the -*ta* and -*te* forms of (H) verbs of the first conjugation.

For example, the more common (standard Tokyo) contractions for *omou* (*o-mo-hu*) 'think' are *omotta* and *omotte*. The usual Kyoto pronunciations have a long *ō* sound, *omouta* and *omoute*.

Even in Tokyo, however, the -*ta* and -*te* forms of the very polite and formal verb *tamau* (*ta-ma-hu*) are *tamauta* and *tamaute*. See introductory Note on Verbs.

2. As a suffix to an adjective root, -*ute* is a common contraction of the standard suffix -*kute*.

For example, in the standard Tokyo dialect we have for the adjective *omoshiroi* 'interesting', the -*ku* form *omoshiroku* and the -*kute* form *omoshirokute,* which corresponds in meaning to "being interesting" or "be interesting and . . . ." The usual Kyoto form is *omoshiroute*.

WA. A postposition, usually written with the *kana* symbol for *ha*.

According to Japanese grammarians its original function was *hai-ta-teki* 'exclusive'. That is, it set what it followed apart from other ideas.

In practice, it is used to show what one is talking about, and so may be considered as marking a "psychological subject," with the rest of the sentence being a "psychological predicate."

It does not, however, in itself show a correspondence to any particular English grammatical relationship. Whether or not the "psychological subject" is also the grammatical subject of a sentence depends wholly on the context. As will be seen from the examples, it may even correspond to a direct object.

Furthermore, *wa* not only sets what it follows apart from other ideas, but in so doing suggests that there is in the user's mind some thought of comparison with ideas in the same class as the idea that has been mentioned.

Wa may be thought of as a sort of oral parenthesis mark, approximating in its effect to an English "as for (this)," or "talking about (this)."

For examples of how *wa* may be used, see not only the following but also under DE WA, -TE WA, NO DE WA, NO NI WA, TO SHITE WA, NI SHITE WA, TOTE WA, and NI WA.

Wa may be used after a word or phrase which is the grammatical subject of a sentence.

Kore wa empitsu desu	This is a pencil.
Anata wa doko e ikimasu ka	Where are you going?

It may be used after a word or phrase which corresponds more or less to a grammatical direct object.

Kono ie wa chichi ga tatemashita	This house my father put up.
Sankōsho nado wa go tsugō no yoi toki ni o-kaeshi negaimasu	As for the reference books, etc., we request (their) return at your convenience. (From a business letter.)
Q. *Kore wo yonda ka*	Have you read this?
A. *Sore wa zutto mae ni yonda*	That? I read it a long time ago.

It may be used after a word or phrase that corresponds more or less to a grammatical indirect object.

Boku wa hito no seishitsu ga yoku wakaru	I have an insight into character. [More literally: . . . (it) is clear to me.]

It may be used after adverbs or adverbial phrases:

Tsukue no ue ni wa empitsu ga aru	On the table there are pencils.
Shiroku wa ikemasen ga	(Making it) white is impossible.

The force of *wa* is perhaps especially clear in phrases where it comes between duplicated words.

Fune wa fune da ga shōsen ka gunkan ka wakaranu	The "ship" is a ship (all right) but it is not clear whether it is a merchantman or a warship.

Mi wa mita ga sukoshimo As for seeing it, I saw it, but
  omoshiroku-nakatta   it wasn't in the least inter-
                               esting.

Inasmuch as *wa* in itself suggests comparison it is natural that it should be often used in compound sentences where one idea is expressly compared to another.

Watakushi wa iku ga ano hito *I* will go, but *he* won't.
  wa ikanai
Asa wa iku ga yoru wa ikanai Mornings (I) will go, but evenings (I) will not go.
Nomi wa shita ga tabe wa (I) have drunk, but (I) have
  shinai   not eaten.

Note that in the last two sentences the subject was not expressed. There is no reason that it should not have been expressed as, say, *watakushi wa,* to give us three *wa* strung together, as:

Watakushi wa nomi wa shita I have drunk, but not eaten.
  ga tabe wa shinai

There is a special use of *wa* after words of quantity or measurement. Its insertion does not greatly affect the sense if the sentence is a positive statement, but it may affect the sense greatly if the sentence is negative.

Sukoshi motte imasu (I) have a little.
Sukoshi wa motte imasu (I) have *a little.*

Kono kotoba wa mina All these words are not clear
  wakaranai   (i.e., I don't understand any of them).
Kono kotoba wa mina wa *All* these words are not clear
  wakaranai   (i.e., I don't understand all of them, but I do understand most. Not all these words are clear).

When *wa* occurs at the end of sentences it may indicate simply an inversion, as:

Demo keshikaranu yatsu da Gracious, he's an outrageous
 ne . . . ano Taguchi to iu fellow, isn't he? . . . that
 otoko wa man Taguchi!

or it may be definitely used as an exclamation, as in:

Kore wa omoi wa This is heavy, ugh!
Kimi ga sonna koto wo iu To think that *you* should say
 to wa such a thing!

THE COLLOQUIAL USE OF "WA" AND "GA" COMPARED

There is, among non-Japanese, a certain tendency to confusion between *wa* and *ga,* owing to the fact that both may be used after the grammatical subject of a sentence, and a short discussion may be useful.

Reference to the article on *ga* will show that the function of *ga* is different from that of *wa.* *Ga* clearly marks a concept as a grammatical subject important in itself, and forms a close link with another concept, either a verb or a substantive (noun). *Wa* marks a "psychological subject" (i.e., "what one is talking about"), forms a rather loose link with a "psychological predicate," and suggests comparison with other subjects of the same class.

There are, of course, times when the functions overlap, and it will make no particular difference which is used, but usually the distinction is quite marked. Take for example the sentences:

(1) . . . *ii n'desu* It is good. (It's all right.)
(2) *Kore wa ii n'desu* As for this one, it's good. (This one is good.)
(3) *Kore ga ii n'desu* This in especial is good.

In (1) there is no subject expressed—a very common state of affairs in Japanese sentences. In (2) the very fact that the subject is named at all lays a certain stress on it. The *wa* suggests a comparison with other things which may not be good. In (3), however, the stress on the subject is deliberate and definite. The *ga* focuses attention on the subject, and does not in itself suggest any comparison with other things.

Consider also the remarks:

(1) *Ii—Warui*   It's good. It's bad.
(2) *Kore wa ii—Sore wa warui* As for this one, it's good. As
                                              for that, it's bad.
(3) *Kore ga ii—Sore ga warui* This in especial is good, that
                                              in especial is bad.

Here (1) could make sense only if accompanied by some motion
of the hand or action of the body. As what one is talking about
has to be expressed, no particular stress is laid on it by the form
of (2), and what stress there is remains with the contrasting
predicate. In (3), however, the stress on the "this" and "that" is
deliberate and definite.

Consider further the phrases:

(1) *Tori ga tobu toki ni . . .*   At the time when birds fly . . .
(2) *Tori wa tobu toki ni . . .*   As for the birds, at the time
                                              when they fly . . .

In (1) a stress is laid on *tori,* and it is closely linked to its verb
tobu. The whole expression *tori ga tobu* therefore modifies **toki**.
But in (2) *tori* is marked as the psychological subject of the whole
following sentence, and is not rigidly linked to *tobu* alone.

Consequently both (1) and (2) may be followed by expressions in which *tori* is the subject, e.g., "they flap their wings this
way." But only (1) may be followed by expressions of which *tori*
is not the subject, e.g., "I always want to fly too."

As a further example one might compare the phrases:

                    (1) *Yoshida kun wa Eigo ga tokui da*

and

                    (2) *Yoshida kun wa Eigo wa tokui da*

They both convey the idea that for Mr. Yoshida English is a
strong point. The difference is that (1) is complete in thought;
(2) suggests some comparison with English, say mathematics or
history, which perhaps may not be strong points.

It may be added that it is usually natural to use *ga* to mark a
subject when it is referred to for the first time, as then a certain

stress on it is usually intended. It is almost always more natural to use *wa* when referring to it later on.

Note also that interrogative pronouns, when used as subjects, can never be followed by *wa*.

Dare ga kimashita ka	Who has come?
Dore ga ii	Which is better?

WAI. An expression used at the end of sentences to indicate that the emotion is strong. It is now apparently confined to rather low-class speech.

Washi nanimo shiran' wai	I don't know a damn thing.

WO. A postposition. It marks a substantive as presented for action to be taken on it.

There are only slight differences in the use of *wo* in bungo and the colloquial. These will be referred to in the discussion.

To a Japanese the use of *wo* is extremely simple. It always gives the feeling "here is something presented for action to be taken on it."

The difficulties found by foreigners arise chiefly from the fact that many Japanese verbs have no exact English equivalents, and that the conceptions of "transitive" and "intransitive" are foreign to Japanese grammar.

There are verbs which indicate a direct action on something else, and which may always be called "transitive," e.g., *toru* 'grasp', *tasukeru* 'save'. With such verbs *wo* marks what corresponds to a direct object.

There are verbs which do not indicate any action at all, and which may always be called "intransitive," e.g., *aru* 'be', etc. With such verbs *wo* cannot be used.

There are verbs which refer primarily to the action of the subject, and which may or may not indicate action "on something else." These may be called transitive or intransitive, according to how they are used. For example, *Kōgun wo yorokonda* 'He enjoyed the marching' (transitive) ; *Yume ka to yorokonda,* 'He rejoiced, wondering if it were not a dream' (intransitive) .

There are verbs which might be called "self-acting," as they

refer to direct action on the subject rather than on anything else,
e.g., *deru* 'come out' or 'out oneself'; *tasukaru* 'be saved' or 'save
oneself'. Such verbs are certainly intransitive, from our point of
view at any rate, yet what they "act on" may be marked with
wo.

The foregoing is of course not a complete classification of
Japanese verbs, but it will serve the present purpose. Such as it
is, it refers to simple verbs only, and not to "passive," "potential,"
"causative," "desiderative," or other compound forms made by
the addition of *-rareru, -saseru, -tai,* etc.

In the following discussion an attempt has been made to give
separate treatment to the various ways in which the word or
phrase marked by *wo* is "acted on" by the various kinds of verbs.
Nevertheless, however various the ways may seem to us, the
student should remember that to the Japanese these ways all
seem much the same, and he should try to get the "feel" of *wo*
in the same way that they do.

1. The word or phrase marked by *wo* may be acted on as if
it were the direct object of a transitive verb. This is the most
common use of *wo,* and presents no difficulties to foreigners.

The real difficulty for the foreigner is that of getting the true meaning
of the Japanese verbs.

Hon wo yonde iru	(He) is reading a book.
Mizu wo nomu	(He) drinks water.
Kare wa ano onna no bōshi wo warau	He laughs at her hat (derides her hat).
Shōri wo yorokonde iru	They are rejoicing at the victory (enjoying the victory).
Natsuyasumi wo asobi ni iku no desu	He has gone to enjoy himself on his summer vacation (. . . to enjoy his summer vacation).
Saki wo arasou	They fight over the front place (. . . contest the front place).
Hito no kuru no wo matte iru	(He) is awaiting the coming of someone.

Note that what precedes the *wo* is necessarily a substantive *in thought,* but not necessarily a substantive *in form.*

Thus in the preceding example the substantival *no* may be omitted without any danger of confusion:

Hito no kuru wo matte iru   (He) is awaiting the coming of someone.

As an example of the difficulty of getting at the full meaning of a Japanese verb, take for example *tasukeru* 'help', 'save', etc. This may always be considered a "transitive" verb, and what is marked by *wo* corresponds to a direct object.

Oboreru hito wo tasuketa   (He) saved a drowning person.

Hito no shigoto wo tasuketa   (He) helped a person in his work (. . . helped a person's work) .

Kore wa seikō wo tasuketa   This contributed to success (. . . helped success) .

Ayaui inochi wo tasuketa   (He) saved an endangered life (someone else's life) .

2. The word or phrase marked by *wo* may be acted on when the verb used is a "self-acting" verb.   (See definition above.)

Japanese grammarians give as the "standard" type of such sentences those in which the subject is in movement, and the *wo* marks the place moved through, on, or away from.

Michi wo aruku   Walk on the street (walk the street) .

Sora wo tobu   Fly in the sky (fly the sky) .

Ie wo deru   Go out of the house (leave the house) .

Kyōto wo tatsu   Start out from Kyoto (leave Kyoto) .

Hashi wo wataru   Cross over the bridge (cross the bridge) .

Ichinichijū daidokoro wo hataraku no desu   All day long I work in the kitchen.

This last is perhaps not "good" Japanese, but it is a type of phrase one is likely to hear.

Note, however, that the "standard" type has in practice been extended to include the time worked through, when it emphasizes the time as in sentences such as:

Kono nagai jikan wo	(I) have been working this
hataraite ita	long time.

Also that it has been extended to include situations moved through or away from. E.g.:

Ayaui inochi wo tasukatta	He escaped a situation where his life was in danger. (Cf. with rather similar sentence in paragraph 1 above.)
Ame no naka wo kasa wo sasanaide dete itta	He went out into the rain without putting up his umbrella.
Osome-Hisamatsu wo ji de yuku	(They) play the parts of Osome and Hisamatsu (in life, not on the stage) .

3. The word or phrase marked by *wo* may be the direct object of a "passive" verb, i.e., one in the *-reru, -rareru* form.

This is because a Japanese "passive" is not the same as an English passive, and may indicate that the subject undergoes an action performed by somebody or something else. The *wo* will then mark what is acted on by what may be called the "root-meaning" of the verb, not the "passive" part of it; e.g., in the following examples, *miru, yaku,* and *tasukeru.*

Watakushi wa tansho wo miru	I see the shortcomings.
Watakushi wa tansho wo mirareru	I undergo the seeing of shortcomings. (I have my shortcomings seen.)

The person who does the seeing in the second sentence is marked by the postposition *ni.* See -NI, part 3, pp. 199-200.

Watakushi wa hito ni tansho wo mirareru	I have my shortcomings seen by others. (I undergo the seeing of my shortcomings by others.)

Kaji de ie wo yakareta hito . . .   People who had their houses burned in a fire . . .

Watakushi wa ano hito ni ayaui tokoro wo tasukerareta   I was saved by him from a dangerous situation.

4. The word or phrase marked by *wo* may be acted on by a "causative" verb. (Cf. under the "causative" suffixes *-su, -seru, -shimu,* etc.) In such sentences the *wo* may be used in two ways.

(a) It may mark the person or thing which is caused to perform the action, as in:

Watakushi wa jochū wo mi ni ikaseta   I sent the maid to see. (I caused the maid to go to see.)

(b) It may mark what is acted on by what may be called the "root-meaning" of the verb, not the causative part of it. In such sentences the person or thing caused to perform the action is marked by *ni* (not by a second *wo*). This device avoids the confusion that might possibly be caused by the presence of two *wo* in the same clause. (Cf. WO SHITE.)

Haha wa ko ni kusuri wo nomaseru   The mother causes the child to drink the medicine (. . . causes the drinking of the medicine by the child).

Note that if the "passive" form of a causative is used the subject undergoes the action of causing, and *ni* indicates the person (or thing) who does the causing:

Haha wa ko ni kusuri wo nomaserareru   The mother is caused by the child to drink medicine (. . . undergoes the causing).

5. The word or phrase marked by *wo* may be acted on by a verb or verb-phrase expressing likes or dislikes, ability or inability. It should be noted that there are certain phrases of this type

in which the use of *wo* is usually avoided.   (Cf. -ERU, -RERU, -TAI.)
E.g.:

Ano hito wa kore ga suki desu	That person likes this.
Biiru ga nomitai	(I) want to drink some beer.
Anata wa kanji ga yomeru ka	Can you read Chinese characters?

However, even in this type of sentence it is possible to use a *wo*, especially if something is very definitely "presented for action to be taken on it." E.g.:

(Q) *Kore wo o-suki desu ka*	Do you like *this?*
(A) *Ha, sore ga suki desu*	Yes, I do like it.

Note that the first sentence places great emphasis on the *kore* (which might well refer to something held out for examination). Similarly:

Kono kanji wo anata wa *yomeru ka*	This Chinese character—can you read it?

The *ga* . . . -*tai* and *wo* . . . -*tai* constructions seem to be running a race for popularity.   It may be said that forms like *biiru ga nomitai* have a head start, and are favored by conservative and careful speakers.   However, forms like *biiru wo nomitai* are apparently gaining favor, especially among the younger generation.

It should perhaps be added that there seems to be a strong tendency to avoid the use of *wo* in negative sentences, so that one often comes across such constructions as:

Sonna hito wa futsū ni *shimbun wa yomanai*	Such people as that usually do not read newspapers.

However, it will be used, even with negatives, if there is any reason for doing so.   In the following sentence, *wo* would naturally be used to give an effect of balance.

Shimbun wo yomu hito mo
    shimbun wo yomanai hito
    mo rajio-fuan desu
	Both the people who read
	newspapers and those who
	do not read newspapers, are
	radio fans.

6. A phrase marked by *wo* may not be acted on by any particular verb. In the colloquial this usually occurs when *wo* follows *no, mono, tokoro,* and similar words. (See also MONO WO.)

In this use the *no, mono,* or *tokoro* is used to substantivize a clause which describes some state of affairs. The following clause then refers to action taken or to be taken in regard to the state of affairs described. If there is no following clause the *wo* simply indicates that here is a state of affairs that calls for action to be taken on it.

Sekkaku kita no wo tada kaesu	He came, with much inconvenience to himself—and they just send him home!
Kore hodo iu no wo wakaranai no ka	I tell you all this (talk up to this extent) —and you don't understand?
Benkyō sureba seikō-suru mono wo naze shinai	If you work hard (at your studies) you will be successful—why don't you do it?

A similar use may occur in bungo without any formal "substantivizing" of the previous sentence.

Yuki furu wo bōshi wo kaburazu	The snow falls, and (yet) he does not put on his hat.

This is sometimes called an "adversative" use of wo, in which the *wo* means "in spite of the fact that." Matsuura, for example, gives the colloquial equivalent of the above example as *Yuki ga furu no ni bōshi wo kaburanai.*

It is undoubtedly true that this is the usual effect of *wo* used in this way. Nevertheless it seems equally true that the "adversative" effect comes from the context, and is not inherent in the *wo* itself. For example, such a sentence as:

Shingen wa abunai tokoro wo tasukatta	Shingen escaped from a dangerous situation.

is probably best rendered as indicated. Compare the discussion under NO NI.

Perhaps two more examples will clear up this use of *wo*. The first is bungo and is not "adversative," that is, there is no suggestion of "in spite of the fact that":

Reman shōgun mo gasu no tame ni chissoku shi itaru wo Doitsuhei ni hakken-seraretari	General Leman also was suffocated by the gas, and (in that situation) was found by the German soldiers.

The next example is colloquial, and is "adversative" in effect, although the *wo* is not preceded by *no, mono,* or *tokoro.*

Toriwake o-isogashii naka wo isshūkan mo o-hima wo itadakimashite makotoni arigatō zonjimasu	I am truly grateful to have received from you all of a week's leave, in spite of the fact that you are particularly busy.

Note that the adversative effect comes from the context, even if, in English, we replace "in spite of the fact that" by a simple "when." Both these examples, by the way, are taken from the Japanese school readers.

Examples of leaving off any following clause and ending with *wo* are:

Benkyō sureba seikō-suru mono wo . . .	If you work hard you will be successful . . . (that is the situation presented to you for action).
Inochi-bakari wa o-tasuke wo Iesusu wa anata ni tanoshimi wo motosaran koto wo	Only spare my life! May Jesus bring you happiness!

This last example was taken from a modern Christmas card. The *-n* of *motosaran* equals a bungo *-mu.*

7. The student should note the Japanese habit of omitting unnecessary parts of a sentence when such omissions are obvious from the context. A few examples where *wo* helps to supply the necessary clue are:

Kore wo kakitome ni negaimasu	I request that you register this.
Ue wo shita e to sawaide . . .	Being excited so that everything was turned topsy-turvy . . .
Watakushi no koto wo kyōjin datte	Talking about me, he said I was a lunatic!

Perhaps one of the best examples is supplied by Yamada, who refers to two famous *haiku* (17-syllable poems). The *wo* indicates action, the *ni* quiescence.

Kome-arau	In front of the washer of rice
mae wo hotaru no	two or three fireflies (flit
futatsu mitsu	by).

Kome-arau	Just in front of the washer of
mae ni hotaru no	rice two or three fireflies
futatsu mitsu	(she sees, on the leaves, not flying).

In these two poems the moods suggested correspond to the scene. The first is almost an omen that the lady's lover is near, and so suggests active emotion. The second suggests quiet thought and longing.

WO BA. An emphasized form of *wo*. (See BA.)

WO MOTTE. See MOTTE.

WO SHITE. A combination of the postposition *wo* and the *te* form of *suru* 'do', 'make', 'act', etc.

In most contexts its meaning is quite clear, but there is a special bungo usage which may bother the student. This is found when there is a special need or desire to point out who or what is "acted on." Particularly in causative sentences (where *wo* and *ni* may be required to mark other words), *wo shite* may be used to mark the "indirect subject," i.e., the person who is caused to act. (Cf NI.) E.g.:

Shujin genan wo shite machi ni shinamono wo kai ni ikasu	The master sends the servant to the town to buy goods (. . . "acting on" the servant causes him to go . . .).
Hito wo shite shiru koto atawazarashimu	(They) make it impossible for a person to know.

It is the custom to use *wo shite* whenever the causative suffix *-shimu* is used, even when the sense would be obvious without the addition of *shite* to the *wo*.

WO YA. A combination of the particles *wo* and *ya*. The *wo* retains its usual effect of "presenting something for action." The *ya* normally has the effect of making the phrase a rhetorical question.

The most common use of *wo ya* is at the end of a phrase which has been introduced by *iwanya* (*iwamuya*). E.g.:

Seijin dani shikari iwanya warera wo ya	Even the saints are like that— how much more we!

The force of *iwanya* being "shall I say it?" or "need I say it?", the "feel" of the final phrase is "Is there any use asking about us?"

The *iwanya . . . wo ya* combination is quite common in the colloquial, and may be rendered by various English idioms.

Kare wa keizaigaku sura yoku wakaranai—iwanya marukusu shugi wo ya da	He knows little even about economics (in general)—to say nothing of Marxism!

In bungo, without an introductory *iwanya*, it depends on the context whether the rhetorical question is one which calls for the answer "No!" or simply one to which no answer is expected.

An example of the first type (from the 8th century Imperial Rescripts) is:

Ame no shita no koto wo ya tayasuku okonawamu	Shall I easily perform the task of (ruling) the whole country?

An example of the second type (from the present school reader, Vol. VIII) is:

Kuni ni haha wo ya	Has he perhaps left a mother
nokosuramu	back home (in his home
	province) ?

YA. A particle with various uses.   (See also WO YA, YA INA YA, -IYA, -NYA.)

It should be noted that in all its uses this particle has a rather soft effect.   There is nothing hard and sharp about it.

THE COLLOQUIAL

The following are the purely colloquial uses of *ya*.

Note that occasionally one may hear other uses of *ya*, such as *ya ina ya*. (See YA INA YA.)   These other uses, however, may be considered as borrowings or quotations from bungo.

1. It may be used as a sort of oral exclamation-mark.   When so used it is somewhat like *yo*, but less sharp and positive.   It may occur:

(a)   After personal names, etc., as a vocative.   This is a quite common use.

Saburō ya saa ikō	Hi, Saburō! Let's go now!

(b)   As an imperative particle, like *yo, ro,* or *i,* but with a somewhat softer effect.

Hayaku koi ya	Come quickly!
Sore (wo) miya	Look at that!
Sonna koto wo suru	Don't do things like that!
na ya	

(c)   After the negative *-nai* and "dubitative" *-u, -yō* forms of verbs.   When so used it seems to have only a slight exclamatory effect.

Boku wa shiranaiya	I don't know!
Motto yomō ya	Let us read more!
Tenisu wo shiyō ya	Let's play tennis!

2. It may be used as a connective, either between substantives or between statements.

(a) In connecting substantives *ya* is somewhat like *to*, but much less precise and exact. It gives the impression that the substantives connected are lumped together in the mind of the writer or speaker; also that there has been no precise enumeration.

Tsukue no ue ni wa hon ya   On the desk there are books
   empitsu ya pen ga aru   and pencils and pens (and
                                      probably other things too).

In the usual colloquial *ya* is not added after the final substantive. It may be so added, however, and in bungo often is.

(b) In connecting statements *ya* is usually followed by *tadachi ni*, or some similar phrase indicating immediacy. (But cf. the corresponding use in bungo.) This indicates that the second statement follows "just as soon as" the first occurred.

This use is similar to that of *to*, discussed under TO, in the colloquial section of part 2. It is much more common in writing than in speech.

Ki-Bei suru ya tadachi ni   Just as soon as (he) arrived
  Ruzuveruto daitōryō ni   home in America he brought
  sono teian wo motarashita   these proposals to President
  (newspaper Japanese)   Roosevelt.

3. *Ya* may be used in place of *wa*. When used in this way in ordinary informal speech it is most commonly found separating a verbal noun [i.e., a Line 2 form (*renyōkei*) of a verb] from a following form of *suru*. Such sentences are definitely emphatic. E.g.:

Yomi wa shinai   (He) does *not* read. (As for
Yomi ya shinai   reading, he doesn't.)

There is at most only a shade of difference between the two Japanese sentences given above, and the colloquial use of *ya* for *wa* may be considered as due to convenience in speech, *ombin*. Compare, however, with the corresponding bungo use of *ya*.

BUNGO

In bungo *ya* has uses corresponding to the colloquial uses, but somewhat wider in scope. It has also at least two further uses.

One is that of expressing doubt or interrogation, which does not occur at all in the colloquial except in one or two stereotyped phrases borrowed or quoted from bungo. The other occurs in poetry, especially *haiku*.

1. It may be used as an exclamatory particle, practically an interjection, which may be introduced into a sentence almost anywhere.

When so used it may be considered as an emphatic particle, with at least a suggestion of connection to other ideas.

Ji ya koko wo saru iku sen ri	My child! Away from here how many thousand miles!
Kokoroshite ike yo ya	Go carefully!
Ureshi ya tanoshi ya	What joy! What happiness!
Naniwa ni saku ya kono hana . . .	These flowers (which bloom in Naniwa!) . . .
Yo no naka wa ika ni ya ika ni	Life is such—is such!

In poetry or rhythmic prose *ya* may be used as an interjection without much meaning in order to give the proper number of syllables to a line. (This does not apply to *ya* after substantives in *haiku*, etc., for which see paragraph 4 below.)

Ōmi no ya	At Kagami Mountain,
Kagami-no-yama ni . . .	in Ōmi. . . .

2. *Ya* may be used as a connective, either between substantives or between statements.

(a) As a connective between substantives *ya* has much the same effect as in the colloquial. It is, however, more common in bungo to add a *ya* to the final substantive.

Ringo ya nashi ya nado wo natsukashige ni motarite kui nado suru	(They) do such things as eagerly take and eat apples and pears and so forth.
Mina hito wa chō ya hana ya to isogu hi mo . . .	. . . and days when everybody runs around talking about butterflies and flowers.

There is also, however, the "dubitative" use of *ya,* which is discussed in section 5 below, which accounts for such a phrase as *oya ya shinrui* having sometimes more the force of "parents *or* relations" than that of "parents *and* relations."

(b) As a connective between statements *ya* indicates that when. the first occurs the second follows. It is not commonly followed, as in the colloquial, by any phrase indicating immediacy.

The final verb of the first statement is properly put in the Line 3A form *(rentaikei)* .

Yo ga saki ni kono shōcho wo	When I previously published
ōyake ni seshi ya saiwai ni	this little book, even though
kōko no kangei suru tokoro	fortunately it happened that
to narishi mo . . .	it was well received by the
	public . . .

3. *Ya* may be used in place of *wa.* In bungo this seems to be always deliberate, not *ombin.* (Cf. the Colloquial, section 3.) ·

The effect, especially in poetry, is to put a particular emphasis on the thought marked by *ya.* (Cf. *ya* in poetry, under section 4 below.)

Haru wa yuku	Spring goes.
Haru ya yuku	Spring! It goes!
Mezurashi to	"Marvelous," I say
Miru mono goto ni	And with each separate
Haru ya yuku	thing I see
	Springtime fades away!

4. In poetry, especially *haiku, ya* performs a special function when it follows a substantive which is not directly connected with a following verb.

In this use it draws special attention to the substantive, and indicates that it is to be thought of in connection with the rest of the poem. This is obviously a not very great extension of the original use of *ya* as an exclamatory particle.

Furu ike ya	An ancient pond!
Kawazu tobikomu	And the plash of the water
Mizu no oto	When a frog jumps in!

Araumi ya	How rough the sea!
Sado ni yokotō	And, stretching off to Sado
Ama-no-gawa	Isle,
	The Galaxy . . .

These two haiku are by Bashō.

5. *Ya* may be used to express doubt, and hence a sort of inter-rogation or "rhetorical question."

In this use the *ya* is much like *yara* 'I wonder', or a rather soft *ka*. This is a special extension of its use as an exclamatory par-ticle, and is usually not found in the colloquial. (But see WO YA and YA INA YA.)

Kore ikanaru sho ni idetaru *koto ni ya*	I wonder in what book this is put down (?)
Kore to ya omou *Kore ya to omou*	I think it is this (but I am not sure) .
Omoiataru koto ari ya nashi ya	I wonder if you remember it or not?

If the context indicates it, the rhetorical question may suggest the answer "No!" as in:

Saru koto arubeshi ya	Are such things to be?
Nan no kanashimu koto ya *aru*	Is there anything to be sad about?

Note that grammarians say that the interrogative use of *ya* calls for the Line 3A form (*rentaikei*) of the final verb or adjective. Thus:

Hana otsu	Blossoms fall.
Hana ya otsuru	Do blossoms fall, I wonder?
Mizu wa kiyoshi	The water is clear.
Mizu ya kiyoki	Is the water clear?

Apparently, however, this rule is not usually observed in modern bungo. And it certainly was not always observed in the earliest texts, such as the Manyōshū.

The question is too complicated to go into here. It seems that the general rule *should* be that *ya* at the end of a sentence would follow a sentence-ending form. After *ya,* not at the end of a sentence, a *rentaikei* would then be a syntactical device, to indicate that the sentence is to be given a rhetorically interrogative sense.

6. There is a special use of *ya* after verb-forms which are neither the *shūshikei* nor *rentaikei* (Line forms 3 or 3A).

After the Line 4 form *(izenkei) ya* gives a certain suggestion of "is it perhaps because?" to a clause used as part of a compound sentence. Apparently this is due to the fact that in the very early language the *izenkei* was used in much the sense of a perfect tense. Cf. the uses of *-ba* and *-do* after the *izenkei.*

Ametsuchi no kami wa nakare	Are there no gods of heaven
ya uruwashiki waga tsuma	and earth (and is it perhaps
sakaru	because of that?) —that I am
	parted from my lovely mate?
Suzushisa no	Is it, I wonder, because it is
Katamari nare ya	one mass of coolness?
Yowa no tsuki	O, midnight moon!
Haru nare ya	Spring has come, and (is it be-
Namonaki yama no	cause of that?)
Asagasumi	— the morning-mist
	round even a nameless hill!

It is perhaps the influence of this usage which has allowed the addition of *ya* to still other verb-forms, as:

Koe ni mina	So! And did it yell
Nakishimaute ya	Till it became all voice?
Semi no kara	Cicada-shell!

Note that the *izenkei* plus *ya* does not give this effect if it ends a sentence. See paragraph 5 above.

Ware wasurere ya	Have I forgotten! (No!)

After a *-mu, -n* form *ya* may convey supposition. Cf. p. 124, para. 5.

-YA, -YĀ.   See also -IYA, -NYA, -KYA.

This may be an informal pronunciation of the sound *-i wa* **or** *-e wa.*

For example, *ni wa* may be pronounced *nya* or *nyā*.
Kore wa may be pronounced *korya* or *koryā*, etc.
It may also be a pronunciation of *-eba*. Cf. -IYA.. E.g.:

nakereba	
nakeriya	if not be
nakerya	

YA INA YA. A combination used both in the colloquial and in
bungo. Here *ina* is a negative, and *ya* expresses a feeling of doubt
or question. (Cf. under YA, p. 346.) Literally the feeling is "...?
or not? ... "

Ari ya ina ya to shimpai su   He is anxious (wondering)
                                    whether there are or not.

Following a statement in verb form, this combination suggests
that it is hard to say whether the action described had or had not
actually taken place.
When directly followed by another statement the effect may be
rendered in English by such phrases as "No sooner . . . than
. . ."; "Hardly . . . when . . ."; "As soon as . . .," etc.

Dekakeru ya ina ya ame ga   No sooner had I gone out than
furidashimashita   it began to rain.
                               I had hardly gone out
                               when . . .
                               Just as I went out . . .

-YAKA. A suffix, added to nouns, including the Line 2 form
(*renyōkei*) of verbs. It may be regarded as a sort of noun (or
adverb) of quality. It is usually, though not always, followed
by *na, ni,* or *sa*. Only a comparatively small number of words
formed with this suffix are in common use.

hana-yaka-na	gay
shinobi-yaka ni	stealthily
mameyaka-na	faithful
shitoyaka-sa	gentleness
adeyaka adeyaka	admirable! admirable!

YARA. A particle, technically confined to the colloquial, but with a special use in poetry, especially *haiku.*

Grammarians trace it from the early Heian *ni ya aramu* (approximately "is it perhaps") through the late Heian (10th century) *yaramu, yaran* and the Kamakura *yarau* (*yarō*) forms.

It expresses doubt, uncertainty, conjecture, etc. It is something like *ka* or *ya,* but is rather softer and vaguer. (Cf. KA and YA.)

It may come before or after most postpositions, and may substitute for *ga* or *wo.* When used with the postposition *no,* however, it always precedes it.

It is sometimes considered a suffix rather than a separate particle.

1. After interrogatives, it makes them indefinites:

Dare yara to kenka shita	(He) quarreled with somebody or other.
Naniyara mite iru	(He) is looking at something or other.
Naniyara wo yonde iru	(He) is reading something or other.
Dare wo yara tsurete kita	(He) brought along somebody or other.
Dare yara no hanashi . . .	A story about someone or other . . .

2. After words which are not interrogatives *yara* indicates uncertainty or conjecture.

Ōsaka e itta yara	(He) went to Osaka, was it?
Ōsaka yara e itta toki no koto da	It has to do with a time (he) went to Osaka or some place.
Akambō wa wakaru no yara niko-niko wazatte iru	The infant is smiling as if (perhaps) he understood.
Saru mono wa hibi ni utoshi yara	"Out of sight, out of mind," perhaps (i.e., the proverb may be true in this case) .

3. *Yara* in sequence gives a sort of "and/or" effect: (Compare
KA . . . KA and YA . . . YA.)

Kabe ni e yara shashin yara ga aru	On the wall were paintings and/or photographs.
Fue yara taiko yara de . . .	What with fifes and drums and such . . .
Utareru yara kerareru yara sanzanna me ni atta	(He) was beaten and kicked and had a terrible time.

4. When used in poetry, especially *haiku, yara* has an added emotional content.

It is not possible to give an exact definition, as the effect varies with the context, but it may be roughly described as a sort of vague "I wonder," suggested rather than expressed.

Tombotsuri	Dragon-fly-catcher
kyō wa doko made	Today to what place
itta yara	Has he gone?

This last poem has been splendidly rendered in English by Thomas Nelson Page:

I wonder in what fields today
He chases dragon-flies in play
My little boy—who ran away.

YA WA. A combination used, especially in bungo, to show that a sentence which is a question in form is not to be taken as a real question, but as an ironical or rhetorical one.

Nadote osoruru koto ya wa aru	There is nothing to fear! [(It) is "why be afraid?"]
Ya wa ka sono mama ni okubeki	What? Leave things in that state?

YASU. A dialect form (Kansai, especially Kyoto) used as a polite imperative, equivalent to *nasai* or *kudasai*.

O-hairi yasu	Come in!
Gomen yasu	I beg your pardon.

YE. Postposition meaning "towards." (See E.)

YO. A particle, used for emphasis. It is a sort of oral exclamation mark, and makes what it follows very sharp and positive.

In the colloquial it seems to be used only at the end of sentences. It may be used:

1. As an imperative particle. (Cf. the section on Imperatives in the introductory Note on Verbs.)

Mi yo	Look!
Tabe yo	Eat!
Mate yo	Wait!
Sonna koto wo suru na yo	Don't do that sort of thing!

2. After statements, which may or may not be grammatically complete sentences.

Watashi wa omae no ani da yo	I am your older brother!
Abunai yo	Danger!
Sore da kara yo	It is because of that!

In bungo the effect of *yo* is the same. It may, however, be used in the interior of sentences as well as at the end. It also may be used as a vocative, as in:

Tomo yo kitare	Friends! Come here!

YŌ. This may be:

1. An emotionally lengthened form of *yo*. (See YO.) It is chiefly used by women and children.

O-kaasan—o-shibai e tsurete	Mother! Do please take me
itte kudasai yō	to the play!

2. It may be the noun *yō* meaning "way," "manner," "appearance," etc. 様 There is no need to go into its use here, as it can be found in all dictionaries, but a few examples are appended.

Ame ga furu yō desu	It looks like rain.
Tanoshii yō desu	(Someone) looks happy.

Hana no chiru no wa yuki no   The falling of blossoms is like
   yō desu   that of snow.
Watakushi no yōna hito   A person like me.

-YŌ. A colloquial suffix added to the *ko* form of *kuru*, the *shi* form of *suru*, and the Line 1 form (*mizenkei*) of all verbs of the second (*ichidan; -iru* and *-eru*) conjugation. E.g.:

> From *kuru* 'come' we get *koyō*.
> From *suru* 'do', 'act' we get *shiyō*.
> From *miru* 'see' we get *miyō*.
> From *taberu* 'eat' we get *tabeyō*.

In *kana* this *yō* is usually written with the symbols for *yo* and *u*.

This suffix is used, like *-u*, to indicate an "absence of positivity." For examples of this use, see under -U.

Katte koyō   I think I'll go and buy it.
   Let's go and buy it!

Mō okiyō ka   I'd better be getting up now.
   Shall we get up?

YŌ NI. This combination of the noun *yō* 'way', 'manner' and the postposition *ni* is often used to express an imperative.

The full form of the imperative would be something like . . . *yō ni shite kudasai.*

Jochū ni isha wo yobu yō ni   Please tell the maid to call the
   itte kudasai   doctor.
Sugu iku yō ni iimashō ka   Shall I tell (her) to go at once?

Yowanai yō ni . . . (nasai)   See that you don't get drunk!

YORI. A postposition, used only after substantives. (Cf. NI YORI.)

Substantives, of course, are usually nouns or pronouns, but may be other words or word-groups acting as substantives.

It marks what it follows as a limit or base from which some action takes place, or beyond which some state exists. This limit

may be regarded as either in space or in time, and may be concrete, abstract, or metaphorical. (See also the note under YOTTE.)

Yori is usually translatable by "from" or "beyond" but may, in
the circumstances noted below, be translated as "by means of."

It is primarily a bungo word, and is little used in the colloquial
except in making comparisons or when it is followed by *hoka ni*.
When it is used in any other way in the colloquial, it has an effect
of formality.

In the following examples, the standard bungo and colloquial
ways of expressing an idea are both given. It will be noticed that
except in comparisons the *yori* is normally replaced by *kara* in
the colloquial.

Note that in comparing the bungo uses of *kara* and *yori* Yamada says
that when *kara* is used it emphasizes the original base, while *yori* emphasizes what takes place beyond it.

Gogo goji yori kaien *Gogo goji kara kaien*	The performance begins at (continues from) five o'clock p.m.
Naga-no tabiji yori kaerikitaru *Nagai ryokō kara kaette kuru*	He has returned home from a long journey.

Tōkyō yori Shanghai
    made . . .
Tōkyō kara Shanghai
    made . . .
	From Tokyo down to Shanghai . . .

Kokoro yori kaigo no jō wo
    arawaseri
Kokoro kara kaigo no jō wo
    arawaseta
	He showed the emotion of re-pentance from his heart.

Sono ie wo idete yori . . . *Sono ie wo dete kara . . .*	After leaving their houses . . .

There is one rather peculiar use of *yori*, in which it indicates
the means by which an action is made possible.

This is connected with the original meaning of the verb *yoru*, discussed under NI YORI.

Hikōki yori kyūkō seri
Hikōki kara kyūkōshita

By means of an airplane (he) was able to make a quick journey.

It may also be used for the purpose of comparison. In bungo, when *yori* is used this way, it is usually followed by *wa* or *mo*. In the colloquial it is often followed by *ka*.

Fubo no on wa umi yori mo
fukaku yama yori mo
takashi
Fubo no on wa umi yori
fukaku yama yori takai

Parental love is deeper (even) than the sea, and higher (even) than the hills.

Zashi-sen yori wa susumite
taoruru ni shikazu
Zashi-suru yori ka susunde
shinda hō ga ii

It is better to go forward and die than to play the part of a mere spectator.

There is a modern use of *yori* modelled on English comparatives, so that one may come across phrases in which the original standard of comparison is omitted, such as:

Yori okii yori utsukushii hana
ga hoshii n'desu

(We) want bigger and finer flowers.

When followed by *hoka ni* it has the feeling of "other than."

Benkyō yori hoka ni seikō no
michi nashi
Benkyō yori hoka ni seikō no
michi wa nai

Other than hard study, there is no road to success.

A few examples of the colloquial uses of *yori* are added:

Kami yori hoka ni wa shiru
hito wa nai
Sore yori ka kore ga ii

Other than God, there is no one who knows.
This is perhaps better than that.

Mikake yori wa omoi ne
Ippan no gakusha ga shinjite
oru tokoro yori mo zutto
furui

Heavier than it looks, isn't it?
It is a great deal older even than most scholars believe it to be.

Ryōshin yori yoroshiku	Best wishes to you from my parents.

YORI MO. There is a special use of *yori mo* which seems to be confined to comparisons in which the *yori mo* is directly followed by an adjective. It occurs in both bungo and colloquial.

Shi yori mo tsuyoshi *Shi yori mo tsuyoi*	(It is) stronger even than death.
Tobu yori mo hayashi *Tobu yori mo hayai*	(It is) even faster than flying.

YOTTE. As a conjunction used at the beginning of a sentence, this word may be translated as "consequently," "as a consequence of that," "hence," etc. (Cf. discussion under NI YORU.)

It refers to some previous statement, and is practically equivalent to *sore ni yotte* 'taking that as a basis'. E.g.:

Yotte kono na ari	Hence this name.

YU. A particle equivalent to *yori*, now used only in poems.

-ZARA, -ZARE, -ZARI, -ZARU. Bungo suffixes, added to the Line 1 form (*mizenkei*) of verbs. They derive from contractions of the negative suffix *-zu* with forms of *-ari* 'be', and have a negative meaning. The conjugation is of course equivalent to that of *ari*. E.g.:

Ware yukazaramu	I shall not go.
Kare yukazariki	He did not go.
Subekarazaru koto nari	It is a thing that is not to be done.
Meisō onajikarazaredomo koto wa sunawachi ichi nari	Even though the names and appearances are not the same, the (essential) matter is actually one.

The main use of these suffixes is to make possible the addition of still further suffixes, especially inflected ones, which cannot be added to negative forms in *-zu*. They are not used in normal colloquial Japanese, except for forms in *-bekarazaru*.

In some dialects, however, these forms may still be found used to a certain extent. Even contracted forms like *shirazatta* 'did not know' may be heard occasionally.

ZE. A colloquial particle placed at the end of a sentence for emphasis.

It is used chiefly with plain and sometimes with semi-polite forms. It is a good deal like the American colloquial "See?" (Cf. zo.)

Sor'ya kimi, sō iu mise wa takusan arimasu ze	Look here (Bill), there are lots of shops of that kind, see?
Mo dekita ze	Aha, through with it.
Gojissen de ii ze	Fifty sen is enough, see?
Kimi wa matteru keredo are wa kesshite konai ze	You are waiting for him but he's surely not coming!

-ZE. See -ZU, -ZURU.

ZO. A particle, with somewhat different uses in bungo and in the colloquial.

BUNGO

In bungo *zo* is purely an emphatic particle. It may come in the middle of a sentence or at the end. It is usually used to emphasize statements, but may strengthen questions as well.

It calls for the use of the Line 3A form (*rentaikei*) for the final verb, or for the *-ki* form of an adjective acting as the final verb. It may be combined with other particles. (Cf. TO ZO.)

Natsu zo atsuki	The summer is hot!
Naka no hitori wa boku naru zo	One among them is I!
Utsubeki toki wa ima naru zo	The time to strike is now!
Chugi ni arazu shite nan zo	If you don't consider this loyalty, what do you consider it? (What is this but loyalty?)

So wa nani zo to iu ni tsugi no shorei no gotoki kore nari	In connection with the question what that is, it is this, which is illustrated in the following examples.
Kawari-yasuki wa onna-gokoro zo	What is easily changed is the heart of a woman!

Note that in the last three examples the "final verb" is omitted.

THE COLLOQUIAL

In the colloquial *zo* is used as a purely emphatic word only at the end of sentences.

Nakanaka omoshiroi zo	It is very interesting indeed.
Kyō iku zo	I am going today!
Sora wa hareru-rashii zo	The sky seems to be clearing!

It must be remembered that of course *zo* may come at the end of a quoted sentence marked as such by *to,* and also that the colloquial may contain quotations from bungo. E.g.:

Kore zo to iu hodo no koto mo nai	There is nothing very special to be said (about her, them, it, etc.) (. . . that calls for saying *Kore zo.*)

Here *kore zo* may be regarded as a quotation taken from bungo.

Zo may be used in the middle of a sentence, but only directly after interrogatives. When so used, *zo* still has an effect of emphasis, but it also serves to turn the interrogative words into indefinites.

Note that when *zo* is used the postpositions *wa, ga* and *wo* are usually omitted.

Dare zo tayoraneba naranu	I must rely on somebody!
Kitto doko zo e asobi ni o-dekake ni natta no deshō	He must surely have gone out somewhere to amuse himself.
Doko zo ni toki wo motomeru ie wa nai ka	Isn't there somewhere a house where one can find food?

Nanzo mitai ka   Would you like to see something?

-ZU. A suffix, added to the Line 1 form (*mizenkei*) of verbs. It indicates a negative.

Zu may also be a sonant form of *su*. (Cf. -ZURU.)

It is used in both the colloquial and bungo, but in slightly different ways.

Japanese grammarians usually combine it with the negative suffix -*nu* to make a partial conjugation. (See -NU.)

		Bungo	Colloquial
Line 1	*Mizenkei*	-zu	-zu
Line 2	*Renyōkei*	-zu	-zu
Line 3	*Shūshikei*	-zu	(-nu)
Line 3A	*Rentaikei*	(-nu)	(-nu)
Line 4	*Izenkei*	(-ne)	(-ne)

It will be noted that the difference is that in the colloquial -*zu* is not used as a sentence-ending form (*shūshikei*).

It is perhaps not strictly correct to say that -*zu* is used as a Line 1 form (*mizenkei*). The only reason for doing so is that it may take the suffix -*ba,* to give the meaning "if not." (See -ZU BA.) It has no other connection with the *mizenkei*.

The most common use of -*zu* in the colloquial does correspond to that of a *renyōkei*. In other words it may act as a connective and also as a noun. Furthermore, like many other nouns (e.g., *toki* 'time') it may act as an adverb, even when it is not marked as such by the addition of the postposition *ni*. This use as an adverb is the commonest use of -*zu* in the colloquial.

Yome mo sezu kake mo senu He cannot read, nor can he write.
Nezu no ban wo suru   (They) keep sleepless watch.
Watakushi ni shirasezu ni itte wa ikenai You must not go without letting me know.

Kasa wo motazu dekaketa   He went out without carrying
Kasa wo motazu ni dekaketa   an umbrella.

The use of -*zu* as a Line 2 form in bungo corresponds to that in the colloquial. In bungo, however, it seems to be much more used as a connective. E.g.:

Natsu atsukarazu fuyu samukarazaru wa waga kokyō nari	Where the summers are not hot and the winters are not cold (that place) is my native place.

The common colloquial equivalent of such a sentence would probably be *Natsu mo atsuku naku fuyu mo samuku nai no wa waga kokyō desu.*

The use of -zu as a sentence-ending form (*shūshikei*) is very common in bungo. It is occasionally found in the colloquial also, but the feeling is always that it is a quotation from bungo.

Nerareneba yume mo mizu	Since I did not sleep, neither did I dream.
Arasoi wo konomu wa ikioi ni arazu	To like disputes is not an integral part of strength.
Muyō no mono hairu-bekarazu	Those without business are not to come in.

In the colloquial the most common use of -zu seems to be in the forms *arazu* and *bekarazu.* The last example given above is often used on signs and corresponds to our "No Admittance except on Business."

It should be noted that in reading Japanese written in the Chinese style, the negative sign 非 is often read *arazu.* In writing ordinary Japanese the words *arazu, arazaru,* etc., may be written with this sign followed by *zu, zaru,* etc., in *kana.* In such words the *kana* is used to show the pronunciation only. No double negative is implied.

-ZUBA, -ZUMBA. A suffix meaning "if not." It is primarily a literary form, and while it is still heard in speech it seems to be obsolescent in the modern colloquial.

It is added to the Line 1 form (*mizenkei*) of verbs. (See -zu.)

Isogi yukazuba chikoku semu	If you don't go quickly you will be late.

When this form is used in speech it seems to be usually pronounced -*zumba.*

It is of course equivalent in meaning to the more commonly used colloquial -*neba* or -*nakereba*.

-ZU, -ZURU. A sonant form of -*su, -suru,* used in both bungo and the colloquial. E.g.:

> *meisuru* becomes *meizuru* 'order', etc.
> *shinsu* becomes *shinzu* 'believe', etc.

In the modern colloquial, this form seems to be more common in Kyoto than in Tokyo. The common Tokyo speech would, for instance, prefer *meijiru*. (Cf. -JIRU.)

It is used in both bungo and the colloquial, and may of course be conjugated in the same way as the bungo *su* or the colloquial *suru*.

			Colloquial	Bungo
Line 1	form	*Mizenkei*	-*ze* (-*ji*)	-*ze* (-*ji*)
Line 2	form	*Renyōkei*	-*ji*	-*ji*
Line 3	form	*Shūshikei*	-*zuru*	-*zu*
Line 3A	form	*Rentaikei*	-*zuru*	-*zuru*
Line 4	form	*Izenkei*	-*zure*	-*zure*

Yo ga koto wo shinzezariki	They did not believe my words.
Mate to meijite kure tamae	Please tell him to wait.

The first of these examples is bungo, the second colloquial. Note that the form *meijite* is the -*te* form of both *meizuru* and *meijiru*.

-ZUTSU. Suffix, added to words of number or quantity.

It corresponds approximately to the English phrase "at a time" when used in counting.

Note, however, that for good English translation the phrase "at a time" is usually best rendered by some other phrase.

sukoshi zutsu	a little at a time (little by *little)
futatsu zutsu	two at a time (two by two)
hitori ni mittsu zutsu	for a single person three at a time (three each per person)

ABCDEFGHI–H–73210/698

Jul 27'70

JY 20'71

PL535 H4 1948
+Handbook of Japa+Henderson, Harol

0 00 02 0151994 9
MIDDLEBURY COLLEGE